Anarchism and the Black Revolution

The Definitive Edition

Lorenzo Kom'boa Ervin

Forewords by William C. Anderson and Joy James

PLUTO PRESS

First published 2021 by Pluto Press
New Wing, Somerset House, Strand, London WC2R 1LA

www.plutobooks.com

British Library Cataloguing in Publication Data
A catalogue record for this book is available from the British Library

ISBN 978 0 7453 4580 2   Hardback
ISBN 978 0 7453 4581 9   Paperback
ISBN 978 0 7453 4575 8   PDF
ISBN 978 0 7453 4579 6   EPUB

This book is printed on paper suitable for recycling and made from fully managed and sustained forest sources. Logging, pulping and manufacturing processes are expected to conform to the environmental standards of the country of origin.

Typeset by Stanford DTP Services, Northampton, England

Simultaneously printed in the United Kingdom and United States of America

Contents

Dedicated to Martin Sostre, my late mentor; JoNina Ervin, my loving wife; Munyiga Ras Nokashere, staunchest comrade of the Black Autonomy movement from the beginning and throughout; William C. Anderson, who pushed me to re-write and to come to Pluto Press for this edition; Bedour Alagraa, of the Black Critique series, and others who helped and encouraged me to write this edition. I also give credit to the Institute for Anarchist Studies, which financed and encouraged me to write the previous edition of the book, and, by extension, this definitive edition. Thank you all.

Foreword

By William C. Anderson

It's not an exaggeration to say that Lorenzo Kom'boa Ervin has changed the world. Countless people have been affected and influenced by his work throughout the years. His story is a testament to the extraordinary possibilities that lie just beneath the surface of the many passing moments of our lives. Unforeseeable, explosive events may erupt just because of someone making the decision to take a chance. Lorenzo decided to do this many times and that's what's led to yet another major event in his life. The first official publication of his legendary book, *Anarchism and the Black Revolution*, is yet another monumental occurrence in a life that almost seems cinematic.

Lorenzo Kom'boa Ervin was born in 1947 in Chattanooga, Tennessee, to a mother who was a domestic worker and a father who was a chauffeur. With two parents working in service to wealthier white people in the apartheid of the Jim Crow South, it wasn't long before Lorenzo intimately understood the risks of being Black. At the age of five, surrounding white community members attempted to burn down his family home. The traumatic near death experience he wouldn't completely understand until he was older runs parallel to his radical trajectory. The symbolism in it shouldn't be neglected because it frames much of what's to come. As recalled by Harry Belafonte, Dr. Martin Luther King, Jr. once said that he believed Black America was integrating "into a burning house." A question that responds to such a statement was raised in James Baldwin's *The Fire Next Time*,[1] "Do I really want to be integrated into a burning house?" Ervin's story answers "no," time and time again.

As a young man, Lorenzo joined the army during the Vietnam War where he became an anti-war activist. This was the year the first U.S. combat troops arrived on the ground in a country that has still yet to recover from all the damage that was done by imperialist forces. At the same time, the USA was embroiled in the Civil Rights movement. The Voting Rights Act was signed this same year that Alabama police assaulted marchers on "Bloody Sunday" in Selma and attacked activists

---

1. James Baldwin, *The Fire Next Time*, Dial Press, New York, 1963.

associated with Student Nonviolent Coordinating Committee (SNCC). This historic movement organization would attract Lorenzo after his anti-war activism saw him court martialed, prosecuted, and ultimately discharged.

He became affiliated with SNCC and was influenced by the organizer Mukasa Dada, formerly known as Willie Ricks who coined the "Black Power" slogan that was popularized by Kwame Ture (formerly Stokely Carmichael) and ultimately the Black Panther Party. Lorenzo had been selling the *Black Panther* newspaper while working with SNCC who had alliances with the party. He eventually started working with the party directly as a member, but he'd eventually grow disillusioned with the leadership style among other aspects of the Panthers. Then his circumstances shifted dramatically after Martin Luther King, Jr. was assassinated. Rebellions and uprising broke out across the country and as a result, Tennessee state officials convened grand juries to investigate and punish Black activists and civil rights groups on felonious charges. Accused of gun running and threatening to bomb a Klan sympathizing judge, Lorenzo fled to Atlanta. He decided to take his flight from the charges levied against him even further and hijacked a plane to Cuba.

At the time of Ervin's departure, hijacking planes and fleeing to Cuba was more common than people may realize. The cases of Black radicals who did so are sometimes romanticized, but Ervin's experience highlights an important distinction. Upon his arrival he stayed with other hijackers who were grouped together before ultimately being imprisoned by the Cuban government and put into solitary confinement. Black Panther Party leader Eldridge Cleaver was already in Cuba himself and had a strained relationship with the government because of ongoing disagreements. The other Panthers there would be affected by the intensity of this situation and it led to Lorenzo getting travel documents before he was deported to Czechoslovakia.

His experience in Czechoslovakia wasn't much better. There he was subjected to harassment and monitoring by government officials before he was ultimately detained again. Despite efforts by Lorenzo to secure safety and solidarity among the African university students he bonded with there, he found himself held by the U.S. consulate in Prague. He'd flee *again*, this time making his way to East Germany which was part of the Eastern Bloc during the Cold War. This was where he was captured by federal authorities who would in turn ship him back to the USA after torturing him in detention.

At the Federal Detention Center in New York City Lorenzo's life was changed by his chance encounter with a jailhouse lawyer and Black radical educator named Martin Sostre. Whether Sostre knew it or not, his meeting with Lorenzo was something that would affect generations to come. It was Sostre who first introduced Lorenzo to anarchism and mentored him which he'd later reflect on in an essay he wrote about Martin:

> He bounced a new word on me: "Anarchist Socialism." I had no idea what he was talking about at the time … He explained to me about "self-governing socialism," which he described as free of state bureaucracy, any kind of party or leader dictatorship. Almost every day he regaled me about "direct democracy," "communitarianism," "radical autonomy," "general assemblies," and other stuff I knew nothing about. So I just listened for hours as he schooled me.

Sostre had already reshaped the prison system through a series of victorious lawsuits around prisoners' rights after his being framed led to his incarceration. He didn't know at the time that his passage of an Anarchist theory and political education to Lorenzo would change the course of politics for many throughout the world. Lorenzo faced trial in the small town of Newnan, Georgia, and was given a life sentence by an all-white jury. He was eventually transferred to the federal penitentiary in Terre Haute, Indiana. This was a facility known for its brutality where the legacy of the Ku Klux Klan resurgence in the early twentieth century remained strong. Black men in the facility he was imprisoned in faced regular torture and brutality at the hands of card carrying klansmen who were prison guards in addition to other positions of authority. It all contributed to the creation of a book that was forged through the aforementioned experiences and the torment of the cell which Lorenzo knew intimately at this point.

Anarchism and the Black Revolution was written in 1979 at a critical juncture where Lorenzo Kom'boa Ervin was politically maturing and applying his newfound interests in anarchism to the life experiences that had led up to a special moment. It was written by hand and had to be kept hidden from prison authorities who might have destroyed it given the chance. He would hide it in different places or pass it to other prisoners to hold if his cell became vulnerable. It was still seized, but luckily it made its way to his lawyer before this short pamphlet was first produced by an Anarchist collective in New York. His case then became an international Anarchist solidarity campaign and eventually led to his release from prison.

Once he was outside of the prison system again, Lorenzo was interested in publishing his autobiography. This was one of several texts he wrote while he was incarcerated including a *Manifesto for the International Anarchist movement* and a *Draft Proposal for an International Working People's Association*. But it was *Anarchism and the Black Revolution* which was already making waves as an underground, revolutionary text that he ended up republishing again in 1988 as a second edition through the Industrial Workers of the World (IWW). The third edition of this text was published in the late 2000s with another IWW press, P&L Printing, based in Denver, Colorado. Now, for the first time in this legendary book's history it will be produced and available to read through a publisher who has the ability to offer it more widespread distribution. To hold this writing is to hold much more than a mere object; it is to hold a movement.

Anarchism and the Black Revolution is *the* definitive writing on Black anarchism in the USA. If it were not for this book, many people in the USA and throughout the world would have significantly different politics. That's not hyperbole because the book outlined the contours of radical changes within and outside of critically important Black struggles. That is to say, this text represents the underappreciated rejection of neat narratives that condense intricate histories into straight lines instead of complicated shapes. His original text and its expanded editions that followed detail a searing critique of the failures of the Black Power and the Civil Rights movements. And it did so as foundational text offering these criticisms from a Black Anarchist perspective.

Lorenzo's work is extremely thorough in its attention to detail. It offers explanations for beginners and detailed analysis that challenges seasoned thinkers. He covers nearly every imaginable aspect he can of the different conflicts that were subjects to arise in his compilation of topics. Comprehensive history and a wide range of perspectives come together to create a mosaic of counterpoints to challenge the dogma of a left stuck in an echo chamber. Unfortunately, the history that Lorenzo's dissident life and work represents is still groundbreakingly relevant thanks to the unresolved repetitions of leftist ideological devotions, hagiography, and the romanticization of state-building. This text was fighting these things many decades ago and the fact that it's still as pertinent as it is represents the prescience of an author and the shortcomings of responses to the issues raised. We'd do well to take longevity of its application as an indictment of our collective approach although this is by no means a holy book.

I had the privilege of encountering Lorenzo as a young organizer in my early twenties, disillusioned with many of the things he has made a name for himself being outspoken about. I had no idea who I was speaking to or what he had accomplished in his life. He told me in passing about *Anarchism and the Black Revolution* when I took interest in his politics after hearing him speak at the workshop I had co-organized. I connected with him and JoNina Abron-Ervin from a place of alienation. I was frustrated with the cultism of the left and the professionalization of activism that I had been encountering for years already. I wanted something more and I had no idea that this book I'd eventually inquire about again and receive in the mail would shake me up the way it did.

I initially contacted Lorenzo later in a meandering message while feeling conflicted about the potential of embracing anything "Anarchist," which I viewed as a white, juvenile set of politics. I had long embraced statism and Black nationalism, but had reached a point of undeniable frustration with the conflicts I encountered among cadres and organizations I was involved with. In a short paragraph Facebook message I wrote, "Hey Lorenzo! Love your posts on Facebook! I have been feeling lately that I might be an anarchist … So, do you have any books or recommendations?" Lorenzo responded, "I recommend *Anarchism and the Black Revolution* by me." By the time I got my copy and read the book, I was convinced that I needed to drastically re-evaluate my politics.

What sets Black anarchism apart from classical or European anarchism is that it was born out of a rejection of the hierarchical, messainic, and authoritarian embraces that limited so many Black movements prior. The Black Anarchist forebears of the era Lorenzo came out of like Martin Sostre, Ashanti Alston and Ojore Lutalo were once what they later criticized while developing this breakaway movement. Lorenzo himself was a Maoist when he hijacked the plane to Cuba. This makes Black anarchism special because it was already doing the terribly undervalued work of internal critique. It was trying to transcend the limitations it identified within and exceed its past and its present formations. Many of its primary criticisms are an invitation for others to join who haven't yet or have no desire to do this.

Lorenzo's *Anarchism and the Black Revolution* insists that yes, the house and the plantation are indeed burning but we do not need to burn with them. As a rejection of reform and statism, Lorenzo challenges us to not simply try to create a new state and paint it red or black. He asks us to think beyond what might have succeeded or failed in the past and think about what needs to happen in the present. He assures us that liberation will not be achieved by mimicking what didn't free us before and it won't be achieved by not interrogating what's happening around us now.

Anarchism and the Black Revolution reappears during a time where the need for upheaval is crucially important. Amid an unrelenting pandemic, ecological crises, and bolstered fascism the nation-state has revealed itself to be more of a problem than a solution for many. Masses of people are realizing overnight that these apparatuses will not protect us much like the prisons, militaries, and police that they use to do their bidding. The proliferation of mutual aid groups in response to what's popularly being criticized as a "failed state" calls into question the entire idea that the state is failing us at all when it's clear it was never meant to serve us. Meanwhile, Black anarchism has certainly become more widely read and embraced than ever before with the help of new writings, collectives, and traditions being cultivated by needed shifts in perspective.

None of this would be the same as it is now were it not for *Anarchism and the Black Revolution*. It set the stage for so much of what's transpiring before us by watering barren fields with the quenching sustenance of visionary politics. This is Lorenzo and his book's *raison d'être*, and now that we're witnessing the growth of the seeds flowering the minds and hearts of many we should give back a bouquet. We can do this by planting seeds of our own and understanding the significance of what we have to offer because of what others offered of themselves before us. This is how revolutionary potential can flourish and radical springs follow the winters that have weighed us down. Not every person or their work deserves the title "revolutionary" but Lorenzo has made as much known about himself through his life's purpose. Readers can decide for themselves if, when, or how they would like to use this legendary offering to break new ground.

Catalyst

By Joy James

For decades, the writings of Lorenzo Ervin have been shared and studied. Since the rebellions of the postwar twentieth century, Lorenzo Kom'boa Ervin as liberation theorist and practitioner has provided essential reading for those who not only care about our worlds but also demand resources, justice, equity, beauty, and care delivered to those worlds and our collective well-being.

At the turn of the twenty-first century, my students at Brown University and I knew, after organizing gatherings of political prisoners to visit campus and converse with students and each other, that it was imperative to anthologize the writings of those who fought and sacrificed in struggles against racism, capitalism, imperialism and (hetero)sexism. We collectively constructed several anthologies. In *Imprisoned Intellectuals* (2003), Ervin is significant as the rare analyst of anarchism who also had organized in various militant organizations and been interred as a political prisoner. *Imprisoned Intellectuals* included twentieth-century rebels, from spiritualists to materialists and pacifists to militarists; the volume centers on the writings of twentieth-century revolutionary political prisoners in the United States. Ervin's work makes an important contribution, in part because so few of us understood the complexity of anarchist thought and the expansive embrace of Black resistance to predation. Ervin synthesized the two. He wrote what he had already seen and experienced, although not as the political norm in rebellion against repression but as the possibility of becoming the norm.

The anthology's introduction centered on the writings of captured US revolutionaries who also function as internationalists in their liberation politics. This reflects the political biography of Lorenzo Kom'boa Ervin:

> Radical organizations garnered wide support based on their ability
> to address the material needs and aspirations, as well as ideals, of
> their communities. For example, reservation, barrio, or urban youths
> were (and are) disaffected by and overwhelmed with frustration

at dead-end jobs, poverty, inferior and disciplinary schooling, and police violence. It is logical then that the Black Panther Party, Brown Berets, Young Lords, Young Patriots, and American Indian Movement would have mass appeal among the young. While the majority media focused on the armed aspect of such groups, it was their free breakfast programs, free medical clinics, freedom schools, and social services that elicited wide support. They offered an alternative to the state; and by their massive appeal in oppressed communities, they presented the government with the real threat of popular insurrection built by revolutionaries.[1]

Our excerpt from the 1979 *Anarchism and the Black Revolution* begins with his paragraph:

Historically, there have been three major forms of socialism—Libertarian Socialism (Anarchism), Authoritarian Socialism (Marxist Communism), and Democratic Socialism (electoral social democracy). The non-Anarchist Left has echoed the bourgeoisie's portrayal of Anarchism as an ideology of chaos and lunacy. But Anarchism, and especially Anarchist-Communism, has nothing in common with this image. It is false and made up by its ideological opponents, the Marxists-Leninists.[2]

Some leftists and progressives would argue that Ervin's assertion is "anti-Communist." However, Ervin develops an analysis on the differences between anarchists and Marxist-Leninists: "Anarchists are social revolutionaries who seek a stateless, classless, voluntary cooperative federation of decentralized communities based upon social ownership, individual liberty, and autonomous self-management of social and economic life".[3]

His key distinction focuses on organizing. Anarchists not only reject what he identifies as the three pillars of "authoritarian socialists": Vanguard party, democratic centralism, dictatorship of the proletariat. Anarchists offer an alternative to the dominant paradigm of "leadership."

---

1. Joy James, ed., *Imprisoned Intellectuals*, Rowman & Littlefield, 2003 (Intro xiii) https://repositories.lib.utexas.edu/handle/2152/7098

2. See this volume, p. 48.

3. *Ibid*, p. 49.

Ervin identifies the "catalyst group" not as a vanguard seeking hegemony and ideological conformity but as an organic collective. Rejecting vanguardism, elitism, and cooptation of power into a central committee, the catalyst group, according to Ervin, becomes the site of theory and action. Ervin's catalyst group suggests the political agency of the masses that distinguishes itself from political elites, as dissected in *Return to the Source* and Amilcar Cabral's analysis: "We recognize the devastations of lack of clean water, adequate food and shelter but the cause of those deficits cannot be remedied through policy. If so, then there is no need for confrontation only accommodation with colonialists and petitions for greater benefit packages."[4]

Ervin writes that "anarchists oppose hierarchical, power-tripping Marxist leadership that suppresses the creative urge of those involved and forces an agenda down their throats."[5] The catalyst group is the antithesis of the celebrity pundit or political leader who becomes the representational figure for the mass yet participates in the revenue streams and prestige accumulations linked to "movement millionaires." Such accumulations are not signs of catalytic changes for liberation from repression and poverty; yet these accumulations are defended by prominent pundits, academics, funded activists.

When I read *Anarchism and the Black Revolution*, I see that Ervin has a community that would not fully agree with his analyses, still their work aligns and intersects with his. The War Resisters League (WRL) shares their pie chart on military spending and taxpayers' resources redirected to predation. Founded in 1923, WRL aligns in ethics with Ervin's resistance to militarism, exploitation and extortion. Putting these two in dialectical dialogue would build the Catalyst Group.

With *Anarchism and the Black Revolution* we can expand our analyses for activist and academic intellectuals to discern how catalyst groups grow despite or become casualties of authoritarianism. Echoes of this can be found in academic writings. August Nimtz asserts that counterrevolutions follow revolutions and that Stalinism was the counterrevolution of the 1917 Bolshevik-led October Revolution, through which workers and peasants briefly led the Soviet Union. For

---

4. Amilcar Cabral, *Return to the Source: Selected Speeches*, Monthly Review Press, 1973.
5. See this volume, p. 50.

Nimtz, Stalinism is a "counterrevolutionary current within the modern workers' movement" as "the dictatorship of the proletariat" became "the dictatorship of the bureaucracy"; and Stalin's 1935 "Popular Front" as "a belated attempt to counter fascism" became an international mandate for workers' movements to partner with the "progressive bourgeoisie" not "independent working-class" activists; thus, in the name of the "Popular Front," the CPUSA became effective operating against a "working-class party independent of the Democratic Party."[6]

We can also rethink "Black Marxism" beyond academic frameworks by placing *Anarchism and the Black Revolution* in conversation with books by other political prisoners, such as radical activists Frank Chapman's *Marxist-Leninist Perspectives on Black Liberation and Socialism.* Chapman writes: "the workers' movement and the Black Liberation movement—emerged separately in the 1800s, when Marx and Engels were developing the theory of scientific socialism ... the struggle for freedom for Black people was central to Marx's analysis of the United States ... showing that the African slave trade was the foundation of mercantile capitalism."[7]

Ervin's work is original and brilliant. I do not agree with all of his analyses. However, I note that his interventions against fascism, whether for the reader they create a corridor as big as an avenue or as slim as a crack in concrete, remain essential reading. His political intellectual thought allows us to think more rapidly and more radically. Flexibility, creativity, communal-centered and catalytic—these are the characteristics we require under crises.

Since we cannot agree on history or destiny, the present moments are best used in building our communities to leverage revolutionary love and grow effective groups and mobilizations. Some variation of the beloved community, catalyst group, return to the source. If we pay more attention to those with painfully accumulated experiential knowledge, such as Lorenzo Kom'boa Ervin, we will better understand what the catalyst is comprised of: ancestor and survivor; elders/youths; activists; intellectuals; rebels; revolutionary lovers. Their and our individual and collective efforts for justice and liberation might be obscured by the

---

6. "Symposium: Is the Term 'Stalinism' Valid and Useful for Marxist Analysis?", *Science & Society*, Vol. 82, No. 4, October 2018, 555–67.

7. Frank Chapman, *Marxist-Leninist Perspectives on Black Liberation and Socialism*, Freedom Road Socialist Organization, 2021, p. 9.

projections of elites and fearful clinging to convention. Still, change is inevitable and *Anarchism and the Black Revolution* is one of the catalysts and resources for those seeking freedom.

Introduction

My name at birth (March 30, 1947) was Lorenzo Edward Ervin, Jr. I am a Black southerner from Chattanooga, Tennessee, a mid-sized city of 175,000, about 100 miles from Atlanta, Georgia. During the 1950s when I was growing up, I was like many Black people in the South. We faced a racially segregated world. We had no rights that the white government was legally bound to respect. No right to vote, discrimination in jobs and housing, no equal rights at all compared to that which white people enjoyed, and in too many instances, no right to life. We were supposed to stay in our place and do what the white folks told us.

But in the late 1950s through the 1960s, a Black insurgent protest movement exploded on to the American social scene which challenged the system of racial segregation in the Southern USA like no other. First, in 1956, the Montgomery, Alabama bus boycott shook segregation in transportation services, and after a year-long boycott forced them to stop the practice. This was the adult, Black preacher-led movement, which brought Dr. Martin Luther King, Jr. to prominence as a Black civil rights leader. This later led to the creation of the Southern Christian Leadership Conference in 1957, which became the best known civil rights group at the time.

However, in three years, it would be superseded by a new Black movement. A youth-based protest campaign broke out suddenly all over the South and Midwest. In less than six months, it hit all the major cities in the South: Nashville and Memphis in Tennessee, Atlanta, Georgia, New Orleans, Louisiana, Charleston, South Carolina, Raleigh and Durham in North Carolina, and 38 others.

This movement, part of the sit-in campaigns as they were first known, was actually radical occupations by students or youth, of white businesses known to engage in racial discrimination. This movement was not led by Dr. King or the adult wing of the civil right movement. It had been created by Black students and youth unaffiliated with Dr. King or the old line civil rights groups, who were fairly conservative and had grave misgivings about the "militancy" of the new protest movement.

By contrast, veteran Black activist and socialist Ella Baker summoned many of the student and youth leaders to Raleigh, North Carolina, in the spring of 1960 to discuss how to sustain and expand the movement. Thus was born the Student Nonviolent Coordinating Committee (SNCC). Throughout the 1960s, SNCC was instrumental in combatting racial segregation and empowering oppressed Black people all over the South. In fact, many campaigns attributed to Dr. King and the Southern Christian Leadership Conference (SCLC) were conducted by the SNCC. The 1963 March on Washington was proposed and organized by SNCC activists but was usurped by the Democratic Party, SCLC and union bureaucrats. The ruling class elements in the Kennedy administration and civil rights establishment were afraid of SNCC's plans, and angered that these youth were on a more radical road. So they plotted with authorities and wrested the leadership into their own hands.

This fear by the Kennedy government actually arose in 1960, especially since they had seen how a street "riot" had allegedly broken out in Chattanooga, Tennessee, a sit-in protest at a series of department stores. This sit-in had been organized by local high school students who were physically attacked by racist students, youth and adults, who spit on the Black activists, and tried to beat them up. Instead of passively submitting to the racist scum, the Black students fought back, and in their resistance beat the racists to a bloody pulp, making them literally run for their lives.

Word of this horrified the Kennedy administration of the federal government. The Chattanooga sit-in protests were like none other in that period. Almost the entire Black community arose after the attempted racist beatings and the arrests by brutal cops.

I was just one of the young people who after leaving our elementary schools marched toward the downtown area, along with many Black working-class adults. We were marching to support the Howard High School students, who started the protests when they took over the customer seating areas of department stores, downtown restaurants, and other white businesses.

The police were desperately holding the line against us entering the downtown area. They sprayed us with high pressure water hoses, threw tear gas bombs in our path, and even used vicious police dogs to drive us back. We were literally going toe-to-toe with police and white civilians until we were ensured the Black students were not hurt or in jail.

These events radicalized me for life, pointing out that Black people could fight back, and could win. The politicians and businessmen, making up the ruling class of that city, had to drop their racist policies or suffer economically. Something as simple as that began to change our world.

SNCC was a truly instrumental group, acting as the foundation of the Black student/youth Civil Rights movement in the early 1960s. By 1965 it produced the Black Power Movement, and by 1966–69 it had united with the up and coming Black Panther Party (BPP). I myself briefly became a member at this time of both SNCC and the BPP.

I am not going to romanticize the Panthers or my brief role in it. In 1967–68, it was just to go 100 miles from my hometown to Atlanta, Georgia, pick up 50–75 Black Panther newspapers, and bring them back to sell or give them away to Black youth. This was years before a Panther chapter would be founded in Chattanooga or in a Southern state. Yet, for just doing that, and continuing to speak out against the Vietnam War, this would put me in fear of my life. Local cops and the FBI harassed me, spied on me, beat me up, and eventually ran me out of town.

What is much more important than me personally, however, is that after uniting with SNCC, the BPP quickly became the central radical political organization in the late 1960s, and lasted over 15 years, even with severe government and police repression. It had no formal status in the Black Power movement, but most today recognize it as being the radical wing.

By 1969, though, I was disenchanted with the BPP and the Civil Rights movement, and began looking for a new political ideology. I felt the New Left and Black Power had been corrupted and become excessively authoritarian. Further, I had seen with my own eyes how both Cuba and Eastern European communist countries were authoritarian states, not to be admired, except for opposing the West, but they provided no real alternatives for socialism. I believed a revolution to put soulless bureaucrats in power, whether East or West, was not enough. I began thinking we needed a whole new culture, civilization, and world ... beyond state socialism, nation-statism and capitalism. We needed more than civil rights for Blacks, or just "rights" for anyone. I didn't know what it was, but I was yearning for anarchism at that very moment.

MARTIN SOSTRE, PRISON REVOLUTIONARY

Everyone has someone who inspired them in life. For me it was Martin Sostre (1923–2015). Even in this generation, many young activists know of George Jackson, aka Comrade George, a Black Panther leader, revolutionary prison writer, and organizer who was assassinated in August, 1971, in the California penitentiary, San Quentin. Sostre was not a writer with a bestselling book like Comrade George.

In the late 1960s and early 1970s, Martin Sostre was every bit as well known as a prison activist, revolutionary, and jailhouse lawyer. He almost single-handedly won democratic rights for prisoners to receive and read revolutionary literature; write books; worship alternative religious faiths; to not be railroaded in unfair disciplinary hearings and held indefinitely in solitary confinement; and to have the right to cultural studies programs. He was the one activist responsible for prisoners being able to organize during the prison struggle in 1967–74. These lawsuits changed prison conditions nationwide.

He had served a prison sentence in Attica, New York, during the early 1960s and went through a political metamorphosis from a Black Muslim in the Nation of Islam to a Black nationalist, and later an Anarchist. In 1966, he got out of prison, came home to Buffalo, New York, and started the Afro-Asian Bookstore in the Black community. This bookstore became a center of radical thought and political education in that city. A Black riot against police brutality of a Black youth broke out at this time in Buffalo, and Sostre was blamed for this rebellion since many youth visited his bookstore.

The city cops and white political establishment chafed at Sostre's organizing and political education and decided to shut him down. They arrested him on July 14, 1967, along with a bookstore co-worker, and charged them with the sale of narcotics, riot, arson, and assault. These were totally frame-up charges, but he was sentenced to 41 years in prison. Recognizing this injustice, an international campaign was begun on his behalf by his supporters and fellow activists.

At one point, he became the best known political prisoner in the world, and his case was adopted in 1973 by Amnesty International, the prisoner of conscience organization. This was a first for U.S. political prisoners and put tremendous pressure on the state of New York and the U.S. government. Finally, his worldwide defense organization pressured the New York state governor to grant Sostre an executive clemency, and he was released in 1976.

HISTORICAL IMPORTANCE OF MARTIN SOSTRE

Sostre's political consciousness and legal activism opened the door for prisoners to have legal and human rights and the ability to organize at a time of civil rights, Black Power, the New Left, radical feminism, and the Vietnam anti-war movements. At one stage, 1970–76, the prison movement became the central protest movement in America, especially after the August 1971 political assassination of George Jackson, and the September 1971 Attica rebellion. The protest at Attica was put down with a bloody massacre by prison and political officials, but it opened the eyes of millions all over the world to American state violence and racism. A mass prison support movement arose almost overnight, which demanded human rights for prisoners. There is no doubt that the prior demands of Martin Sostre, in his writings and prisoners' rights lawsuits, who had been imprisoned at Attica some years previous, played a role ideologically. Sostre's struggle inside as a political prisoner was clearly bound up with what later became the Attica Rebellion. He was not at Attica at the time of the rebellion itself, but his earlier organizing provided the spark. The radical ideals that he fought for, prisoners had civil and human rights, incited a prison rebellion.

Contrary to prison officials' accounts which claimed that the so-called Attica prison "riot" had taken place because of a "gang of criminals" who took guards hostage for no good reason, the truth is New York State officials refused to listen to Sostre or even the federal courts, which over the years had ordered an end to brutality, racism, and mistreatment of the men inside. The prisoners took matters into their own hands, demanding human rights and an end to racist abuse with the 1971 rebellion, which shook America and the entire world.

MARTIN SOSTRE AND ME

I met Martin Sostre at the Federal Detention Center in New York City in August/September 1969. I had just been brought back to the USA from Berlin, Germany, for hijacking a plane to Cuba earlier that year. He had sued prison officials and been transferred to federal prison to await a court hearing. I didn't know who he was at the time, but someone said he was an activist prisoner and a jailhouse lawyer. They told me that I should talk to him.

A scowling, powerfully built Black man, he looked like a teacher, which in many ways he was, just a revolutionary teacher. So, I went up and introduced myself, and we started talking about prison generally. He was interested in my case and how the CIA had captured me, and we started talking about that. He was concerned that I could be sentenced to death by an all-white Southern jury.

He knew it was a political case, and so we talked about what I could do about it. Almost every day that I saw him, we would go over my case, and he would give me legal advice. Somewhere along the line, we started talking about revolutionary politics generally, and he bounced new words on me, Anarchist socialism. I had no idea what he was talking about at the time. I had just come from Cuba, Czechoslovakia, and East Germany, which called themselves socialist republics, so I thought I knew all about it. I was wrong. He explained self-governing socialism, which he described as free of state bureaucracy, any kind of party or leader dictatorship. Almost every day he regaled me about direct democracy, communitarianism, radical autonomy, general assemblies, and other stuff I knew nothing about. So I just listened for hours as he schooled me.

The initial ideas for Black Autonomy, within the overall Anarchist movement, came from these sessions. As a Black Puerto Rican, Sostre felt alienated from his community, and since much of the analysis about Black oppression and socialism was by white radicals, he had originally gravitated into Black nationalism. It was only later during his time in prison that he gravitated into Anarchist socialism. He told me endlessly that socialism and anarchism were for all people, not just Europeans and well-to-do intellectuals. It was universal. At first, I had serious doubts about all this, as it seemed just more white radical student ideology. They were not sympathetic to the Black struggle, and they were not working class or poor. Sostre's ideas, however, were that Anarchists of color must build their wing of the Anarchist movement. He didn't call it Black Autonomy, but that is what it was.

I did not even consider myself at the time as an Anarchist, and did not fully understand what he told me. But I had seen firsthand Soviet socialism and was not impressed. It was elitist, authoritarian, and oppressive. I could say the same thing about Marxist-Leninist Maoism, which helped to destroy the 1960s New Left and the radical wing of the Black Power movement, with a cult of personality, middle-class snobbery, manipulation, and opportunism.

Even before meeting Martin Sostre, I was definitely already looking for something new and willing to consider anarchism. He explained what that something was.

But only after a few years later, serving two life terms in prison, did I really start Anarchist political education in earnest. As Sostre suggested, I started reading Anarchist books and papers, and started corresponding with Anarchist figures and groups all over the world.

These discussions with Martin Sostre were invaluable in broadening my thinking about radical political alternatives. I also found out about many unknown revolutions in Africa, Russia, China, Spain and other parts of the world, as well as early Anarchist labor/radical tendencies among Eastern European immigrants, especially in the USA (1860s–1900s). The stickler is that the Anarchist movement generally had no ties or solidarity to the Black population in the USA, the UK or the colonized people of color in the Third World. It was essentially a white European movement for most of its history. I set out to do something about it.

Like Sostre had said, we must manufacture our own Anarchist of Color "school" of thought and revolutionary practice. Nobody can truly speak for us and fight in our name. Black Autonomy means independence of thought, culture and action. We are not racial separatists or ethnic purists, but we must be sure that we are strong enough to insist on our politics, leadership, and respect within any broader universal movement. We have been sold out, left out, betrayed, and tricked too many times by internal racism inside majority white coalitions and movements. Black voices matter!

Martin Sostre has been lost to history because the white left and Anarchist radical tendencies have had no regard for him or his legacy. He literally opened the doors for radical prisoners, Anarchist tendencies of color, and radical praxis. Yet not one institution or movement today is named after him. This is an outrage which must be recognized or corrected now.

I became an Anarchist, a jailhouse lawyer, and a prison activist during the 1970s because of Martin Sostre. In fact, it was a result of observing Martin's international defense committee and seeing how he was able to put pressure on the state government that encouraged me to create the Free Lorenzo movement, which resulted in my own freedom in 1984 from two life sentences. I owe him a tremendous personal debt. I spoke to him less than a month in a prison cell, but it changed my life. He had a similar impact on many others who never met him but benefitted from him standing up for their rights.

We don't have him here today in the flesh, but we can at least honor his memory and never let it die!

HOW I BECAME AN ANARCHIST AND WHY I WROTE THIS BOOK

I wrote *Anarchism and the Black Revolution* while a political prisoner at the maximum security hellhole prison in Marion, Illinois. The year was 1979, and I wanted to write a book with wholly new subject matter for Anarchist readers and Black activists. It was at the end of the Black Power era, and within a deep crisis for state socialist countries grouped around the Warsaw Pact military alliance with Russia, state socialism was starting to sputter and to die. After decades of Stalinism and statist repression, it ceased to have a reason to exist and was gone by 1991. I had seen this develop with my own eyes in 1969 after the invasion of Czechoslovakia in 1968, and I was on the run from the USA. One by one, countries withdrew from the Warsaw Pact. After the 1979 invasion of Afghanistan, which led to the end of the USSR, it was literally the beginning of the end for state socialism as a dominant political theory and formations of the left.

By 1979, I had been an Anarchist for a decade, stretching back to when I first met Martin Sostre. It was his influence at a time when I was looking for new radical theories and was totally disenchanted with American and European radicalism. I had been a Maoist, Black nationalist, and civil rights activist. I had seen them all crash and burn by 1969. Sostre opened my eyes to new possibilities with Anarchist communism in that New York City jail cell. Further, years after my political education with Martin, I continued my studies in every prison I was in. Even though I was sentenced to two life sentences and might have never gotten out of prison, I held fast to Anarchist political theory.

I even started to teach it to other prisoners, and started study groups to talk about it.

After I had been an Anarchist for ten years, it was time for me to speak up and try to challenge the whiteness and closet idealism of Anarchist thought and practice in the 1960s and 1970s.

So I wrote a pamphlet, *Anarchism and the Black Revolution*, that tried to change things and let Anarchists all over the world know that anarchism was not just a white European movement and theory. Certainly, I was one of the few Anarchists of color anywhere in the world. It was not just a matter of racist exclusion, but rather Anarchist movements simply didn't support Black radical and Civil Rights struggles, which had shaken the U.S. establishment to the bone.

Not surprisingly, Black activists did not join Anarchist groups due to the lack of recruitment activities of white Anarchists. Further, the white Anarchist groups were not too supportive of the stray Black Anarchist sympathizer who walked into their building. These groups seemed more inclined to discourage these participants. One thing I do know is that Black people won't just join hostile white activist spaces and will leave on their own when they discover them.

This is why years later, after I had been released from prison and had many frustrating years working with white Anarchist groups, I began to put my energies toward creating a Black Anarchist federation, the Black Autonomy Federation, which was founded in 1994 by myself, a group of Black college students at Clark College, and a few Black community activists in Atlanta, Georgia.

This small Black Anarchist federation organized in the city of Atlanta, and after a brief period spread to ten other cities which started chapters. Over the years, it eventually spread abroad to Canada, the UK, and had interest in Europe and Africa.

It was not greeted with open arms by white Anarchist tendencies. Anything but. We were accused of being anti-white, narrow race nationalists, and were subject to all manner of diatribes by many of the existing Anarchist collectives. Yet our group held on for a number of years despite the hostility and lack of support from the overall Anarchist movement. It is now even reorganizing, and making contacts with the new wave of Black Anarchists in 2021.

Sadly, I am being told, many old school Anarchist groups are still hostile to the new Black Anarchist groups, created within the last five years. Some of the young people in the Black anarchist "second wave" have complained about the inhospitable actions of many white Anarchists, much like I experienced after 1994 when we started our Black Anarchist federation. This will have to stop, and these white radical forces will have to get over it. Black Anarchist tendencies are here to stay.

I want to make this point here, the same as I did years ago. I am united with other Black Anarchists on the proposition that we have the right to be here as Anarchists, and to have our unique ideas heard. Even if you do not politically agree with us, we have the right to build the kind of Black autonomous tendencies as we'd like.

Historically, Russians, Italians, Lithuanians, Germans, Yiddish language Jews, and other European groups have freely built their own Anarchist and cultural tendencies in the USA. No one can then tell us that Black people cannot do the same. It should not even be an issue in 2021, except that too many of these white activists want to control the entire radical scene and lock Black Anarchists out or somehow delegitimize us. The Black Anarchists do not have to culturally conform to what white radical Anarchists or their groups would like us to be. Black Anarchists should be free to build their own movements and ideology. That is what motivated me in 1979 to write the first edition of this book and to create the first Black Anarchist federation.

Black Autonomy is the original ideology for Black anarchism. It is based on anarchism as libertarian socialism, rather than culture, lifestylism or individualism. The Black Autonomy Federation was formed in 1994 and was the first Black Anarchist federation ever formed in North America. Since it was the first to be created, it is the foundation of all Black Anarchist tendencies, even though an individual group may have their own beliefs and group structure. The original ideas have been outlined for over 40 years in my book.

TEN REASONS FOR THE CONTINUING IMPORTANCE OF ANARCHISM AND THE BLACK REVOLUTION[1]

Most important to me is the lasting relevance of the book. I had no idea that what was started as an 84-page stapled pamphlet in 1979 (the first edition of *Anarchism and the Black Revolution*) would be published three more times as separate editions. Why? It still speaks to many with new ideas, and it challenges orthodoxy in both society and the Anarchist movement to this day. This fourth edition (called the definitive edition) is being published by a major radical press, Pluto Press of the United Kingdom, rather than a small Anarchist collective or International Workers of the World (IWW) print shop, as was done with the editions up to this point. Now everything changes for the reach of the book, and many more will be able to read it.

The book, even as a small press edition by a collective, still managed to sell. I would take 200 copies at a time on one of my speaking tours,

---

1.   *Anarchism and the Black Revolution* was first published in 1979 and lasted until 1993, the 2nd edition came out in 1988 and lasted until 2008, the 3rd edition was published in 2012. This 4th edition is slated for October 2021. Each edition builds on the ideals of the last one, and is designed as political education for Anarchists and a form of counter logic to conventional wisdom found in political theory.

and sell every one at whatever price I wanted to. In addition, tens of thousands of copies were distributed free to prisoners. In all, if you count the editions sold over these years, over 10,000 were sold. That makes this book an underground bestseller, a classic work, and a book of long-term historical importance. I never dreamed that 42 years after its 1979 appearance, I would be putting it back in print in 2021 for a fourth time. Why would there be this much interest in a book of this sort?

1. *The book, from the first, has been political education for Anarchists.* This book is a full-throated defense of Anarchist communism, revolutionary syndicalism, and Black autonomous political ideas. It gives a rational explanation, in class terms, of what anarchism really stands for, rather than government, corporate, and authoritarian left propaganda and caricatures claim it is madness personified. Reading the book has always given a down-to-earth explanation of Anarchist principles, as well as the different factions of this broad-based theory.

2. *The book was the first one to raise Anarchist theory and politics in relation to the Black struggle.* Anarchism was strictly a white radical space before the book challenged the configuration and orientation of the movement as a whole and its dismissal of racism and oppression of Africans in America. There is no question about it. Racism was not even being discussed in Anarchist circles, and the clumsily organized anti-racist movements had no clue. Even the Anti-Racist Action and Antifa, later organized with Anarchist support, did not effectively deal with racism until this book (and myself as a highly vocal Black Anarchist critic) in their midst made them deal with it.

The decolonized political theory, which surfaced in Anarchist and radical circles during the contemporary period, can be partially credited to *Anarchism and the Black Revolution*, where an analysis of racism and internal colonialism first surfaced.

The reason the book was written in the first place was because there were no Black people in the Anarchist movement when I joined it. I was basically the only Black member in 1969 until the early 1980s. This was the beginning. If you really want to understand what I experienced, read the book.

3. *The book tried to create a more radical prison movement.* Because the book was written by an activist prisoner, rather than a detached middle-

class college professor, it was harsh, authentic, and gave a sharp focus on the prison system in this country. This book is one of the first to discuss the prison system as a tool of racist repression of Black people in America and a concentration camp of the poor.

Now, the USA has the largest prison system in world history, with enough prisoners (2.2 million) to become a nation in its own right. Yet, the Anarchist prison movement has never stopped to analyze the mass imprisonment today as a new form of attack by the state, and yet another step toward an outright fascist regime. More people are in prison today in the USA than all the past concentration camps run by bloody dictatorships in Mao's China and the Nazi or Stalinist concentration camps combined.

The Anarchist Black Cross (ABC) groups in North America have failed to build a militant fightback movement against mass incarceration, even though the book is literally a prison manual to guide prison activists to raise such issues. We Black Anarchists need to pressure the current Anarchist prisoner support movements into a fight against mass prison slavery as well as the abolition of prisons generally. These ABC groups in North America are still locked into the past, the political prisoner ideals of the 1970s and do not seem to realize that the world has changed. They cannot continue to split prisoner populations into *political* and *social* prisoners. This is a serious ideological error. They won't listen to me even though I have tried to explain it to them many times.

In the 1970s when I was in prison, there was still a revolutionary left anarchism wing and a powerful post-Attica mass prisoner support movement in the USA, Canada, and Europe. Because so many had seen the Attica Prison rebellion transpire and be bathed in blood by prison guards and state troopers, two things happened: (a) The majority of prisoners were radicalized and up in arms with their own struggles against racist and repressive prison conditions. (b) In cities and towns all over the country, there were now hundreds of thousands, if not millions, of prisoner rights supporters. At the time there were only 350,000 prisoners in the entire country. If we compare that to today's two million, we clearly can see that this deserves its own struggle at this time.

Mass imprisonment, racial profiling, and paramilitary policing have changed everything since that time. Millions are in prison. Now, ordinary Black and Latin X civilians are being gunned down in the streets over traffic stops and misdemeanor cases. The police have become a paramilitary death squad, just as the book and Black Autonomy explained and predicted would happen. It's clear that we need a new type of prison movement, one linked to the Black struggle and communities of color.

4. *The book created an Anarchist radical critique of authoritarian socialism at a deeper level, but more accessible than most Anarchist books, which were dry academic or even outdated.* It provided analysis of both Marxism and anarchism, making all complicated theories plain for the non-academic audience.

For example, it explained that although academic Marxists criticize the *natural violence* of anarchism, in point of fact their ideology has resulted in much more violence when it assumed control of the state. Leninist practice in Russia resulted in hundreds of thousands of workers dead or imprisoned as a result of their methods of dictatorship. They were not killed or imprisoned because they were counter-revolutionaries, but because they were political rivals or critics of the state. This *dictatorship of the people* believed in the primacy of the political party and naked state power, not the power of the people and their rights to freedom under socialism and communism. This is how Anarchists were outlawed and driven into exile, if not outright executed or imprisoned. Of course, Lenin was deeply authoritarian in his own right, but Stalin was even more brutal and established an outright cult of personality and party dictatorship. He even killed and imprisoned fellow party members.

This Stalinist regime resulted in the oppression, arrest, and murder of massive numbers of peasants and workers under the most authoritarian socialist regime. It was a literal reign of terror. This type of regime was run by the most soulless bureaucrats and secret police operatives. The Soviet state, which ruled over Russia for 70 years, was the main form of state socialism during the twentieth century and influenced most activists of that period.

Even though Anarchists ideally believed in anti-statism and opposed authoritarian socialism or communism, they had not developed deep political theories or strategies to combat it ideologically. The book gave it to them, all in one place, even placing Anarchist history and political ideals before young or inexperienced Anarchists.

The book was considered an Anarchist political science class, as one young reader told me. It allowed the book to do for others what had been done for me: open my eyes to political history, ideals, and to explain tasks I would otherwise not be exposed to.

The fact that anarchism is a broad-based theory, with many different factions, spokespersons, history, and beliefs really opened my mind in the early days and made me want more. Its long history as an alternate stateless form of self-governing socialism, as opposed to Marxist-Leninist-Maoism and its state socialism, made me understand how and why I had been lied to all these years. This was in the early stages of my political development, and I would never be the same.

This was especially the case when I read about Anarchist radical development and social revolutions in Spain, Russia, and other countries. When I read about the treachery of the Bolsheviks or Stalinists which put down burgeoning Anarchist social revolutions within larger revolutions, I finally understood. This taught me that state socialism with its stage of *people's dictatorship* could not be trusted to lead to any stateless socialism. Marxists have given lip service to a "withering away" stage when the state would be eradicated. In actual practice, there is no real evidence that they ever accepted anything but the primacy of the state. If it did not happen after 70 years of their political rule in Russia and other countries, we can best believe that it will never voluntarily happen. All we have now is dictatorships with some democratic features, like the right to go through the act of voting for whatever soulless bureaucrat administers the state. Authoritarian dictatorships can never lead to freedom, whether they are imposed from the left or right.

As an example, through my studies, I also learned that prison systems in all societies are just slavery by the state, and that most sections of the left in Western countries sought not to destroy the prisons, but instead would use them, if they should somehow obtain state power, against the mass of workers and the poor. We must prevent this entire tragic history of Leninist, Stalinist and Maoist cultism and political party rule from taking over the left again. We have to ideologically defeat such movements. We must save the people from falsely believing in the authoritarian form of socialism by making them see that it has bathed them in blood, hid them away in prisons, and imposed dictatorship instead of direct democracy.

5. *The book pushed cooperative radical politics which has influenced understanding of mutual aid today, especially for Black Anarchists in the urban core.* From the second edition onwards, the book talked about the Poor People's Survival Movement (PPSM) started in 1996, in both Atlanta, Georgia, and Chattanooga, Tennessee, to feed the poor, start

food cooperatives or a cooperative buying club to obtain organic, Kosher foods to give Black inner city families access to better food overall.

The PPSM was created by the Black Autonomy Network of Community Organizers (BANCO) to organize the poor to fight grocers and agribusinesses (corporate farming by rich white businesses). Through a series of articles in Black newspapers, the *Black Autonomy* magazine and mass meetings, we were also able to educate poor neighborhood programs to take membership in the PPSM to organize a fight to create an Atlanta Transit Riders Union and resist the city of Atlanta's Metro Atlanta Rapid Transit Authority from raising the transit fares, and eliminating routes in poor Black areas of the city, in an attempt to exploit riders from the inner city when the 1996 Olympics was held in Atlanta.

The book (and PPSM) campaigned for affordable inner city housing programs and worked with residents to prevent city officials from destroying Capitol Homes, a large downtown Atlanta housing project that real estate developers coveted. They wanted to gentrify the entire downtown area and drive poor people out.

The book was the first Anarchist publication that campaigned for radical community autonomous zones where it was "no go" for cops and other government agents. The book openly agitated for armed expropriation of government financial resources, in addition to steady pressure to win our demands over the long term.

More than anything, the book discussed using such a strategy to try to build a survival program as the foundation of a pre-revolutionary or stateless socialist economy. To build a consideration of such an alternate economy, it is necessary to project it in an actual urban environment. In the essay "Let's Organize the 'Hood: Urban Inner City Programs," the book discusses methods of building local mutual aid programs and food survival programs, including a trucking and distribution cooperative.

This was a decade before they appeared in 2020 during the COVID-19 pandemic and actually began to reach millions of unemployed poor people. Mutual aid today, just like the original survival programs of the BPP in the 1960s, is not a form of charity that emanates from the rich or the government. It is about unity, self-determination, and resistance to the system that makes us poor and wrecks our communities.

Today's radical mutual aid is just a road map to radical economic policies which can lead us to Anarchist socialism, which is a form of self-governing stateless socialism. It is a door to a new form of economy if we keep building and engaging in widespread struggle. Of course, we must build our campaigns in the cities. The possibilities are there during this crisis.

The U.S. economic system is in collapse, and millions of people are suffering from lack of basic human needs. As a result, all over the world, activists are serving their neighbors, community, or cities, especially senior citizens, the chronically ill, and urban poor communities. An entire radical service network has arisen due to the lockdowns, unemployment, and sickness from the virus. Yet, it is just the disaster stage of capitalism, not a fatal collapse. Capitalism will not die. It must be killed by the masses of its victims.

Working and poor people will have to organize and fight back. We need such a movement to be autonomous, and its fight for community economic development must be based on community control of the economy and all social life. This cannot be used to empower the government, bankers or non-profit front groups. The poverty pimps associated with the system are always present to sell us out or to try to convince us that we no longer have to fight. Community control of industry and of utilities has to place self-management power in the hands of the people until total power can be obtained through self-governing socialism over the whole of society.

But don't believe any of this will happen just because we want it to. We will have to organize and fight hard for it. We will have to create and train groups of revolutionary community organizers like the Black Panther Party did in the 1960s (which, although not an Anarchist group, was an autonomous mass radical tendency). We will have to create people's general assemblies to bring the poor and workers together so they can massively decide on such matters in urban areas and suburbs of low-income communities. Mutual aid programs created during the pandemic can be further developed into a transitional survival economy,

Instead of the rich profiting from our misery, we can build local and regional programs to rebuild our communities and force the government to provide our communities with unrestricted funds under total community control until we can build our own financial base. We can even call this reparations if we choose to do so.

This capitalist crisis of 2020–21 can only be resolved fully by socialism, but until then we can begin to build survival programs pending revolution, as put forth by the original Black Panther Party and other movements historically.

We will have to fight those in power by any means necessary as they will not voluntarily relinquish resources or power. At every juncture we must seek to put power and control in the hands of the people directly, not government bureaucrats, police agencies, city politicians, or entrepreneurs.

Especially at a time of even more entrenched white supremacist politics and violence, we must create a counterweight, just as we did in the 1960s: Defend yourself and your community with a *Black Partisan* militia as part of a general revolution.

It is clear that the state is wedded to the capitalist model, and that activists and poor communities need to adopt community control of utility services and industries. This community control has to be based on a radical Anarchist survival program not to just fill in for the state's failures to provide adequate programs or services or corporate greed but to create a radical program to prefigure a survival economy. It is not socialism yet, but it certainly opens the door for socialism to be built.

If the government or corporations will not do it, the movement must create a new public sector entirely to meet the needs of the people. This can be done by taking over existing institutions or by creating something totally new.

Radical Anarchists are anti-capitalists by nature, with anarchism referred to historically as libertarian socialism or Anarchist socialism, that is, all without the state or a statist corporation.

Total Anarchist socialism would mean the destruction of the capitalist system itself and can be created by social revolution, spontaneously or in transitional stages. We do not know how it will be imposed exactly. We just know it will not be given to us or arise on its own. We will have to fight and defeat the rich and their institutions while in the process of creating a new society, including a new economy for people's needs, rather than for profit.

Here is the two-page handbook for community based mutual aid:

Mutual Aid and Organizing 101

A. Empower communities to meet their own needs, and build community control. We must begin to solve our own social problems. Rather than charity from the rich, we are starting grassroots survival programs that the poor people can take over themselves. The main thing is no longer relying on external structures (like government or corporate foundations) to solve problems. They controlled us in the past but no more.

- A mutual aid program starts with addressing material needs and may grow into collective action and grassroots organizing, building long-term trust, dual power and direct democracy. We especially need to understand how to build a neighborhood general assembly in opposition to city hall politicians and the government structure itself.
- We are opposed to corporate non-profits, capitalist banks, politicians and government, major business corporations, and inherited wealth. These forces have always benefitted from our poverty and misery and are part of the structure that oppresses us.
- Organizing is not just "issue" activism or protesting poverty but constructing mutual aid and survival programs to feed, house or serve poor and working people facing life altering or life threatening conditions. Issues come and go, but the community is still there.
- Mutual aid is inherently antiauthoritarian, bringing us together on equal terms to solve the problems of the community, society, and our lives. It puts power in our hands instead of the elite.

LET'S ORGANIZE THE 'HOOD MUTUAL AID: HOW TO DO IT

Neighbor-based Organizing

Do research on urban area neighborhoods, including low income suburbs. If it's your neighborhood, all the better. Since you can't organize the whole city, you should choose a name and geographical boundary.

Create an outreach program—electronically and through flyering. Do old school door to door organizing.

Stay Connected with activists and the community. Have meetings and other get-togethers.

Bring folks together in the mutual aid organizing group using technology.

Keep checking in with organizers to see how they are holding up and if they need any specific help right now.

How are you going to get involved?

You and/or your group have to decide what kind of organizing you are willing to commit to and the best way to find out is ask the people what they need or research the conditions of the community historically.

6. *The book made one of the first radical critiques of the existing Black social justice movement which came after the Civil Rights and Black Power eras.* Beginning with the publication of the second edition of the book, a class analysis of the movements by the author exposed the petty bourgeois nature of the leadership forces dominating the 1980s post-Civil Rights movements: Jesse Jackson, Al Sharpton, and others, which led to a more conservative and politically controlled movement, which continues to this day.

These forces were in bed with the left liberal wing of the Democratic Party. In 1986, with the passage by Congress of the new tax code, charitable foundations were freed to pour money into so-called social justice movements of the left, to continue the mop-up operation against 1960s militant left movements and replace them with more moderate, pro-government elements. This campaign included outright corporate donations and financing by numerous foundations of protest groups in the 1960s. These new groups were totally hostile toward militant, anti-capitalist groups of the 1960s and the 1970s.

Although during the 1960s there had been charitable and corporate financial donations to civil rights groups, these funds could never totally control civil rights groups like they later could in the 1980s and onwards down to this period. Now we are talking about political pimp groups totally dependent on corporate grants for their entire budgets. The political approach of the new movements was based upon what the corporate foundations wanted, not what the Black community wanted from such a movement.

Since 2013 and the founding of the Black Lives Matter (BLM) movement by three Black women activists, Alicia Garza, Patrisse Cullors, and Opal Tometi, the group has dominated protests against police terrorism of Black communities. They created the first mass national movement against murderous police violence since the 1966 founding of the Black Panther Party, the October 22nd movement of 1996, and the present Anarchist-created International Day Against Police Brutality founded in 1997.

Black Lives Matter and the Black Panther Party were two totally different organizations. The Black Panther Party was founded as a Black community armed militia, which after the first year became a revolutionary political party. The BPP did not live off of corporate grants or function as a Democratic Party front group. It fought for revolutionary socialism and a radical form of Black nationalism.

The BPP was an anti-establishment movement from inception, and though it later made political errors, it did not sell out to capitalist grants and donations like Black Lives Matter has clearly done. Although Black Lives Matter, with its grassroots base, has fought a radical fightback in this period, its misleadership and founders have undermined them at every turn.

In 2021, all of this came to a head with a massive scandal of $90 million in corporate donations allegedly mishandled by Black Lives Matter leadership. These funds were given to Black Lives Matter to stave off the 2020 nationwide protests over the televised police lynching of George Floyd in Minneapolis on May 25, 2020. Those protests involved a reported 15–25 million people and terrified the entire ruling class. Reportedly, 2,500–3,000 cities in the USA and worldwide saw such protests, and neither the cops nor the military could stop them, despite brutality and repression. Although most corporations had said nothing about the police murders and brutality of thousands of Black people over decades, they overnight suddenly declared themselves an ally of Black Lives Matter and financed the movement to the tune of $90 million. This was bribery, but the donations were made nevertheless and accepted by the leadership. The controversy has erupted over the alleged mismanagement of these donations, especially after it became known that Patrisse Cullors, a Black Lives Matter leader and founder, owned four homes that she bought in recent years.

We can only look at all this as corporate control of left liberal forces, and their continuing to do the bidding of major corporations, high-ranking Democratic Party leaders, and the foundations who underwrite them. Corporations see the job of Black Lives Matter leadership as to take control of these protest campaigns and ensure they will not become ungovernable. Demand "radical" reforms, yes, but not revolution.

The purpose of the corporate-funded movements in this period is to prevent another period like the 1960s. The ruling class will use the iron fist (of the police and military) and the velvet glove (of liberal politicians and their social justice groups) depending on circumstances. That is the leadership of Black Lives Matter in this period, taking on the mantle of other poverty or political pimps from the past.

I am not saying that everyone in Black Lives Matter is corrupt, or on the take. I am especially saying that the grassroots activists have done good work, and have not mismanaged funds like the national leadership has apparently done. These contradictions usually signal the collapse. I don't think this group can survive this scandal and political split. The group may have done its entire program in 20 years. I don't know. The NAACP has been around for a century and has been a husk of itself since the 1960s.

We clearly need a new type of Black anti-cop and anti-fascist movement, with genuine revolutionary ideals about transforming society and dismantling racial capitalism. We need revolutionary Black Autonomy/ anarchism leading us to stateless socialism, not more reforms.

Some activists propose an alternative to Black Lives Matter: community control of the police. But I say lipstick on a pig shows us reformism will not win and won't stop police murder of Black people.

The BPP and its 1968 Community Control of the Police (CCP) referenda process was a failure in Berkeley, California. Over the years since that time, various radical or liberal demands raising these types of reforms also failed all over the country. Criticism surfaced in the 1960s and 1970s that CCP was a useless political demand amounting to lipstick on a pig, but it persists due to the idealism of the left-liberals.

Why does it keep failing? The capitalist political establishment supports the murderous actions of the police, which makes prosecution of the police almost impossible and reform a fascist joke.

The police now have their own unions and the support of police foundations, which makes it impossible to make any significant reforms despite public outrage. They pressure the politicians and local government to go along with their fascist program.

Neither CCP, Defund the Police, and other demands can be won at a time when the government continues to give the police full impunity to commit their murderous crimes. For leftists to give the political authorities the right to offer their so-called reforms to city hall is just another false hope. They will likely give us an even worse outcome: an autonomous police authority controlled by the police agencies themselves, which are totally immune to civilian control and which give total impunity to police crimes. The police are a white supremacist death squad, not a law enforcement agency for the good of society.

A third position exists to oppose both the reform camps of defunding the police and CCP: Black anti-fascism. In the 1960s Black anti-fascism was personified by the BPP throughout its existence. They taught us that police can only be disbanded during or after a revolution, not by reform legislation from the government. Black people are fighting against state-sponsored racial genocide, not just suppression of civil rights. Black community-based armed self-defense; anti-capitalism and building a socialist society; a transitional survival economy to feed the people; community control over utilities and public corporations; and the end to police state fascism and racist vigilante and militia groups lay the foundation to widespread anti-capitalist resistance.

After the defeat of the 1968 electoral CCP campaign in Berkeley, California, the BPP held a mass conference in 1969 which created a Black-led anti-fascist movement, the National Committee to Combat Fascism (NCCF), for both solidarity and anti-fascist activism. They seemed to have learned from the earlier electoral error. Unfortunately, it was too late to save the BPP from police and FBI repression, which ultimately destroyed the movement. However, the NCCF does provide us with another example of resistance.

We can still build a broad-based anti-police movement as the BPP did in the 1960s, but we need to understand that police terrorism is not just misbehavior by bad cops, but that they are death squads doing the bidding of the rich. We are now at the stage of civil war and revolution, past that of protests. Protests now, even radical protests, are just a form of radical democracy, an attempt to work within the system. It will not work, and cannot transform this racist society.

THE BOOK WAS THE FIRST TO CRITIQUE
WHITE RADICAL ANTI-FASCISM

7. *The usual definition of fascism is of Mussolini's corporate state, the merger of capital and labor under centralized state control.* Yet, fascism's development is not the same in all countries, and every authoritarian regime is not a fascist government. Some regimes have had a racist government and a virtual dictator but were not part of the international fascist movement. It seems that the development of fascist regimes is built on the basis of a particular nation-state at a certain point in history, and depended on the crisis conditions of world history at that time. For instance, the capitalist Great Depression of the 1930s created the conditions for fascism in a number of countries, such as Germany and Italy, but again was not successful in every nation-state during that time.

The deep economic crisis and other social conditions, along with other factors such as racism and nationalism, also fueled fascist movements in countries that they were not able to successfully take power in, even though they had a mass base. It even happened in the USA, which had the fascist Ku Klux Klan and the German-American Bund during the 1920s and 1930s, who could not seize power despite building mass pro-fascist movements containing millions.

Most importantly with my analysis, the liberal left social commentators in the USA and other countries have created an anti-fascist mythology based on a racist fallacy. This fallacy states that because whites are not subjected to the kind of economic pillage or ethnic and racial persecution as historically had happened to colonized peoples in Africa, Asia or Latin America, it was only fascism when it happened to Europeans. This exceptionalism is why anti-fascist ideology is linked to such a degree to the European history of the 1920s to the 1940s, and historical crimes by their colonial governments is redefined or excused. This has been used by many commentators to say, in practice, if not in words: "It's only fascism when it happens to white people."

For many years in the colonial departments of the major Western imperialist powers, Britain, Germany, France and the USA, there was a long history of slavery, genocide, waging aggressive wars, brutal colonialism, and other policies more brutal than Hitler's crimes against Europeans leading up to World War II. Most of the liberal left commentators don't want to recognize this suffering by non-whites because they don't want to equally humanize Africans in the Congo, Namibia, or other colonized peoples also killed in the tens of millions, forced into slave labor, starved and systematically brutalized for Western capitalist enterprises or colonial power like those Europeans killed in World War II.

African descended residents in the USA and other Western countries have historically been murdered by lynch mobs and are still routinely mass murdered by either police or vigilantes today. They have been robbed for centuries of their labor, debased as human beings, and worked to death on slave plantations, in prisons, or factories. They disproportionately live in poverty in the USA, the UK, and other countries, because of racial discrimination and capitalist exploitation. Those countries were only enriched and fully developed because of New World slavery and their colonial exploitation of Africa, Asia and Latin America. There are still many white radical tendencies that deny this.

Black people understand that when it comes to fascism, we are fighting against racial genocide, new forms of colonialism, and hyper-exploitation of our labor in prisons, which is the new form of slavery by the state. It is not just a question of only ending prison as an institution, but ending all form of slavery permitted by the state and capitalist definitions of criminality. We are also fighting against the mass psychology and ideology of fascism, which gives rise to the white supremacy beliefs so widespread in the USA.

It's not an academic or political debate. We are being systematically killed today, and neither the cops nor the government will take any action on our behalf to stop it. For those of us who are Black libertarian socialists, we have to not just fight against capitalism; we have to fight for the lives of ourselves and our own people as an oppressed group. We need to build our own self-defense organizations if we are to even survive attacks by cops, racists, and fascist militias in this period. Black people are routinely brutalized, colonized, starved, murdered, and singled out for all manner of terror by the state and vigilantes. Left liberals call it denial of civil rights, discrimination, or "systemic racism," the latter of which seems to be in vogue right now.

In the USA, the white radicals don't want to recognize that it is the political state, which was founded as a white racist republic and slave empire, which provided the foundations of American capitalism. This is why nothing fundamentally changed in mainstream political opposition among American white radical anti-fascists in 2020 despite massive numbers of protesters. Why? White supremacy is not just "bad ideas" swimming around the heads of white people. It is a system built on the economic exploitation and oppression of Africans in America and of other oppressed peoples of color.

Today's milquetoast radicalism by the liberal left as an activist front within the Democratic Party is a real thing. Because they are still linked to reformism or electoral politics, these people are demanding the defunding of the police agencies and other reforms, with no hope of that happening, short of a civil war or revolution. It is the corporations buying time and the government giving cops license to commit their crimes, while still pretending they care about civil rights.

Black people cannot depend on the police, government, or white radicals to defend us. We must defend ourselves against all forms of fascist repression, whether from the state, corporations, or fascist paramilitary forces. When they roll in on our communities, we have to be able to turn them back and create a permanent "no-go" zone for cops and neo-fascists by any means necessary. This is a life and death struggle for Black people and the poor. We still don't know what the white workers would do to help defend us, even though they mobilized in May 2020.

For Black people in America, so-called African Americans, we must say that we have been building toward this moment when the only choices have been socialism or barbarism, genocide or complete freedom, for a long time. It's obvious that a new Black anti-fascist tendency beyond white radicalism is in order. We will call it All Power to the People, and will unite all forces of every race and nationality to join us to beat back fascism.

We must make choices in our own interests, not because someone tells us that we have to follow them because only the white radicals have all the answers, or that they are born to rule over us: the inferior people and the despised class. We need a new mass anti-fascist movement which will be more militant than either Antifa or Black Lives Matter. We need to correctly identify the capitalist state, corporations, and the government as constituting the greatest danger of the fascist threat, rather than either fascist street punks or the Republican Party alone. Then we must form a mass coalition to smash them all!

8. *The book is based upon the Black radical tradition, Black activism, and resistance.* It's about anarchism, yet it's "colorized." The book always has included a different way of thinking about anarchism that makes us think of radicalism as extending beyond Eurocentrism and the white working class, to dealing with the oppressed and colonized Blacks and other peoples of the world as a central force.

From the very beginning in 1979, *Anarchism and the Black Revolution* recognized that slavery and the slave system built America, and that slavery was the antecedent and the foundation of capitalism. It was a recognition that slave and colonial labor had long been ignored as a major factor, if not misunderstood by Anarchist activist groups or institutions.

The book forces the condition of Black people upon the Anarchist movement, just as Black people have forged their own movements to resist and win power for their people. It has refused the subjectivity and obscurity of Blacks in an intellectual ghetto. Black Autonomy says: We won't be pushed into the side pockets of white radicals, and we won't wait to fight for our own freedom.

I am not an academic or a traditional intellectual, nor am I a Marxist, but I accept much of Cedric Robinson's critique of Marxist ideology, derived from Marx himself. Racial capitalism, as Robinson defines it, is a much deeper critique of Marx's entire radical perspective of the white working class as a revolutionary force. Robinson exposed it as Eurocentric, even chauvinistic. The plantation economy was the backbone of capitalism, not European labor.[2]

True, I had accepted Marx's theory of "primitive accumulation" in stating that slavery was the "pedestal" upon which capitalism rested, even though I accepted little else. However, Cedric Robinson went much further by saying capitalism itself is based on a racist regime. Further, he pointed out that Marx almost wholly ignored the non-European historical models. Thus, colonial oppression, the middle passage, and the history of slavery was glossed over, as was the predicament of Black workers by Marx's followers. In talking about the American Civil War, Marx made an attempt to talk about slavery in the USA and gave another rather weak perspective, not championing Black Liberation, but rather an integrated, white-led movement for socialism. This is the usual white radical approach even today of the white working-class hero: "Follow me and I'll set you free!" Contrary to the entire Eurocentric ideology and the revolutionary social practices of the white radicals, Blacks have had their own struggles, not as an adjunct of the white working-class struggle, but fighting for our own liberation and conceptions of a socialist society.

It has been a reflection that Black people cannot wait on white people to emerge as meaningful allies before beginning to fight for our liberation. From the beginning of the white slavers' republic called the USA, we could not blindly accept the idea that white people in any large numbers would fight next to us in solidarity if we did not first build our own movement. There have been few historical examples of this happening on its own. We had to fight, whether on the slave ship, in the penitentiary, or in the racist society, to prevent our lynching in the past or our murder by the police today, which carry out the same function as the lynchers.

We have built our own movements and embarked on resistance campaigns worldwide from the beginning to the present day. If we did not speak up or rise up against slavery, segregation, colonialism, or other forms of oppression, nobody would on our behalf, whether Marx or

---

2.   Cedric J. Robinson, *Black Marxism*, Zed, London, 1983.

any other white people. Of course, some did, like radical anti-slavery guerrilla, John Brown, who died for the anti-slavery cause, the result of the Harpers Ferry, Virginia, raid on a military depot to obtain arms for a slave revolt.

When the Civil War began in 1861, the Union intervention only became a full-fledged anti-slavery and revolutionary civil war when over 100,000 Blacks enlisted and fought on the Union side. In fact, Lincoln would not have won that war against the South, organized as the Confederate States of America, without those Black troops. They fought for and won their own liberation against slavery, not to preserve the Union. This is just an historical example.

The white left still refuses to recognize our right to build autonomous radical movements. True to form, every so often a white radical organization will criticize the Black Panther Party of the 1960s because it referred to the urban lumpen proletariat as its base, as if this dismisses its entire legacy. The error here is that Marx's bias against the European super-poor of his day would not even apply to Blacks in the USA. These Black urban lumpen forces were not just retrograde elements, déclassé, vagrants, or gangsters. They were instead workers subjected to permanent unemployment and systemic poverty. Black workers were always on the bottom due to the legacy of slavery, racial discrimination, internal colonialism and even super-class exploitation resulting in mass imprisonment today. There has never been equal employment or equal rights under capitalism for Black people. I think Cedric Robinson is absolutely right by labeling capitalism as a racial project not limited to the white working-class experience.

Even the majority white labor unions had engaged in racial discrimination for many years: blocking union memberships, not supporting Black workers for union posts, functioning for years as white job trusts, even encouraging violent racist acts by white workers. Only after the rise of the Civil Rights and Black Power movements became unstoppable did many unions begin to relent in the 1970s. Yet, the white left then and now continues to pretend that it is the labor unions which are the backbone of a radical workers' movement, if it could just be reformed or radicalized. Some claim that unions are a class vanguard. This nonsense about these business unions is just another example of leftist lack of political logic. The trade unions will not lead a revolution, nor will they be part of a non-capitalistic society. They can fight for workers' rights and working conditions under capitalism now. Once again, this familiar concept of the white working-class hero is used over and over by white radicals to justify domination of social change movements. This means what is projected as universal liberation is sectarian activism and opportunism.

What changed the white-dominated labor unions was not just civil rights legislation or lawsuits, but during the 1960s Black auto workers in Detroit and other cities formed their own labor unions and Black caucuses to fight racism and class discrimination in their plants. They are hardly talked about by white radicals, but these workers organized into the League of Revolutionary Black Workers, and were the backbone of the unauthorized strike waves against Ford and other corporations, and challenged the corruption of the United Auto Workers union. They were not long-lasting but were as significant in the 1960s as the IWW or the anarcho-syndicalists of their day.

I am not opposed to united struggle, but it must be based on principled solidarity. The ideals of solidarity are distorted and cynically subverted if they are not led by the oppressed peoples of color themselves at the center of the struggle. The Black radical tradition just means that Black people and other peoples of color have had to fight against slavery, genocide, capitalist exploitation, police terror, and other crimes of the state, whether white workers united with them or not. We have to understand and celebrate our autonomous struggles, whether white activists ever do.

Over the course of 500 years in the USA, Brazil, Oceania, and Africa, and during the current internal colonialism in the West, Black people have fought, built communities of resistance, alternate cultures, and many fightback movements against racial capitalism in all its forms. Yes, this entire system is racist and must be dismantled. We can dismantle racial capitalism and the white racist republic which calls itself the United States of America. Our lives depend on our struggles. We have to push anarchism, Marxism and all radical political tendencies to support our Black struggles and tendencies, whether inside or outside their ranks.

I am not here to save America or anarchism as a white radical movement. I am one of the gravediggers of capitalism, of which there are millions more born and fighting each day. Black anarchism is part of the Black radical tradition.

9. *Anarchism as a Mass Movement for Direct Democracy and Dual Power.* Anarchists need a practical way to challenge capitalism and government and the institutions they use to maintain power. It is not as simple to function as a mere propaganda society, but rather a mass movement

made out of ideals like Anarchist direct democracy and dual power as a competitor to electoral politics and representative government.

If anarchism is going to ascend to the next stage, then it must assume political relevance in the lives of masses of people. We need to go beyond protest to ungovernability, and then build neighborhood general assemblies to take us onward to libertarian socialism. If not, we'll be trapped in conventional politics and reformism.

To me, one of the most exciting and serious features of anarchism is urban general assemblies as an alternative to the existing political state and a way to radically educate and mobilize the people on a broad scale. The cities have tremendous opportunity as a testing ground, even the possibility that they can be subverted to mass urban communes.

In the USA, the Anarchist movement has not taken this road and is currently mired in protests as primary acts of resistance. In my mind, this is problematic.

I have said for many years that although we must resist and fight the state, we cannot forever be captured in the stage of protest. We must build libertarian socialism as a stage to a whole new society of Anarchist communism. We have to challenge and defeat layers of the state all the way. Even though we have to enter into a long-term period of ungovernability, we have to present a plan to broad layers of the people in order to draw them into the struggle. Macho radical posturing is not enough, nor is sectarian dogma. You've got to have programs for freedom, not just an ideological cult or a club, to put power into the hands of the people.

Every radical talks about socialism, but we have to talk about socialism as freedom, not another strait-jacket or pair of handcuffs. Stateless socialism is self-governing socialism by the people themselves, not by a dictator, political party, or a rich class of rulers like we have now. Let's organize in the streets and communities to make it happen!

CONCLUSION

10. *I was an Anarchist before anarchism was (suddenly) cool.* It amazes me how over recent years a cultural trend has started where damn near everybody is calling themselves an Anarchist today. I have even heard of prosecuting attorneys who are allegedly Anarchists. I'm not here to tell you that they are not people with firmly held beliefs. I'm just saying that when popular culture unites with political theory, almost anything is possible, good or bad.

For over 150 years, anarchism has been held in scorn, fear, and almost total social disapproval by governments, corporations, and political rivals. Yet a subculture of white youth, accompanied by punk rock and other musical forms sustained and encouraged the genre for several decades, after it almost went extinct as a political movement. Combat boots, black hoodies, and black jeans added to the more modern illusion of the black-robed bomb thrower from the distant past. Yet, much of that is a mere illusion, culture shock.

None of that attracted me to anarchism, and I'll tell you why: I am not concerned with lifestylism or radical chic culture as much as over-turning capitalist society with social revolution. But the actual ideals of anarchism are less known than its style in this period.

For over 50 years since I have been an Anarchist, I have seen style dominate political substance generally, especially in North America during the 1960s and 1970s. Anarchism was totally dominated by middle-class forms of white radicalism. The Yippies were just one of the Anarchist tendencies that existed in that period. They were radical satirists, pranksters, as well as radical lifestylists. Personally, I loathed these types of groups, and were it not for meeting Martin Sostre and then receiving his daily Anarchist political education lectures, I would likely not ever have been attracted to anarchism at all.

To me, political ideology was about political education, and life and death struggles. It was always about class warfare and fighting "the man," as the representation of the power struggle. It should be no great surprise that my first analysis about anarchism is related to power structure research, more precisely, the analysis of prisons, social control, and racism. Without seeing state power and prison firsthand, I may never have known the mortal dangers of nation-statism.

When I got into prison, I started immediately writing articles about prisons for the various Anarchist and prisoner rights publications, and more importantly, for the Anarchist groups all over the world. I needed, and found, an explanation for why the government was consistently locking up young Black men like myself. After reading and correspond-ing with Anarchist groups and individuals worldwide, I found my commitment to fight state terror as an Anarchist.

This communication with Anarchists internationally was crucial in breaking my isolation from the outside and giving me an education in Anarchist theories that I could never get in a state college at the time. The authorities would dismiss it as mere mindlessness, misdirected violence, or chaos. But because of popular culture, even that has now changed. There is a new-found acceptance of Anarchist ideology. For the last 25 years, there has been an actual course of Anarchist studies for students in universities all over the world. This is, of course, a good thing if it is used to break up the simplistic lies, distortions, propaganda, and slandering of its adherents and leading figures by politicians, governments and other authoritarians worldwide. The history of anarchism would make a compelling subject, even if it has been distorted by authority figures or political rivals everywhere. It is so powerful that no amount of condemnations and hated rhetoric have been able to kill it.

I was taught Anarchist theory by Martin Sostre in prison, rather than a college or a university. Yet, the effect was still the same. It raised my consciousness to new heights and filled me with confidence. It replaced my doubts and false beliefs with clarity and understanding. It would be great if prisoners and university students could be told the real history and ideals of this broad-based theory without fear or statist lies. Some of the greatest intellectuals of the world have been Anarchists. It's not just nihilists or terrorists in the ranks.

In fact, most violence is performed by governments and other radical tendencies like nationalism or Marxism. Hitler was not an Anarchist. Neither were the warmongers who started World Wars I or II, which killed hundreds of millions of people. Neither the American CIA or the Russian KGB is an Anarchist group. A very small history of Anarchist individual violence has been used to slander the entire 150-year-old movement. These Anarchist studies could be used to correct and expand the record, as well as deepen the appreciation of the movement.

I would like to see Anarchist studies be made into a major field of study, but it needs to include the work of Black Anarchists and the works of Anarchists of color. In general, work by academics needs to be redefined to include self-taught intellectuals and independent thinkers like myself and others who have produced a body of work like this book. Activists must have a voice, not just academics. It is important that such autodidacts have the ability to interact with traditional university lecturers. I believe without such equal contacts and memberships in Anarchist studies associations, we will just reinforce professional and class snobbery. That's what's wrong with academia and capitalistic educational culture in the first place.

Like many radical organizations and intellectuals, it was a life of oppression and fightback which produced myself and any intellectual gifts I may have. The ability to understand a racist society and provide rationale for resistance against it was something I had at a young age. Also being held in inferior status, and then it largely being assumed by the "master race" that I had no such intellectual ability and could only be a slave, made me highly motivated to learn, whether traditional schooling gave it to me or not. Whatever I learned would be used as a weapon against the state and white supremacy.

The fact that I am an Anarchist is not coincidental. My entire previous life led me here, and I have tried to make the largest impact I could. This book, *Anarchism and the Black Revolution*, is my life's work. This book first came out 42 years ago. I never dreamed that I would be talking about its contents and relevance in 2021. I never expected to even live this long. Whatever intellectual breakthroughs or errors there are in the book can be attributed to the mind of a living, breathing Anarchist dealing with life's twists and turns and the desire for universal freedom. We all make mistakes when dealing with complicated theories, but without critical thinking we can't move forward.

Now, Black anarchism is one of the hottest radical tendencies in the whole Anarchist movement, and anarchism is now the most popular movement of the left. It drew the ire of the fascist former U.S. President Donald Trump, who threatened to put New York City and other cities under martial law because they were considered to be "Anarchist jurisdictions" and were out of control. He even sent fascist thugs and stormtroopers to shoot up Portland, Oregon, and lock people up at random. It's crazy, but we are seeing all kinds of things, and we have just gotten started. My prediction is all the racist and oppressive stuff that has been used against Black people for years and years will now be used against white people as well to keep this system in power.

Where we go from here, I don't know. Anarchists are not soothsayers or mind readers, but we are not going away either. We are part of it, and will see it through to the end.

Love and struggle, and hope you enjoy reading the book.

Power to the People.

1

Anarchism Defined: A Tutorial on Anarchist Theory and Practice

The popular impression of an Anarchist—as a person or group of individuals as "bomb throwers" only interested in destruction for its own sake and opposed to all forms of organization and society—persists to this day. Further, the belief that Anarchy is chaos, a reign of rape, murder and total disorder, is widely believed by the public. That is really nihilism, something very different from anarchism, a doctrine of social progress and transformation.

Because these lies have been consciously promoted for years, such impressions are believed. All who aspire to oppress, exploit and gain power will always be threatened by anarchism because Anarchists uphold struggle against authority and coercion. To Anarchists, a capitalist "democratic" government is no better than a fascist or communist regime since the ruling class only differs in the violence it authorizes the police and army to use and the degree of rights to allow, if any. In fact, Anarchists want to get rid of the greatest perpetrator of violence throughout history: governments. Through war, repression, social neglect and political repression, governments have killed millions of people, whether trying to defend or overthrow a government. Anarchists want to end this slaughter and build a society based on peace and freedom.

The aim of this chapter is to discuss the major elements of Anarchist thought and to give examples of what some Anarchists think. Anarchists and anarchism have historically been misrepresented to the world.

WHAT IS ANARCHISM?

Anarchism is free or libertarian socialism. Anarchists are opposed to government, the state and capitalism. Therefore, simply speaking, anarchism is a non-governmental form of socialism called libertarian socialism.

In common with all Socialists, the Anarchists hold that the private ownership of land, capital and machinery has had its time; that it is condemned to disappear and that all requisites for production must and will become the common property of society and be managed in common by the producers of wealth.

—*Anarchist-Communism: Its Basis and Principles,*
by Peter Kropotkin[1]

Feminism, Black Liberation, gay rights, the ecology movement and others have lent new awareness to the philosophy of anarchism over recent years. Such influence has helped advance anarchism as a social force in modern society. These influences ensure that social revolution will be as all-encompassing and democratic as possible and that all people will be fully liberated, rather than just affluent, straight, white males steeped in the dogma of the last century alone.

There are different types of Anarchists with many points of agreement and disagreement. Principal debates between Anarchists relate to forms of organization and strategies. For instance, significant differences concern the economic organization of future society. Some Anarchists reject money and substitute a system of trade in which work is exchanged for goods and services. Others reject all forms of trade or barter or private ownership as capitalism and believe all major property should be owned in common.

There are Anarchist groups opposed to violence, advocating pacifism and non-violent direct action. Some accept it only in self-defense or during a revolutionary insurrection. In addition, there are those who believe in guerrilla warfare, including assassination, bombings, bank expropriations, etc., as a means of revolutionary attack on the state. Yet, there also are Anarchists who believe almost exclusively in organizational, labor or community work. Some are animal rights activists, some do prison support work and others are feminists. There is no single type, nor do they all agree on strategy and tactics.

Anarchists believe social revolution is the process through which a free society will be created.

Let me point out a social revolution is wholly different from a political revolution. In the former, the issue is to put the people in command.

---

1. Peter Kropotkin, *Anarchist-Communism: Its Basis and Principles,* Freedom House, London, 1913.

In the latter, the leadership commands the people. Anarchists believe people themselves must be in command, not leaders. Self-management will be established in all areas of social life, including the right of all oppressed races of people to self-determination.

Anarchists believe only peasants, workers and farmers can liberate themselves and that they should manage industrial and economic production through workers' councils, factory committees and farm cooperatives, rather than via a party or government. When communist dictators like Joseph Stalin and Mao Tse-Tung tried to force collectivization of agriculture and industry on their peoples, millions died from starvation. Others were imprisoned or executed for resistance. These were not criminals, mercenaries or counter-revolutionaries. They were workers and peasants idealized in communist theory, but harshly oppressed in practice.

By their own initiative, individuals and communities will implement their own management of social life through voluntary associations. They will refuse to surrender self-direction to the state, political parties or vanguard sects since each of these merely aid in establishing or re-establishing domination. Anarchists believe the state and capitalist authority will be abolished by direct action, such as wildcat strikes, slowdowns, boycotts, sabotage and armed insurrection. We recognize our goals cannot be separated from the means used to achieve them. Hence, our practice and the associations we create will reflect the society we seek.

ECONOMIC AND SOCIAL ORGANIZATION

Since it is where everyone's interests converge, crucial attention will be paid to the area of economic organization. Under capitalism, we have to sell our labor to survive and feed our families. After an Anarchist social revolution, the wage system and institution of private and state property will be abolished. In its place, the communist principle of "from each according to ability, to each according to need" will direct the production and distribution of goods.

Voluntary associations of producers and consumers will take common possession of the means of production and allow free use of resources to any voluntary group, provided such use does not deprive others nor entail the use of wage labor. Food and housing cooperatives, cooperative factories, community-run schools, hospitals, recreation facilities and other important social services are examples of such associations. In turn, these groupings will federate with one another on both a territorial and functional basis to facilitate common goals.

Federalism is a form of social organization in which self-determining groups freely agree to coordinate their activities. Federalism is not a type of anarchism, but it is an essential part of anarchism. It is the joining of groups and peoples for political and economic survival and livelihood. The only social system that can possibly meet the diverse needs of society, while still promoting solidarity on the widest scale, is one that allows people to associate freely for common needs and interests. Federalism emphasizes autonomy and decentralization, fosters solidarity and complements groups' efforts to be as self-sufficient as possible. Groups can then be expected to cooperate so long as they derive mutual benefit. Contrary to the capitalist legal system and its contracts, in an Anarchist society, if such benefits are not considered mutual, any group will have the freedom to dissociate. A flexible and self-regulating social organism will be created, always ready to meet new needs by new organizations and adjustments.

Anarchists have an enormous job ahead of them. They must be able to work together for the benefit of the idea. The Italian Anarchist Errico Malatesta said it best when he wrote:

> Our task is that of pushing the "people" to demand and to seize all the freedom they can to make themselves responsible for their own needs without waiting for orders from any kind of authority. Our task is that of demonstrating the uselessness and harmfulness of the government, or provoking and encouraging by propaganda and action all kinds of individual and collective initiatives ... After the revolution, Anarchists will have a special mission of being the vigilant custodians of freedom, against the aspirants to power and possible tyranny of the majority ...
> —*Malatesta: His Life and Times*, edited by Vernon Richards

Therefore, this is the job of the federation, but it does not end with the success of the revolution. There is much reconstruction work to be done and the revolution must be defended to fulfill these tasks. Anarchists must have their own organizations. They must organize the post-revolutionary society and this is why Anarchists create federations.

In a modern independent society, the process of federation must be extended to all humanity. The network of voluntary associations—the Commune—will know no borders. It could be the size of the city, state or nation, or a society much larger than the current nation-state under capitalism. It could be a mass commune encompassing all the world's peoples in several continental Anarchist federations, say North America, Africa or the Caribbean. Truly, this would be a new world! Not a United Nations or "one world government," but a united humanity.

Overcoming our opposition is formidable. Each of us has been taught to believe in the need for government, in the absolute necessity of experts, in taking orders, obeying authority. Thus, for some of us, the principles of anarchism are all new. Nevertheless, when we believe in ourselves and decide we can make a society based on free, caring individuals, that tendency within us will become the conscious choice of freedom-loving people. Anarchists see their job as strengthening that tendency and show that there is no democracy or freedom under government—whether in the United States, China or Russia. Anarchists believe in direct democracy by the people as the only kind of freedom and self-rule.

TYPES OF ANARCHISTS

However, Anarchists cannot be expected to agree on everything. Historically, these differences have led to distinct tendencies in Anarchist theory and practice.

Individualist Anarchists hope for a future society in which free individuals do their social duty and share resources according to the dictates of abstract justice. Generally speaking, Individualists are philosophers rather than revolutionary activists, more likely to be middle class and academic, or right-wing libertarians, although there were some European radical groups in the nineteenth century engaged in armed self-defense and attacks on the state. In the modern period, Individualists are civil libertarians who want to reform the system to make it work "fairly." They were prevalent in the 1960s and are still seen in "counter-cultural" Anarchist formations and even among right-wing "Monetarist" libertarians, who believe in "limiting" the role of government to ensure a laissez-faire "free market" capitalist economy.

Mutualists are Anarchists associated with the ideas of nineteenth century Anarchist philosopher, Pierre-Joseph Proudhon, who based his future economy on individuals and small groups possessing (but not owning) the means of production and bound by mutual exchange and mutual credit (instead of money) to ensure each individual the product of her or his own labor. This type of anarchism synthesizes when Individualists put their ideas into practice and wish to reform capitalism to make it "cooperative." Right-wing libertarians and advocates of a minimized role for the state are often inspired by mutualism. Karl Marx attacked Proudhon as an "idealist" and "utopian philosopher" for the Anarchist concept of mutual aid.

Collectivists are Anarchists who follow the ideas of Michael Bakunin, the Russian Anarchist and best-known advocate of Anarchist theory. Bakunin's collectivist form of anarchism replaced Proudhon's insistence on individual sovereignty with the idea of mutual aid by voluntary institutions, class confrontation by Anarchist workers' movements and the right to the enjoyment of the individual product of her or his labor. This type of anarchism involves a direct threat to the class system and the capitalist state and is the view that society can only be reconstructed when the working class seizes control of the economy, destroys the state apparatus and reorganizes production on common ownership and control by associations of working people. This form of anarchism is the ideological basis of Anarchist-syndicalism, or revolutionary labor unionism.

Anarchist-Syndicalists are Anarchists active in labor and working-class movements. Anarchist-syndicalism is a form of anarchism for class-conscious workers and peasants, for militants and activists in the labor movement and for libertarian socialists who want equality as well as liberty. As pointed out, this philosophy is based heavily on the ideas of Bakunin, although its organizing techniques stem from the French and Spanish CNT trade union movements (called "Syndicates"), in which Anarchists were heavily involved. The Industrial Workers of the World (IWW) in North America, which led the fight for the eight-hour workday, was heavily influenced by Anarchist-syndicalism.

Anarchist-syndicalism is based on the view that a revolutionary form of economic warfare called the General Strike must topple the capitalist state and that the economy must afterward be based on industrial unions under the control of the working class. An Industrial Union Congress would handle political matters, while workplace matters would go to a factory committee elected by the workers and under their direct control. This type of anarchism has great potential in North America if it raises contemporary issues like the shortened workweek, factory councils, the current depression and fighting the bosses' offensive against the working class worldwide.

Anarchist-Communists are revolutionary Anarchists who believe in the philosophy of class struggle, an end to capitalism and all forms of oppression. Anarchist-Communists do not take the mechanical view of class struggle taken by Marxist-Leninists. Anarchism does not hold that only the industrial proletariat can achieve socialism and that victory led by a party represents our ultimate goal. Nor do Anarchists accept the idea of a workers' state presided over by a party and its leaders, such as the case of the former Soviet Union.

Anarchist-Communist philosophy is based on the theories of Peter Kropotkin, another Russian Anarchist of the nineteenth century. Kropotkin and his fellow Anarchist-Communists not only envisaged the commune and workers' councils as the proper guardians of production, but also attacked the wage system in all its forms and revived the ideas of libertarian communism. This type of anarchism is also known as libertarian socialism and includes most left libertarians opposed to the state, dictatorship and party rule, but are not Anarchists.

Since the 1870s, the principles of Anarchist-communism have been accepted by most Anarchist organizations favoring revolution. Anarchist or libertarian communism must not be confused with communism based on state ownership of the economy, control of both production and distribution and on party dictatorship. Such authoritarian communism is based on oppression and slavery to the state, while Anarchist-Communists favor a free, voluntary communism of shared resources. Libertarian communists are not Bolsheviks and have no connection with or support for V.I. Lenin, Stalin, Leon Trotsky or Mao. Anarchist-Communists do not seek state or private control over the essentials of life. They oppose all forms of dictatorship by either a political party or the government. Anarchist-Communists seek to foster the growth of a new society in which freedom to develop as one sees fit is integrated to the fullest extent with social responsibility to others.

Autonomism arose in the mid-1980s in Germany as groups of autonomous leftists broke away from Marxism and Leninism and it later spread to other countries in Europe and North America. Students, intellectuals and disaffected young workers made up this tendency originally, but there are also Anarchists who call themselves Autonomists to imply they are not doctrinaire or "purist" in their ideological perspectives or organizing styles. Like libertarian socialists, they seem to draw their ideology from both aspects of Marxism and some tenets of Anarchist philosophy (like Anarchist-communism), but they tend to be more independent and very meticulous about explaining this different identity.

Platformism is a type of Anarchist-communism created by Ida Mett, Petr Makhno, Peter Arshinov and others in Paris during the 1920s after the defeat of the Anarchist section of the Russian Revolution by the Bolsheviks. Platformists call for an Anarchist/left alternative to Leninism, a tight political organization with agreed-upon points of unity, collective responsibility, organizational discipline and federalism or free association. Like Syndicalists, they believe in work through labor unions, but unlike Syndicalists, Platformists believe in independent political action as well. After years of dormancy, new movements appeared on the scene in several countries during the 1990s that adopted "The Platform of Anarchist Communists."

Primitivism is a radical new school of anarchism, based partly on neo-Luddite theory and a new radical environmentalism. Primitivists believe and organize around anti-civilization and anti-technology themes. A large part of the concept is that, with the onset of the industrial age, modern humanity lost the "wildness" which allowed survival free of domineering institutions. So-called primitive peoples, as this philosophy goes, have been less corrupted by industrial society and are thus much nobler than "civilized" peoples. Many Primitivists seek to transform human life from industrial civilization to the new/old stage of human relations: hunter-gatherer clans. Since the mid-1990s, primitivism has become a worldwide movement in its own right. It was one of the more militant wings of the anti-globalization movement and a strong voice in the radical environmentalist movement.

Anarchist-feminism, to bring together the Anarchist and feminist ideology goes back to the 1936 Spanish Revolution, and was given new life in the Women's Liberation explosion of the 1970s.

This is one way to describe the different tendencies in Anarchist thought and practice. There may be many other ways to do it and describe the historical development of each tendency. That, however, is beyond the scope of this book.

Anarchists hope for, construct theories about and act to promote the abolition of government, the state and the principle of authority central to contemporary social forms and to replace them with a liberated social organization. Voluntary cooperation between free individuals will replace oppressive institutions. All Anarchist tendencies, except the Individualists (and to some extent, the Mutualists), in the past period believed this future society should be based on an organic network of mutual aid associations, workers' and consumers' collectives, communes and other voluntary alliances, organized into regional non-authoritarian federations. Such units would share ideas, information, technical skills and large-scale technological, cultural and recreational resources. All that we can say now is that ideally Anarchists believe in freedom from hunger and want and are against all forms of oppression and political manipulation by a nation-state or authority.

Although it is not really an Anarchist movement or ideology in itself, something needs to be said here about the anti-globalization movement, which has recently come into prominence. Although the impetus for anti-globalization came out of peasant struggles over the last 30 years, and was particularly inspired by the EZLN (Ejercito Zapatista de Liberacion Nacional) of Mexico, the movement made its own history when it disrupted the World Trade Organization meeting in Seattle, Washington. Anarchists were clearly the most militant tendency in the movement and pushed it ever further to the ultra-left. It still uses direct action tactics to disrupt meetings by the world's wealthy nations as they plan their attacks on underdeveloped poor nations and oppressed peoples in the Western world.

WHY I AM AN ANARCHIST TODAY

The Anarchist movement in North America is overwhelmingly white, middle class and for the most part, a pacifist movement. So the question arises: why am I a part of the Anarchist movement, since I am none of those things?

Well, although the movement today may not be what I think it should be in North America, it was once a movement of the poor and working class. I visualize a mass movement with hundreds of thousands, perhaps millions of Black, Chicano and other non-white workers in it. It will not be a Eurocentric Anarchist movement that Black workers and other oppressed people will just "join." It will be an independent movement with its own social outlook, cultural imperatives and political agenda. It will be Anarchist at its core, but will also extend anarchism as no previous European social or cultural group ever has done.

I am certain many of these workers will believe, as I do, that anarchism is the most democratic, effective and radical way to obtain our freedom, but that we must be free to design our own movements, whether it is understood or "approved" by North American Anarchists or not. We must fight for our freedom. No one else can free us, but they can help us.

Student Nonviolent Coordinating Committee

The early years of the Student Nonviolent Coordinating Committee were a contrast in many ways to any Black freedom group to come before or after. SNCC was one of the most militant organizations to come out of the Black Civil Rights movement. Although most of the SNCC activists were middle-class college intellectuals, with a small number of working-class grassroots activists, they developed a working style that was very anti-authoritarian and unique to the Civil Rights movement. Instead of bringing in a national leader to lead local struggles, as Dr. Martin Luther King, Jr. and his group, the Southern Christian Leadership Conference, tended to do, SNCC sent in field organizers to work with the local people, develop their leadership and help organize, but not take over local struggles.

SNCC organizers placed their faith in the ability of the people to determine an agenda and lead themselves to obtain their goals rather than being told what to do by a SNCC leader. SNCC itself had no strong leaders. Even though it had people in decision-making authority, they were accountable to membership boards and the community in a way no other group in the Civil Rights movement ever was.

SNCC was a secular organization, in contrast to SCLC, which was formed by Black preachers who adopted an organizing style from the Church, with a religious authority figure who gave orders to the troops. Today, most political commentators or historians still do not want to give full credit to the effectiveness of SNCC, but many of the most powerful and successful struggles of the Civil Rights movement were initiated and won by SNCC, including most of the voting rights struggles and the Mississippi freedom movement.

I learned a lot about internal democracy by being a part of SNCC—how it could make or break an organization and how it had so much to do with the morale of the members. Everyone was given an opportunity to participate in decision-making and felt part of a great historic mission, which would change our lives forever. We were right.

Even though SNCC gave some lifelong lessons to all of us involved, it crumbled to an authoritarian style in later years.

The Black Panther Party

In the 1960s, I was part of several Black revolutionary movements, including the Black Panther Party, one of the most important revolutionary movements of that period. It was probably the single most powerful Black poor, working-class revolutionary movement to ever arise on the scene, actually "a son" of Malcolm X. If the Civil Rights and Black Power movements had a "baby," then this was it, a transformation of those movements, along with a small dose of Chinese "Maoism." Though it pushed the entire left wing of that period and directly challenged the fascist government, police brutality and racism, it was as a Black revolutionary organization where it really shook the whole of U.S. society. Its survival programs really touched the Black working class, when it began to feed, clothe, house and protect the Black community, winning over a large number of supporters to its program. Enough support that the FBI labeled it "the greatest threat to the internal security of the USA." It was a threat because it taught Black people and millions of others that they could stand up to the system, and work toward a new world.

The Black Panther Party, I feel, failed in part because of the authoritarian leadership styles of Huey P. Newton, Bobby Seale and others on the Central Committee. This is not a recrimination against those individuals, but many errors were made because of that.

National leadership was divorced from chapters in cities all over the country and therefore engaged in "commandism" or leaders dictating work to local branches. The Marxist-Leninist structure of the organization created numerous contradictions as well. Limited internal democracy and unquestioned leadership meant Central Committee members, not members or community organizers, setting all organizational policies, and when there was internal dissent, those leaders began resorting to repressive actions when contradictions came up. These were very troubling. Purges became commonplace, and good people were expelled simply as "enemies of the people" because they disagreed with leadership on specific issues. Overemphasis on central leadership was ultimately demonstrated by the national organization being liquidated entirely and shipped back to Oakland, California, for its last days.

Of course, the BPP was a young organization and was under intense attack by the state. I do not want to imply internal errors were the primary contradictions that destroyed the BPP; armed FBI and police attacks did that. However, had the BPP been more democratically organized, it might have weathered the storm.

My period in the Panthers, though very brief, was very important because it taught me about the limits—and even the bankruptcy—of leadership in a revolutionary movement. It was not a question of a particular leader's personality defect, but rather a realization that many times leaders have one agenda, while followers have another. Corruption or megalomania can have serious repercussions for any organization.

This is no mindless criticism or backstabbing attack. I loved the party, and no one will ever take away from the tremendous historical role the BPP played in the Black Liberation movement. However, we must look at our organizations, warts and all, so we do not repeat the same mistakes.

Anarchism

I began on a political rethinking process after I was forced into exile from the United States and into Cuba, Czechoslovakia and other socialist bloc countries. In the 1960s, Marxist state communism was put forward as the kind of society for which revolutionaries should fight. However, even though many significant reforms and material advances had been made, these countries were police states. Along with the denial of basic democratic rights and poverty on a scale I would not have thought possible, I observed that racism existed in those countries. While the workers were mere wage slaves, corruption was rampant among Communist Party leaders and well-off state administrators. I thought to myself, "There has to be a better way!"

There is.

I started to hear about anarchism when I was captured in Eastern Europe and heard more when I was eventually thrown into prison in the United States. Prison is a place where one continually thinks about her or his past life, including an examination of new or even contrary political ideals. I began to consider what I had seen in the Black movement, along with my mistreatment in Cuba, my capture and escape in Czechoslovakia and my final capture in East Germany. I replayed all this repeatedly in my head.

I was first introduced to anarchism in 1969, immediately after I was brought back to the United States and was placed in the federal lock-up in New York City. I met Martin Sostre, a Black Puerto Rican Anarchist, who proved to be a major influence on my life. Sostre told me all about how to survive in prison, the importance of fighting for prisoners' democratic rights and about anarchism as a political ideology. This short course in anarchism did not stick, however, even though I greatly respected Sostre, because I did not understand the theoretical concepts and associated them with white radicals. I just could not believe any society could exist without a central government, politicians and a bureaucracy. I guess I was like most people who hear this for the first time.

Around 1973, after I had been locked up for about three years, I started receiving Anarchist literature and correspondence from Anarchists who had heard about my case. It was from my readings of Anarchist books that I began my slow metamorphosis to becoming a confirmed Anarchist.

During the late 1970s, I was adopted by Anarchist Black Cross-United Kingdom, and a Dutch Anarchist group called HAPOTOC (Help a Prisoner Oppose Torture Organizing Committee) organized an international defense campaign for me. HAPOTOC's newsletter, which was distributed internationally in numerous languages, brought my case to millions. This proved crucial in ultimately getting people all over the world to write to the U.S. government to demand my release and incited demonstrations, riots and even guerrilla actions over the conditions of my confinement.

While in prison, I wrote a succession of articles for the Black prisoners' rights and Anarchist press and was a member of the Social Revolutionary Anarchist Federation, the International Workers of the World (IWW) and several other Anarchist groups in the United States and around the world. However, I became disheartened by the North American Anarchist movement's failure to fight white supremacy, the few people of color in Anarchist groups, and its lack of class struggle politics. Therefore, in 1979 I wrote a pamphlet called *Anarchism and the Black Revolution* to act as a guide to the discussion of these matters by our movement. In those days, the hippie influence was still strong, along with old line labor syndicalism, which I found to be conservative, especially on race issues.

Finally, in 1983, I was released from prison, after having served almost 15 years.

After my release, I fell away from the Anarchist movement in disgust, even though I still considered myself an anti-authoritarian activist. It was not until 1992 when I was working in my hometown, Chattanooga, as an anti-racist community organizer that I became active in the international Anarchist movement again. I soon learned that, for all these years, the pamphlet I wrote in 1979 had influenced a considerable number of anti-racist Anarchists who wanted a more class struggle-oriented approach than the "lifestyle Anarchist" movement then afforded.

What I Believe

All Anarchists do not believe the same things. There are differences in theory and tactics. Many times those differences can coexist and be respected. I do not know what others believe; I just know what I believe, and I will spell it out simply, but thoroughly.

I believe in Black Liberation, so I am a *Black revolutionary*. I believe that Black people are oppressed both as workers and a distinct nationality and will only be freed by a Black revolution, which is an intrinsic part of a social revolution. I believe Blacks and other oppressed nationalities must have their own agendas, distinct worldview and organizations of struggle. This is *Black Autonomy*, which will be discussed elsewhere in this book.

I believe in the destruction of the world capitalist system, so I am an *anti-imperialist*. As long as capitalism is alive on the planet, there will be exploitation, oppression and nation-states. Enslaving and exploiting others cannot achieve freedom. Capitalism is responsible for the major world wars, numerous brush wars and the starvation of millions of people for the profit motive of the rich countries in the West.

I believe in racial justice, so I am an *anti-racist*. The capitalist system created and is maintained by the enslavement and colonial oppression of African, Asian, Latino and other people of color. This continues today with various forms of discrimination and oppression. I believe before there will be a social revolution, white supremacy must be defeated.

I believe Africans in America are colonized and exist as an internal colony of the United States. I believe white workers must give up their privileged status, their "white identity," and must support racially oppressed workers in their fights for freedom and national liberation.

I believe in social justice and economic equality, so I am a *libertarian socialist*. I believe society and all parties responsible for production should share the economic products of labor. I believe capitalism and the state both should be overthrown and abolished. I accept parts of the economic critique of Marxism, but not its model for political organizing.

I accept the anti-authoritarian critique of anarchism, but not its rejection of the class struggle.

I do not believe in government and so I am an *Anarchist*. I believe government is one of the worst forms of modern oppression and must be overthrown. Anarchism means we will have more democracy, social equality and economic prosperity. I oppose all forms of oppression found in modern society.

Destruction of Western Civilization

Although not a Primitivist, I am for the destruction of Western Civilization and the dismantling of the nation-state. I am not for the preservation of the so-called "industrial state," any more than I am for the capitalist welfare state. This so-called civilization is based on the enslavement, exploitation and genocide of large groups of the oppressed people of color and indigenous peoples of the world. Unequal trade, military dictatorships and political manipulation maintain colonialism, fascist genocide, racial slavery and other forms of dreadful oppression are still operative today. Working people are made cogs in the machine, slaves of a wage structure.

Such a society cannot possibly claim it is based on social justice. It is a polluting, poisoning, deadly, oppressive institution leading us toward a planetary catastrophe. It clearly must be junked and something else must be found. I am not prepared to go backwards to a hunter-gathering or primitive stage, but I know this thing has to go. It cannot be rescued, reformed or retooled any more than cures for cancer should be saved to treat future patients. We must kill it before it kills us.

I believe in a future society, but cannot provide any precise model I completely agree with just yet. I think whatever society is built will be *practopian* (i.e., a practical society with utopian features), rather than *utopian* or unattainable in a practical sense. I need to write more about this at another time.

But having said this, I also am convinced that primitivism is not the way either. We should not seek to return to a stage when people were forced to fight to stay alive, and had primitive levels of social organization. The creation of such a state of affairs, with an abrupt destruction of all industrial production, even that controlled by people after capitalism, would result in mass starvation, complete collapse and disorganization. This is not what any Anarchist or social revolutionary should seek.

We need to preserve those things which need to be preserved in mass society during a transitional stage to Anarchist socialism. I do not mean preserve the state as any form of institution, but rather allow masses of people to create cooperatives to produce food, housing, and other social needs on a mass scale for themselves and others, not just by a social cult disconnected from the rest of society, or "tribes" that might prey on and even kill each other.

Until we can build an Anarchist society, we need to build a transitional approach. Although not perfect, we see examples of this with the "solidarity economies" of Latin America, where poor and working peoples have created their own economic institutions. The various community currencies also carry some promise, the ideals of a Participatory Economy (also known as "Parecon") by Michael Albert and Robin Hahnel are plausible and being widely discussed. The Mondragon cooperative system in the Basque Country of Spain stands as one example by an embattled people, and other smaller scale alternative economic alternatives exist all over the world. Even the 38 survival programs of the Black Panther Party could be seen in this light, as the beginning stages of having built a Black solidarity economy in the United States during the 1960s.

ANARCHIST VERSUS MARXIST-LENINIST THOUGHTS ON THE ORGANIZATION OF SOCIETY

Historically, there have been three major forms of socialism: libertarian socialism (Anarchism), authoritarian socialism (Marxist communism) and democratic socialism (social democracy). The left has echoed the bourgeoisie's portrayal of anarchism as an ideology of lunacy, even claiming the capitalist economy was based somehow on "Anarchist principles," which is absolute nonsense. Anarchism and especially Anarchist-communism have nothing in common with this image concocted by its ideological opponents, the Marxist-Leninists.

It is very difficult for the Marxist-Leninists to make an objective criticism of anarchism as such, because by its nature anarchism undermines all the suppositions basic to Marxism. If Marxism and Leninism, its variant which emerged during the Russian Revolution, is held out to be "the" working-class philosophy and yet the proletariat cannot owe its emancipation to anyone but itself, it is hard to go back on it and say that the working class is not yet ready to dispense with authority over itself as well. Lenin came up with the idea of a "transitional state," which would "wither away" over time, to go along with Marx's "dictatorship of the proletariat." The Anarchists expose this entire line as counter-revolutionary and sheer power grabbing. Over 75 years of Marxist-Leninist practice has proven us right.

These so-called "socialist states" produced by Marxist-Leninist doctrine only produced Stalinist police states where workers had no rights, a new ruling class of technocrats and party politicians emerged and the class differential between those the state favored, over those it didn't, created widespread deprivation and injustice among the masses. This was another class struggle of privileged bureaucrats against the common people.

We do not support a Soviet-style state as some Leninists still call for. They are political revolutionaries, who merely want to remove one ruling class for themselves; we have had years of their practices, and see it as no solution. The state communists merely shot, imprisoned and starved millions of workers and peasants into following their governmental authority. The reality is Anarchists are social revolutionaries, who seek a stateless, classless, voluntary, cooperative federation of decentralized communes based on social ownership, individual liberty and autonomous self-management of social and economic life. The political demands of the masses must take priority, not that of a political cult of middle-class activists.

The Anarchists differ from Marxist-Leninists in many areas, but especially in organization building. But they especially differ from the authoritarian socialists in primarily three ways: they reject the Marxist-Leninist notions of the "vanguard party," "democratic centralism" and "dictatorship of the proletariat." The Anarchists have alternatives to each of them. The problem is almost the entire left, including some Anarchists themselves, is completely unaware of anarchism's tangible structural alternatives of the catalyst group, Anarchist consensus and the mass commune.

The Anarchist alternative to the vanguard party is the catalyst group, an anti-authoritarian political action group. The catalyst group is merely an Anarchist-Communist federation of affinity groups in action. This catalyst group or revolutionary Anarchist federation would meet on a regular basis, or only when necessary, depending on the wishes of the membership and the urgency of prevailing social conditions. It would be made up of grassroots representatives from the affinity group, with full voting rights, privileges and responsibilities. It would set both policies and future actions to be performed. It would produce both Anarchist-Communist theory and social practice. A catalyst group believes in the class struggle and the need to overthrow capitalist rule and opposes Marxist-Leninist communist state tyranny as well. It organizes in the communities and workplaces. It is democratic and has no authority figures like a party boss or central committee.

Anarchists oppose hierarchical, power-tripping Marxist leadership that suppresses the creative urge of those involved and forces an agenda down their throats. Members of such communist political cult-type groups are mere servants and worshippers of the party leadership. Although Anarchists reject this type of domineering leadership, they do recognize that some people are more experienced, articulate ideals better and have superior administrative skills, so they become facilitators who will play leadership action roles. Such facilitators are merely a temporary force and can be removed by a vote of the people or organization members at any time. They can never be an entrenched leadership, like the usual politicians in the capitalist or communist states.

There is a conscious attempt to rotate routinely this responsibility and to pass on these skills to others, especially to women and people of color, who would ordinarily not get the chance. The experiences of these facilitators, who are usually veteran activists or better qualified than most in the movement, can help form and drive movements forward and even help crystallize the potential for revolutionary change in the popular movement. What they cannot be allowed to do is take over the initiative of the movement itself. The members of these groups reject hierarchical positions—anyone having more "official" authority than others. Unlike the Marxist-Leninist vanguard parties, the Anarchist groups will not be allowed to perpetuate their leadership through a dictatorship after the revolution. Instead, the catalyst group will be dissolved and its members, when they are ready, will be absorbed into the new society's collective decision-making process. Anarchists are not leaders or dictators, but merely advisors and organizers for a mass movement and freedom of the people to govern themselves.

We know after watching years of Marxist-Leninist excesses that we don't want or need a group of authoritarians "leading" the working class as if they are sheep going to slaughter and then establishing themselves as a centralized decision-making command. Instead of "withering away," Marxist-Leninist nation-states have perpetuated vicious authoritarian institutions (the secret police, gulags, labor bosses and the Communist Party) to maintain their power. The apparent effectiveness of such organizations ("we're just as efficient as the capitalists") masks the way that such "revolutionaries" who pattern themselves after capitalist institutions become absorbed by bourgeois values and completely isolated from the real needs and desires of ordinary people.

The reluctance of Marxist-Leninists to accept Anarchist ideals of revolutionary social change is above all seen in Lenin's conception of the party. It is a prescription to seize power and put it in the hands of the Communist Party. The party Leninists create today, they believe, should become the (only) "Party of the Proletariat" in which the class could organize and seize power.

In practice, however, this meant personal and party dictatorship, which the Marxist-Leninists felt gave them the right and duty to wipe out all other parties and political ideologies. Both Lenin and Stalin killed millions of workers and peasants, their left-wing ideological opponents and even many members of the Bolshevik Party itself. This bloody and treacherous history is why there is so much rivalry and hostility among Marxist-Leninist, Maoist and Trotskyite parties today and it is why the "workers' states," whether in Cuba, China, Vietnam or Korea, are such oppressive bureaucracies over their people. It is also why the petty bourgeoisie and ordinary citizens overthrew most of the East European Stalinist governments in the 1980s. Maybe we are witnessing the eclipse of state communism entirely; since it has nothing new to say and will never get those government seats of power back again.

While Anarchist groups reach decisions through Anarchist consensus, the Marxist-Leninists organize through so-called democratic centralism. Democratic centralism poses as a form of inner party democracy, but is really just a hierarchy by which each member of a party (ultimately of a society) is subordinate to a "higher" member until one reaches the all powerful party central committee and its chairman. This is a very undemocratic procedure, which puts the leadership above criticism even if it is not above reproach. It is a bankrupt, corrupt method of internal operations for a political organization and sets the stage for murderous repression by a government.

You have no voice in such a party and must be afraid to say any unflattering comments to or about the leaders. If you challenge any of their decisions, you will be severely punished, perhaps even expelled. Even worse, in previous times, when such political parties assumed state power as Stalinist regimes, they would have you "purged," and then imprisoned for life as an "enemy of the state" or even shot by the secret police. This is not the kind of society for which we are fighting.

In Anarchist groups, members (none of whom has authority over the other) talk out proposals, dissenting minorities are respected and each individual's participation is voluntary. Everyone has the right to agree or disagree over policy and actions and everyone's ideas are given equal weight and consideration. No decision can be made until each individual member or affiliated group that will be affected by that decision has had a chance to express opinions on the issue. Individual members and affiliated groups shall retain the option to refuse support to specific federation activities, but may not actively obstruct such activities once they are approved. In true democratic fashion, decisions for the federation as a whole must be made by many of its members, with the consent of its minority.

Sometimes, there is no real need for formal meetings to make major decisions. What is needed is coordination of the day-to-day actions of the group. Of course, there are times when a major decision has to be made and sometimes very quickly and the facilitator and the organization staff must take swift action without full consultation with the entire membership. This will be rare, but sometimes it is unavoidable. The consensus, in that case, would then have to be among a much smaller circle than the general membership of hundreds or thousands. However, ordinarily all that is needed is an exchange of information and trust among parties and a decision reaffirming the original decision will be reached if an emergency decision had to be made.

Of course, during the discussion, there will be an endeavor to clarify any major differences and explore alternative courses of action. And there will be an attempt to arrive at a mutually agreed upon consensus between conflicting views. As always, if there should be an impasse or dissatisfaction with the consensus, a vote would be taken and with a two-thirds majority, the matter would be accepted, rejected or rescinded. Consensus can be blocked to ensure a new discussion on the matter, not for purposes of petty disruption, but to make sure all views are known and everything is fully considered.

This is all totally contrary to the practice of Marxist-Leninist parties whose central committees unilaterally set policy for the entire organization and arbitrary authority reigns. They would steamroll over all minority opposition and may even penalize or censure them. Anarchists reject such centralization of authority and the concept of a central committee. All groups are free associations formed out of common people, not "professional" revolutionaries disciplined by fear of authority in a political party.

When the size of the work-groups (which could be formed around labor, fundraising, anti-racism, women's rights, food and housing, etc.) becomes cumbersome, the organizations can be decentralized into two or more autonomous organizations, still united in one large federation. This enables the group to expand limitlessly while maintaining its anarchic form of decentralized self-management. It is somewhat like the scientific theory of a biological cell, dividing and redividing, but in a political sense.

However, Anarchist groups are not necessarily organized loosely or haphazardly. Anarchism is flexible and so its structure can be practically non-existent or very tight, depending on the type of organization demanded by the social conditions being faced. For instance, during military operations or heightened political repression organization would tighten but be more flexible at other times.

Treacherous History of Stalinism

Anarchist-Communists favor the mass commune and reject the Marxist-Leninist concept of the "dictatorship of the proletariat" and a so-called "workers' state." Unlike members of Leninist parties, whose daily lives are generally similar to present bourgeois lifestyles, Anarchist organizational structures and lifestyles, through communal living arrangements, urban tribes, affinity groups, squatting, etc., attempt to reflect the liberated society of the future. Anarchists built all kinds of communes and collectives during the Spanish Revolution of the 1930s, but were crushed by both the fascists and the communists. Since the Marxist-Leninists do not build cooperative structures, the nucleus of the new society, they can only see the world in bourgeois political terms of a nation-state. They just want to seize state power and institute their own dictatorship over the people and the workers, instead of crushing all forms of bureaucratic power and replacing it with a free, cooperative society. Of course, the party, they insist, represents the proletariat and there is no need to organize outside the party.

Yet, even in the former Soviet Union, the Stalinist Communist Party membership only represented 5 percent of the population. This is elitism of the worst sort and even makes the capitalist parties look democratic by comparison. What the Communist Party was intended to represent in terms of workers' power is never made clear, but in true 1984 "doublethink" fashion, the results are years of political repression and state slavery, instead of an era of "glorious communist rule." They must be held politically accountable for these crimes against the people and revolutionary political theory and practice. They have slandered the names of socialism and communism.

We Anarchists reject the dictatorship of the proletariat because it is unbridled oppression and the Marxist-Leninists and Stalinists must be made to answer for it. In addition, millions of peasants and workers were murdered by Stalin in the name of fighting an internal class war and millions more were murdered in China, Poland, Afghanistan, Cambodia and other countries by communist movements which followed Stalin's prescription for revolutionary terror. We reject state communism as the worst aberration and tyranny. We can do better than this with the mass commune, a people's commonwealth.

The Anarchist mass commune (sometimes also called a workers' community council, although there are some differences) is a national, continental or transnational federation of economic and political cooperatives and regional communal formations. Anarchists look to a world and a society in which real decision-making involves everyone who lives in it—a mass commune—not a few discipline freaks pulling the strings in a so-called "proletarian dictatorship." Any dictatorship is bad; it has no redeeming social features, yet it is what the Leninists tell us will protect us from counter-revolution. While Marxist-Leninists claim that their dictatorship is necessary to crush any bourgeois counter-revolutions led by the capitalist class or right-wing reactionaries, Anarchists believe this argument is itself part of the Stalinist school of falsification. A centralized apparatus, such as a state, is a much easier target for opponents of the revolution than is an array of decentralized communes. These communes would remain armed and prepared to defend the revolution against anyone who militarily moves against it. The key is to mobilize the people into defense guards, militias and other military preparedness units.

The Leninists' position of the necessity for a dictatorship to "protect" the revolution was certainly not proven in the Civil War that followed the Russian Revolution. In fact, without support of the Ukrainian Anarchists and other left-wing forces, along with the Russian people, the Bolshevik government would have been defeated. True to any communist dictatorship, it then turned around and wiped out the Russian and Ukrainian Anarchist movements, along with the left-wing opponents like the Mensheviks and Social revolutionaries. They were imprisoned or shot by the secret police. Even ideological opponents in the Bolshevik Party were imprisoned and put to death. Lenin and Trotsky especially killed millions of Russian citizens right after the Civil War when they were consolidating state power, preceding Stalin's even bloodier rule. The lesson is that we should not be tricked into surrendering grassroots people's power to dictators who pose as our friends or leaders.

We do not need the Marxist-Leninists' solutions; they are dangerous and deluding. There is another way, but too much of the left continues to espouse the old dogma. To many ordinary people, the choice has always appeared to be capitalism/fascism or the Marxist/Leninist/Maoist "communist" parties, however dogmatic and dictatorial. This is primarily the result of misunderstanding and propaganda. Anarchist ideology provides feasible organizational structures and a valid alternative revolutionary theory, which, if utilized, could be the basis for organizations just as solid as the Marxist-Leninists (or even more so). Only these organizations will be egalitarian and truly benefit the people rather than the communist leaders and a new class of new intelligentsia.

However, instead of meeting such criticisms head on, Marxist-Leninists have not concentrated their attacks on the doctrine of anarchism, but instead on particular Anarchist figures, especially Bakunin, an ideological opponent of Marx in the First International Socialist movement in the last century. Yet, anarchism is not confined to the ideas of a single theoretician and it allows individual creativity to develop in collective groupings, instead of the characteristic dogmatism of the Marxist-Leninists. Therefore, not being cultist, it encourages innovation and experimentation, prompting its adherents to respond realistically to contemporary conditions. It is the concept of making ideology fit the demands of life, rather than trying to make life fit the demands of ideology.

Therefore, in laying out the final distinction between Marxism-Leninism and anarchism, we can say that Marxist-Leninists believe in a political revolution to empower revolutionary politicians, while Anarchists believe in social revolution to empower the masses of people. Anarchists build organizations to build a new world, not to perpetuate domination over the masses of people. We will build an organized, coordinated international movement aimed at transforming the globe into a mass commune. Such a movement would be a great forward leap in human evolution and a gigantic revolutionary stride. It would change the world as we know it and end the special problems long plaguing humankind. It would be a new era of freedom and fulfillment. Now, let's get on with it. We've got a world to win!

GENERAL PRINCIPLES OF ANARCHIST-COMMUNISM

Since Anarchist-communism (regardless of what it is called these days) is still one of the most important and widely accepted forms of anarchism, more needs to be said about this dynamic revolutionary doctrine. First, because of years of anti-communist indoctrination, the ideals of communism are repugnant to all "good Americans." So, if you say the social revolution you are in favor of is based in any way on communism, the average person will reject it out of fear and loathing. Again, Anarchist-communism has nothing to do with state communism as existed in the former Soviet Union and still exists in China. We are talking about the classical ideals of power to the people, rather than to dictators and politicians.

Anarchist-communism is not primarily based on Marxist theory, but developed as an independent theory. While accepting certain tenets of Marx's economic critique of capitalism, Anarchist-Communists, unlike Marxist-Leninists, do not worship Marx as an infallible leader whose ideas can never be critiqued or revised. Instead, anarchism-communism is based on a conception of society that harmoniously unites individual self-interests and social well-being.

Although Anarchist-Communists agree with Marx and many Marxist-Leninists that capitalism must be abolished because of its crisis-ridden nature (here we reject the false term "anarchy of production") and its exploitation of the working class, we do not believe capitalism is an indispensable, progressive precondition for the transition to a socially beneficial economy. Nor do we believe that the centralized economic planning of state socialism can provide for the wide diversity of needs or desires. We absolutely reject the idea of the need for a state or the false idea that it will "wither away" of its own accord. Nor do we need a political party to "boss over" the workers or "stage manage" the revolution. That is very undemocratic.

Anarchist-Communists believe the "personal is political and the political is personal," meaning that one cannot divorce one's political life from one's personal life. We do not play bureaucratic political roles and are divorced from the results of our decision-making.

Anarchist-Communists recognize people are capable of determining their own needs and of making the necessary arrangements to satisfy those needs, provided they have free access to social resources. Since it is always a political decision whether those resources are to be freely provided to all, Anarchist-Communists believe in the credo of "from each according to (their) means, to each according to their needs." This assures that all will be fed, clothed and housed as normal social practice, not as demeaning welfare clients or that certain classes will be better provided for than others because of favoritism by political leaders.

When not deformed by corrupt social institutions and practices, the interdependence and solidarity of human beings results in individuals who are responsible both for themselves and to the society that makes their well-being and cultural development possible. Therefore, we seek to replace the state and capitalism with a network of voluntary alliances embracing all of social life: production, consumption, health, culture, recreation and other areas In this way, all groups and associations reap the benefits of unity while expanding the range of their freedom. Anarchists believe in free association and federating groups of collectives, workers' councils, food and housing cooperatives, political collectives, with others of all types, rather than dictating to people how they must live their lives.

As a practical matter, Anarchist-Communists believe that we should simultaneously build the new society and fight to crush the old capitalist one. We wish to create non-authoritarian mutual aid organizations (for food, clothing, housing, funding for community projects and others), neighborhood assemblies and cooperatives not affiliated with either government or business corporations and not run for profit, but for social need. Such organizations, if built now, will provide members with a practical experience in self-management and self-sufficiency and will decrease dependency on welfare agencies and employers. In short, we can begin now to build the infrastructure for the communal society so people can see what they are fighting for, not just the ideas in someone's head. That is the real way to freedom.

CAPITALISM, THE STATE AND PRIVATE PROPERTY

The existence of the state and capitalism are rationalized by their apologists as a "necessary evil" due to the alleged inability of the greater part of the population to run their own affairs and those of society, as well as being their protection against crime and violence. Anarchists realize, quite to the contrary, the principal barriers to a free society are the state, the government bureaucrats and the institution of private property. It is the state that causes war, police repression and other forms of violence and it is the government that carries it out. Further, it is private property owned by the rich or the state that creates the lack of equal distribution of major social wealth causing poverty, which in turn causes crime and deprivation.

But what is the state? It is a political abstraction (really a socio-political corporation), a hierarchical institution by which a privileged elite strives to dominate the vast majority of people. The state's mechanisms include a group of institutions containing legislative assemblies, the civil service bureaucracy, the military and police forces, the judiciary and prisons and the sub-central state apparatus. The government is the administrative vehicle that runs the state. The purpose of this specific set of institutions, which are the expressions of authority in capitalist societies (and in so-called "socialist states"), is the maintenance and extension of domination over the common people by a privileged class, the rich in capitalist societies, the so-called Communist Party in state socialist or communist societies like the former Union of Soviet Socialist Republics.

However, the state is always in an elitist position between the actual socio-economic rulers and their order-givers and order-takers all the way down the line to the economic haves and have-nots. The state's top elite is not just the rich and the super-rich, but also those people who assume state positions of authority—high-ranking politicians and judicial officials, presidents, prime ministers and Supreme Court justices. Thus, the state bureaucracy itself, in terms of its relation to ideological property, can become an elite class in its own right. This administrative elite class of the state is developed through dispensing privileges by the economic elite and by the separation of private and public life— the family unit and civil society respectively—and by the opposition between an individual family and the larger society. It is sheer opportunism, brought on by capitalist competition and alienation. Bourgeois society is a breeding ground for agents of the state.

The existence of the state and a ruling class, based on the exploitation and oppression of the working class, are inseparable. Domination and exploitation go hand-in-hand and, in fact, this oppression is not possible without force and violent authority. This is why Anarchist-Communists argue that any attempt to use state power as a means of establishing a free, egalitarian society can only be self-defeating because the habits of commanding and exploiting become ends in themselves. This was proven with the Bolsheviks in the Russian Revolution (1917–21). The fact is officials of the "communist" state accumulate political power much as the capitalist class accumulates economic wealth. Those who govern form a distinct group whose only interest is the retention of political control by any means at their disposal. The institution of capitalist property, moreover, permits a minority of the population to control and to regulate access to and the use of all socially produced wealth and natural resources. You have to pay for the land, water and the fresh air to some giant utility company or real estate firm.

This controlling group may be a separate economic class or the state itself, but in either case, the institution of property leads to a set of social and economic relations, capitalism, in which a small sector of society reaps enormous benefits and privileges at the expense of the laboring minority. The capitalist economy is not based on fulfilling the needs of everyone, but on amassing profit for a few. Both capitalism and the state must be attacked and overthrown, not one or the other, or one then the other, because the fall of either will not ensure the fall of both. Down with capitalism and the state!

No doubt, some working-class people will mistake what I am speaking of as a threat to their accumulated property. No, except for the excessively rich, Anarchists recognize the distinction between personal possessions and major capitalistic property. Capitalistic property is that which has as its basic characteristic and purpose the command of other people's labor power because of its exchange value. The institution of property conditions the development of a set of social and economic relations, which has established capitalism and this situation allows a small minority within society to reap enormous benefits and privileges at the expense of the laboring minority. This is the classic scenario of capital exploiting labor that most socialists accept.

Where there is a high social division of labor and complex industrial organization, money is necessary to perform transactions. It is not simply that this money is legal tender used in place of the direct bartering of goods. That is not what we are limited to here: capital is money, but money as a process, which reproduces and increases its value. Capital arises only when the owner of the means of production finds workers on the market as sellers of their own labor power. Capitalism developed as the form of private property that shifted from the rural agricultural style to the urban, factory style of labor. Capitalism centralizes the instruments of production and brings individuals closely alongside others in a disciplined work force. Capitalism is industrialized commodity production, which makes goods for profit, not for social needs. This is a special distinction of capital and capital alone.

We may understand capitalism and the basis of our observations as capital endowed with will and consciousness. That is, as those people who acquire capital and function as an elite, moneyed class with enough national and political power to rule society. Further, that accumulated capital is money and with money the elite claims to control the means of production, defined as the mills, mines, factories, land, water, energy and other natural resources. The rich know this is their property. They do not need ideological pretensions and are under no illusions about "public property."

An economy, such as the one we have briefly sketched, is not based on fulfilling the needs of everyone in society, but instead is based on · the accumulation of profits for the few, who live in palatial luxury as a leisure class, while the workers live in either poverty or one or two pay checks removed. You see, therefore, that doing away with government also signifies the abolition of monopoly and personal ownership of the means of production and distribution.

ANARCHISM, VIOLENCE AND AUTHORITY

A big lie about Anarchists is they are mindless bomb-throwers, cutthroats and assassins. People spread these lies for their own reasons: governments, because they fear being overthrown by social revolution; Marxist-Leninists, because it is a competing ideology with a different concept of social organization and revolutionary struggle; and the Church, because anarchism does not believe in deities and its rationalism might sway workers away from superstition. It is true that these lies and propaganda are able to sway many people primarily because they never hear the other side. Anarchists receive bad press and suffer a scapegoat of every politician, right or left wing. These lies have had to be told that Anarchists are killers, rapists, robbers, mad bombers, unsavory elements and the worst of the worst.

A social revolution is an Anarchist revolution, which not only abolishes one exploiting class for another, but all exploiters and the instrument of exploitation, the state and capitalism. It is a revolution for people's power, instead of political power; it abolishes both money and wage slavery. Anarchists are for total democracy and freedom, instead of politicians to represent the masses in Parliament, Congress or the Communist Party. Anarchists are for workers' self-management of industry, instead of government regulation. Anarchists are for full sexual, racial, cultural and intellectual diversity, instead of sexual chauvinism, cultural repression, censorship and racial oppression.

Let's look at the real world and see who is causing all this violence and repression of human rights. Wholesale murder by standing armies in World Wars I and II, the pillage and rape of former colonial countries, military invasions or so-called "police operations" in Korea and Vietnam—all of these have been done by governments. It is government and state/class rule which is the source of all violence. This includes all governments. The so-called "communist" world is not communist and the "Free" world is not free. East and West, capitalism, private or state remains an inhuman type of society where the vast majority is bossed at work, at home and in the community. Propaganda (news and literary), policemen and soldiers, prisons and schools, traditional values and morality all serve to reinforce the power of the few and to convince or correct the many into passive acceptance of a brutally degrading and irrational system. Such authoritarian rule is at work in the United States of America, as well as the "communist" governments of China or Cuba; this is what Anarchists mean by authority being oppression.

> What is the thing we call government? Is it anything but organized violence? The law orders you to obey and if you don't obey, it will compel you by force—all governments, all law and authority finally rest upon force and violence, on punishment or fear of punishment.
> —Alexander Berkman, in *ABC of Anarchism*[2]

There are revolutionaries, including many Anarchists, who advocate armed overthrow of the capitalist state. They do not advocate or practice mass murder like the governments of the modern world with their stockpiles of nuclear bombs, poison gas and chemical weapons, huge air forces, navies and armies who are hostile to each other. It was not the Anarchists who provoked two world wars where over 100 million people

---

2. Alexander Berkman, *ABC of Anarchism*, Vanguard Press, New York, 1929.

were slaughtered; nor was it the Anarchists who invaded and butchered the peoples of Korea, Panama, Somalia, Iraq, Indonesia and other countries who have sustained imperialist military attacks. It was not the Anarchists who sent armies of spies all over the world, like the CIA, KGB, MI6, or other national spy agencies, to murder, corrupt, subvert, overthrow and meddle into the internal affairs of other countries, nor use them as secret police to uphold their home governments or puppet dictatorships in various countries, no matter how repressive and unpopular the regime. Further, if your government makes you a police officer or soldier, you kill and repress people in the name of "freedom" or "law and order," or you will not have a job.

> You don't question the right of the government to kill, to confiscate and imprison. If a private person should be guilty of the things that the government is doing all the time, you'd brand him a murderer, thief and scoundrel. But as long as the violence committed is "lawful" you approve of it and submit to it. So it is not real violence that you object to, but people using violence unlawfully.
> —Alexander Berkman, in *ABC of Anarchism*

If we speak honestly, we must admit everyone believes in violence and practices it, however much they may condemn it in others. Either they do it themselves or they have the police or army to do it on their behalf as agents of the state. In fact, all governmental institutions we presently support and the entire life of this society are based on violence. America is the most violent country on earth, or as one SNCC comrade, H. Rap Brown, was quoted as saying: "Violence is as American as apple pie (!)" The United States goes all over the world committing violence; it assassinates heads of state, overthrows governments, slaughters civilians in the millions and makes a prison out of captive nations, such as it is doing in Iraq and Afghanistan today. Americans are expected to passively accept these crimes of conquest of other peoples. That is the hallmark of a good citizen.

Anarchists have no monopoly over violence. When they used it, it was in so-called "propaganda of the deed" attacks against tyrants and dictators, rather than against the common people. These individual reprisals—bombings, assassinations, sabotage—have been efforts at making those in power responsible for their unjust acts and repressive authority. I do not advocate such violence, but I do understand it.

Honesty should compel us to say Anarchists, socialists, communists and other revolutionaries, as well as patriots and nationalists and even reactionaries and racists like the Ku Klux Klan and neo-Nazis, have all used violence for a variety of reasons. Who would not have rejoiced if a dictator like Hitler had been slain by assassins and thus spared the world ethnic genocide and World War II? Further, most transfers of power and almost all revolutions are violent because the oppressing class will not give up power and privileges without a bloody fight. We have no choice anyway. We must fight for a new world.

We would all choose to be pacifists if that were possible. Like Dr. Martin Luther King, Jr. counseled, we would rather resolve our differences with understanding, love and moral reasoning. We will attempt these solutions first, whenever possible. In the insanity that reigns, however, our movement acknowledges the utility of preparedness. It is too dangerous a world to be ignorant of the ways to defend ourselves so we can continue our revolutionary work. Being acquainted with a weapon and its uses does not mean you must immediately go out and use that weapon; but if you need to use it, you can use it well. We are forced to acknowledge the American progressive and radical movements have been too pacifist to be truly effective. We also realize open groups that proposed cooperative change and were non-violent, like the IWW, were crushed violently by the government. Finally, we have the unfortunate example of Dr. King, who was assassinated in 1968 by a conspiracy of agents of the state, most likely the FBI.

Understand the more we succeed at our work, the more dangerous our situation will become because we will then be recognized as a threat to the state. Make no mistake: the insurrection is coming. An American Intifada will destabilize the state. We are talking about a spontaneous, prolonged, uprising of the vast majority of the people and the necessity to defend our social revolution. Although we recognize the importance of defensive paramilitary violence and even urban guerilla attacks, we do not depend on war to achieve our liberation, for our struggle cannot be won by the force of arms alone. No, the people must be armed beforehand with understanding and agreement of our objectives, as well as trust and love of the revolution. Our military weapons are only an expression of our organic spirit and solidarity. Perfect love for the people, perfect hate for the enemy!

The governments of the world commit much of their violence in repressing any attempt to overthrow the state. Crimes of repression against the people have usually benefitted those in power, especially if the government is powerful. Look what happened in the United States when the Black revolution of the 1960s was repressed. Many protesting injustice were jailed, murdered, injured or blacklisted—all set up by the state's secret police agencies. The movement was beaten down for decades as a result. Thus, we cannot only depend on mass mobilizations or engage in underground offensives if we want to defeat the state and its repression. Some mid-place between the two must be found. For the future, our work will include the development of collective techniques of self-defense and underground action while we work toward social revolution.

ANARCHISTS AND REVOLUTIONARY ORGANIZATION

Another lie about Anarchists is that they are nihilistic and do not believe in any organizational structure. Anarchists are not opposed to organization. In fact, anarchism is primarily concerned about analyzing the way in which society is presently organized (i.e., government). Nihilists want to destroy power and all social organizations. Anarchists are frequently confused with them, but we do not at all agree with the nihilist concepts.

Anarchism is all about organization, but it is about alternative forms of organization to what now exists. Anarchism's opposition to authority leads to the view that organization should be non-hierarchical and that membership would be voluntary. Anarchist revolution is a process of organization building and rebuilding. This does not mean the same thing as the Marxist-Leninist concept of "party building," which is about strengthening the role of party leaders and driving out those members who have an independent position. Such purges are methods of domination that the Marxist-Leninists use to beat all democracy out of their movements, yet they facetiously call this "democratic centralism."

To Anarchists, organization means to organize the needs of the people into non-authoritarian social organizations so they can take care of their own business on an equal basis. It also means the coming together of like-minded people to coordinate the work both groups and individuals feel necessary for their survival, well-being and livelihood. Because anarchism involves people who come together for mutual needs and interests, cooperation is a key element. A primary aim is that the individuals should speak for themselves and that all in the group be equally responsible for the group's decisions—no leaders or bosses here!

Many Anarchists would even envisage large-scale organizational needs in terms of small local groups organized in the workplace, collectives, neighborhoods and other areas, which would send delegates to larger committees to make decisions on matters of wider concern. The job of delegates would not be full time; it would be rotated. Although their out-of-pocket expenses would be paid, each delegate would be unpaid, recallable and would only voice the group's decisions. The various schools of anarchism differ in emphasis concerning organization. For example, anarcho-syndicalists stress the revolutionary labor union and other workplace formations as the basic unit of organization, while the Anarchist-Communists recognize the commune as the highest form of social organization. Others may recognize other formations as most important, but they all recognize and support free, independent organizations of the people as the way forward.

The nucleus of most Anarchist-Communist organizations is the affinity group. The affinity group is a revolutionary circle or "cell" of friends and comrades who are in tune with one another both in ideology and as individuals. The affinity group exists to coordinate the needs of the group, as expressed by individuals and by the cell as a body. The group becomes an extended family; the well-being of all becomes the responsibility of all. Many times this precedes any larger formal organizations.

Autonomous, communal and directly democratic, the (affinity) group combines revolutionary theory with revolutionary lifestyle in its everyday behavior. It creates a free space in which revolutionaries can remake themselves individually and also as social beings.

—Murray Bookchin, in *Post-Scarcity Anarchism*[3]

We could also refer to these affinity formations as "groups for living revolution" because they live the revolution now, even though only in seed form. Because the groups are small—from three to fifteen—they can start from a stronger basis of solidarity than mere political strategy alone. The groups would be the number one means of political activity of each member. There are four areas in which affinity groups work:

---

3. Murray Bookchin, *Post Scarcity Anarchism*, Ramparts Press, Menlo Park, CA, 1971.

1. Mutual Aid: This means giving support and solidarity between members, as well as collective work and responsibility.
2. Education: Besides educating the society-at-large to Anarchist ideals, this includes study by members to advance the ideology of the groups and to increase their political, economic, scientific and technical knowledge.
3. Action: This means the actual organizing and political work of the group outside the collective, where all members are expected to contribute.
4. Unity: The group is a form of family, a gathering of friends and comrades, people who care for the well-being of one another, love and support each other, strive to live in the spirit of cooperation and freedom, void of distrust, jealousy, hate, competition and other forms of negative social ideas and behavior. In short, affinity groups allow a collective to live a revolutionary lifestyle.

A big advantage of affinity groups is that they are highly resistant to police infiltration because the group members are so intimate; it is very difficult to infiltrate agents into the group. Even if a group is penetrated, there is no "central office" to give an agent information about the movement as a whole. Each cell has its own politics, agenda and objectives. Therefore, an agent would have to infiltrate hundreds, maybe thousands, of similar groups. Further, since the members all know each other, he could not lead disruptions without risk of immediate exposure, which would blunt an operation like the COINTELPRO used by the FBI against the Black and progressive movements during the 1960s. Furthermore, because there are no leaders in the movement, there is no one to target and destroy the group.

Because they can grow as biological cells grow, by division, affinity groups can proliferate rapidly. There could be hundreds in one large city or region. They prepare for the emergence of a mass movement; they will organize large numbers of people to coordinate activities as their needs become apparent and as social conditions dictate. Affinity groups function as a catalyst within the mass movement, pushing it to higher and higher levels of resistance to the authorities. They are ready-made for underground work in the event of open political repression or mass insurrection.

This leads us to the next level of Anarchist organizations, the area and regional federation. Federations are the networks of affinity groups who come together out of common needs, which include mutual aid education, action and any other work deemed necessary for society's transformation from the authoritarian state to anarchism communism.

The following is an example of how Anarchist-Communist federations could be structured.

- First, there is the area organization, which could cover a large city or county. All like-minded affinity groups in the area would associate themselves in a local federation. Agreements on ideology, mutual aid and action to be undertaken would be made at meetings in which all can come and have equal voice.
- When the local area organization reaches a size where it is deemed too big, the area federation would initiate a Coordinating Consensus Council. The purpose of the council is to coordinate the needs and actions defined by all the groups, including the possibility of splitting and creating another federation.
- Each local area's affinity group would be invited to send representatives to the council with all the viewpoints of their group and as delegates they could vote and join in making policy for the group at the council.
- The next federation would be on a regional basis, say the entire South or Midwest. This organization would take care of the whole region with the same principles of consensus and representation.
- Next would come a national federation to cover the USA and the continental federation, the latter of which would cover the continent of North America.
- Last would be the global organizations, which would be the networking of all federations worldwide. As for the latter, because Anarchists do not recognize national borders and wish to replace the nation-state, they thus federate with all other like-minded people wherever they are living on the planet earth.

For anarchism to really work, the needs of the people must be fulfilled. The first priority of Anarchists is the well-being of all; thus, we must organize the means to fully and equally fulfill the needs of the people.

First, the means of production, transportation and distribution must be organized into revolutionary organizations that the workers and the community run and control themselves.

The second priority of the Anarchists is dealing with the needs of the community. This means organization. It includes cooperative groups to fulfill such needs as health, energy, jobs, childcare, housing, alternative schools, food, entertainment and other social areas. These community groups would form a cooperative community, which would be a network of community needs organizations and serve as an Anarchistic socio-political infrastructure. These groups should network with those in other areas for mutual aid education and action and become a regional federation.

Third, Anarchists would have to address social illness. Not only do we organize for the physical needs of the people, but must also work and propagandize to cure the ills sprouted by the state, which has warped the human personality under capitalism. For instance, the oppression of women must be addressed. No one can be free if 51 percent of society is oppressed, dominated and abused. Not only must we form an organization to tackle the harmful effects of sexism, but work to ensure patriarchy is dead by educating society about its harmful effects. The same must be done with racism. In addition to the re-education of society, we must work to alleviate the social and economic oppression of Black and other non-white peoples and empower them for self-determination to lead free lives. Anarchists need to form groups to expose and combat racial prejudice and capitalist exploitation and extend full support and solidarity to the Black Liberation movement.

Finally, Anarchists would deal with areas too numerous to mention here—science, technology, ecology, disarmament, human rights and so on. We must harness the social sciences and make them serve the people while we co-exist with nature. Authoritarians foolishly believe it is possible to "conquer" nature, but that is not the issue. We are just one of many species which inhabit this planet even if we are the most intelligent. However, other species have not created nuclear weapons, started wars in which millions have been killed, or engaged in discrimination against the races of their sub-species—all which humankind has done. Therefore, who is to say which one is the most "intelligent?"

THE AMERICAN GOVERNMENT: THE BEST ARGUMENT FOR ANARCHISM!

In the United States of America, authoritarian conditioning in the family, schools, the Church and other social institutions is stronger than anywhere else on earth. The "work ethic" (which capitalists use to drive workers to death), militarism, racism, sexism, violence, sexual repression and other negative values are constantly drummed into the psyche of the populace by the American government, corporations, media and the dominant culture. America is undoubtedly the most violent, mentally sick country on the face of the globe and the most powerful and dangerous, with millions of guns among the populace and tens of thousands of nuclear weapons wielded by the U.S. military establishment.

It would be a real test of the worth of Anarchist ideals if we can finally change the social and economic structure and the cultural atmosphere of this country, which is the most important and powerful empire in history. If anarchism is established in the United States, as first a mass movement and then takes over the political and social life of the people of this territory, it can be established anywhere!

LAW AND GOVERNMENT IN AMERICA

The American government (like all governments) says it is based on the rule of law, rather than of men and that laws are allegedly meant to protect society. Neither is true. The American state is not society, the people or the nation. It is the coercive apparatus (police, army, courts, etc.) while government is the political and administrative apparatus of the state. Laws are not meant to protect society but to protect capitalist property and to repress the working class. Law is an instrument of class rule; it is how the rich rule over the poor and workers.

Politicians, judges, police officers and other public officials are chosen for their trustworthiness to the "rule of law." They are not neutral arbiters but direct agents of the state and only do its bidding, even if they have any personal qualms about whether it's right or wrong. That is why the argument about the "good cop" is a joke. All cops are hired to repress the poor and working class, not just to protect society; their job makes it possible for the capitalists to have a stable social environment so that they can make their profits.

The officials of the state have been able to build an aura of integrity, unquestioned social acceptance and fear and respect among the common people. This facade has been tarnished in recent years, as the crimes and corruption of these officials have been exposed to all and sundry. In just the last 40 plus years, there have been major exposés like Watergate,

COINTELPRO, government drug running, bribery, rape, robbery, fraud, drug dealing, conspiracy, illegal wiretapping, spying, burglary, even contract murder and cases of political corruption. Along with crimes by local police, these cases have badly shaken the system like nothing before that have been exposed in the last few years. Capitalism is inherently corrupt; it is a system based on exploitation and theft.

The truth is that any government, British, Russian, Chinese, Cuban, French or American, is based on crime, corruption and organized violence. Since America says it is the leader of the "free world" and the world's policeman, then we can surmise it is more corrupt than most.

The institution of the state itself is the ultimate crime; government is a gigantic con game and it goes something like this: the capitalists are the pimps, the politicians are the whores, the cops are the enforcers and the workers are the "tricks." We're the ones being ripped off daily and it's time we said "down with government and all nation-state oppression!"

THE ANARCHIST CASE AGAINST
REPRESENTATIVE GOVERNMENT

The United States claims to be a democratic government and proudly boasts that since its people can vote for politicians that are put forward by the establishment, they are "free." The obvious criticism against this so-called "free" representative government is that rather than direct democracy, someone must rule in the citizen's name. The people have no political power and can only vote for someone to be their "advocate" in the Presidency, the U.S. Congress, the state legislature or City Hall. This leaves bureaucrats, who are not elected and career politicians with the ultimate power to determine life and death issues affecting us all. This is a corrupt, ineffective system and when the politicians or bureaucrats become unresponsive or sell out to big business and its lobbyists, their constituencies can only cry foul and wonder where they "went wrong." The truth is they were going to sell out to big business all along; it was just a matter of their price.

The capitalists use government and its representatives to act as a buffer between them and the working class. Government officials will use money and power to stay in control for years, regardless of what their constituents want, say, or can even do about it. In fact, except for civil disobedience or to "vote the scoundrels out" and elect another one, there is nothing we can do. This is a gigantic shell game where the pod is kept in the con man's pocket.

Some liberal reformers say that if we start "citizens' groups" or "third parties" that have many voters, we can influence legislation and the behavior of politicians. However, if all the public can do is engage in lobbying by so-called "public interest" groups, then we have no serious recourse to change our political destiny under this system. For the most part, this lobbying by citizens' groups never works because it is an unequal contest; the big business corporations and wealthy capitalists have far more money to sway politicians through contributions and influence-peddling than the public and with the rise of Political Action Committees, elections and politicians are being openly bought and sold. In such a situation, "interest" groups lose out.

The conclusion we must reach is that political government is an absurdity we cannot afford; it is just a mechanism the system uses to beguile the workers and keep the rich in control. It is no "fairer" than any other state dictatorship is fair, which is to say not at all. Representative government is a form of Western capitalist class rule made more palatable to the people, but it is oppression nevertheless. Many people do not realize this until they are railroaded to prison, have seen their loved ones shot down in the streets by police, or had the government confiscate their home and/or property to satisfy taxes. This American representative government is nothing more than a benevolent dictatorship of the wealthy, which at any time of mass discontent or severe economic crisis threatening the stability of the system will be discarded for a fascist dictatorship to ensure continued control by the wealthy. Then they suspend their vaunted Constitution and hurriedly jettison civil rights and liberties with it to establish the strongest emergency police state. This is exactly what the Bush administration did after the September 11, 2001 terrorist attacks in New York and Washington, D.C.

Contrary to liberal law professors and a large segment of the naive public, the capitalists have no misty-eyed outlook or romantic attachment to the democratic capitalist economic structure. If they have to rule through open terror and turn the whole country into a prison to ensure the continued flow of profits and stability of the capitalist system, then that is what they will do. It may not be what they want to do because it is far easier to rule by using the "Matrix" and promote democratic illusions among those who are ruled over and who give the system some political legitimacy by their consent. If necessary, it will be done with a gun pointed to our foreheads as well.

Another Anarchist criticism made against representative government is that it does not represent certain classes of citizens very well, or even at all. When the United States was founded in the late 1700s, only white male landholders could vote. A rich man's version of the U.S. Constitution, establishing a federal republic, was adopted and only the rich had any democratic rights. This was challenged after the Revolutionary War, with events like Shays' Rebellion of 1786, which was really a class war of the landless against the landowners. Although many democratic rights were subsequently won, the voting franchise was still almost exclusively kept for the well-to-do.

This changed with the election of Andrew Jackson as president in the early 1800s, a period referred to as "Jacksonian democracy." All-white males of every class could now vote and the government was radically changed to allow this new voting system. Women, Blacks, Native Americans and immigrants still had no rights, including the right to vote and it would take a bloody civil war and decades of political agitation before they obtained the rights of equal citizenship under the law. In fact, it was not until modern times that Blacks could vote in the Southern United States without risking their lives. Only with the passage of the Civil Rights Act of 1964 was the right to vote recognized by the government. This accounts for the modern emphasis on "civil rights" by the American capitalist state.

However, even in the late stages of the twentieth century, African Americans, Latinos, women, gays, other racial and cultural groups and the economically poor classes were virtually powerless and openly discriminated against in society. In addition, although it had been over 100 years since Congress and the President passed the original civil rights laws during the Civil War, these statutes and their progeny are not being properly enforced and are, in fact, under attack. This government protective legislation does not really protect peoples of color and women very well. In fact, only through filing expensive lawsuits and marching in the streets have peoples of color, the poor and women won any victories at all. Women are also now being covered by the civil rights laws, but that coverage is very weak and the attempt to pass an Equal Rights Amendment to ensure equal pay on the job was defeated in the 1980s by conservative politicians and a strong right-wing fundamentalist Christian movement.

Also, consider that it took gay people years to persuade Congress to pass national homosexual rights legislation to protect them from job, housing and other social discrimination.

Even though federal civil rights laws cover them, racial discrimination, economic exploitation and racist "English Only" legislation has been passed in several states which are victimizing immigrants, particularly Latinos.

All this and more, such as widespread racial discrimination in voting during the 2000 Presidential election, ensuring the coronation of George W. Bush, should convince one that a large portion of the population is almost wholly locked out of the political system. What should be basic protection of all minorities and women is instead a privilege bestowed by the rich and politicians, and only when they are effectively challenged. It is a way to stave off a wider degree of public dissatisfaction with the system, maybe even a revolution. Politicians grant rights that are more democratic when the heat is on them and constrict them when they are on the offensive or now have the favorable balance of political forces. Thus, representative government in America is clearly a sham that only works for the rich, white upper classes.

However, a cottage industry of attorneys and other professionals to "fight for the rights" of different groups has arisen in American politics. Therefore, it is lawyers, judges and politicians who determine your degree of civil rights and civil liberties, and what individual rights the state can allegedly be circumscribed from invading. If someone "grants" you human rights, then you really have no rights at all because those same forces can take them away or violate them at will, just as soon as they have the political power to do so. There has to be a better system than this and there is. The alternative is not just to reform the system by making it easier to vote, or through lawsuits or political protests to force the government to grant more rights in a wider area of American life. Even most Anarchists will admit that civil rights and liberties are important for workers and the poor while the capitalist system still exists, but stronger medicine is needed to transform this society.

The answer is to junk the capitalist political and economic system entirely! Anarchists believe in direct democracy by the people instead of a representative government and reject both national political parties, the Republicans and the Democrats (which claim to be dramatically different in program and personalities, but are in fact two sides of the same coin: liberal and conservative). Whenever one party is in power, the other serves as the "loyal opposition," or seeks to undermine the other just for partisan political advantage. It is just a case of "tweedle-dee and tweedle-dum," or better yet, as described by Malcolm X in one of his speeches, the Republican "wolf" and the Democratic "fox," both of which are carnivorous beasts and will eat you alive!

Direct democracy means that democracy can only stem from the bottom to the top, instead of the other way around. For instance, it calls for the creation of neighborhood assemblies, community unions and other local associations united in a form of "neighborhood government." This grassroots level is where all the most important decisions about social and political life are made and then emanate from there to higher and higher social levels until encompassing all society. From the neighborhood assembly to the city-wide assembly, region-wide assembly and from there to national and international levels, none of which use professional politicians. Representatives at these various levels are not permanent fixtures, but rather subject to immediate recall at any time there is a question of impropriety or dereliction of duties. Instead of elections on the important issues facing the people or in talk shops like the U.S. Congress or state legislatures, such important issues would be decided by direct vote of the people at the local level, in a national referendum, or through another means which guarantees democratic rights.

In this way, we eliminate the "middle man," "the sleazy career politician," and also eliminate the need for a humongous government administration. The people would select their own and, as long as there were checks and balances in the system to protect racial and ethnic groups and gender rights, this would work well and efficiently. Popular prejudices by the majority could not hold sway; issues concerning basic human rights could never be put to a vote. There would have to be a consensus on the basic rights of human beings across gender, race, class and cultural lines, which would be inviolate, for this particular model to work.

We do not know what precise form direct democracy will take in America; we just know it would be a vast improvement over the current system. But even this is not enough to reform the current system because it is the entire system that is at fault. Let's look further, shall we? I am not putting this forth as an example of an Anarchist society, on the contrary, just a transition from that corporate-dominated government which exists now, a way, in fact, to popularize direct democracy and use it against the capitalist government which exists now. I believe that people are ready to end the rule of politicians, but that an alternative which can be adopted now must be proposed and created on the local levels. If we do not present an alternative, one capable of being adopted now and which destabilizes the regime, we cannot move forward to empower the people, and just provide another example of useless idealism.

THE AMERICAN BUREAUCRATIC STATE

Although all governments are bureaucratic, the United States has raised bureaucracy to a new level, with thousands of administrative agencies at the federal level and thousands more at the state, county and city levels. There is endless duplication and waste, corruption and malfeasance in this system. The U.S. Constitution enshrined a bureaucratic structure from the early days of the Republic, a development that accelerated during the "Great Depression" of the 1930s. President Franklin Roosevelt's administration massively increased the size of the federal government and signed into existence thousands of pieces of legislation, each of which created its own enforcement agency. Sometimes that agency subdivided into other agencies until we are now at the stage of massive regulation of almost every aspect of American life.

Although many Marxists, democratic socialists and liberals approve of big government as the only solution to a vast array of social problems, Anarchists and radical libertarians believe it is a massive waste of resources and patently unfair to the masses of people, who are forced to pay higher and higher taxes to get fewer and fewer benefits. America has created a citizenry that is dependent on the government for everything and that is less likely to take personal or political responsibility for the social environment. Strangely, instead of blaming the corrupt political system, it seems almost everyone scapegoats the poor on welfare and complains about the elderly on Social Security as though they were responsible for all the economic and political problems of this country. This is why politicians can so easily take advantage of the people; under such a system, we make them feel needed.

Delivery of government services by bureaucracy also means a professional civil service of agency bureaucrats, imbued with the ideology of government control and surveillance. It means the government has files on everyone, so that if you apply for any government program, all your life history is revealed. This is a loss of privacy that civil libertarians are constantly grappling with. This government surveillance is extremely dangerous and makes it much easier for the secret police to target and retaliate against those with anti-government sentiments.

Bureaucracy does not improve the efficiency of government service delivery. In fact, it makes it more difficult. With so many centers of power with overlapping and repetitive authority, countermanding orders about the same claims are inevitable. That is why people complain about having to go to five or ten different agencies or individuals to perform the simplest of functions or to obtain government benefits. This rigid control and the bureaucracy is necessary if government is to be "efficient," so say the defenders of the system. Anarchists say we need to decentralize the system of social benefits, not centralize them under the current system. Even the capitalist apologists admit that they are now in favor of decentralization of industry, if not the institutions of government and social life. Here I will quote the late Sam Dolgoff from his booklet *The Relevance of Anarchism to Modern Society*:[4]

> Bourgeois economists, sociologists and administrators like Peter Drucker, Gunnar Myrdal, John Kenneth Galbraith, Daniel Bell and others, now favor a large measure of decentralization, not because they suddenly became Anarchists, but primarily because technology has rendered anarchist forms of organization "operational necessities."

The point is that the capitalist apologists only seek reforms or "workarounds" to the problem, rather than a way to solve the matter completely. Let Dolgoff explain in the next quotation:

> But the bourgeois reformers have yet to learn that as long as the organizational forms are tied to the state or capitalism, which connotes the monopoly of political and economic power, decentralization will remain a fraud—a more efficient device to enlist the cooperation of the masses in their own enslavement.

Clearly, this same argument can be effectively made about the American capitalist government, which the apologists recognize is too large and omnipresent. President Ronald Reagan was elected to office promising to "downsize government" and to "get the government off the

---

4.   Sam Dolgoff, *The Relevance of Anarchism to Modern Society*, Libertarian Analysis, New York, 1970.

people's back," even though what he did was to deregulate big business and make it freer to exploit the workers and make larger profits without antitrust, environmental, labor and other regulatory controls. Likewise, in the final years of the Clinton administration, we also saw former Vice President Al Gore talking about "reinventing government" by eliminating certain repetitive and wasteful federal agencies, by simplifying government paperwork and controlling the greediness of political action committees (PACs) and business lobbyists, among other "reform" measures. Virtually none of this was implemented and he was defeated at his run for the Presidency in the 2000 elections.

There is no way to "reinvent" the American federal government to make it more manageable, less bureaucratic and oppressive. Bureaucracy has a built-in defense mechanism. Cut off the head of one federal agency and two more will magically appear. They don't die, they multiply! These so-called "reformers" have appeared since the early days of the Republic, when then President George Washington talked about the same thing and was no more successful. Today's military-industrial complex, business lobbyists and bureaucrats will outlive and outmaneuver any government reformers. The truth is they have created a monster; a dinosaur that is eating everything and everyone in sight and its name is big government. Save yourself and hide the women and children because it demands a sacrifice both in war and peace!

Do you really believe that government bureaucrats are the best thing to happen to you, or that this capitalist system was "ordained by God," as many of the conservative televangelists tell millions of people? This system is based on slavery and oppression and its existence is maintained by violence and exploitation against the lower classes. No amount of government programs or benevolent facade will change this basic fact. There is no freedom in America and we have got to stop pretending there is. We must tell the truth and let the truth set us free from such mythology. No more lies, for our children's sake and our own!

DOWN WITH THE GOVERNMENT!

Although Anarchists must persuade the average person of the futility and harmfulness of government, we will only be effective when we explain it in very simple terms. Anarchism stands for more freedom, not less, because we are talking about a system without a government, unless it is self-government at the community level. We want direct democracy by the people so that they cannot be manipulated, oppressed or ruled over by anybody. Certainly we Anarchists do not ourselves seek power or some sort of political control of the people. Anarchists are the utmost advocates of liberty and individualism. So what is anarchism? It is a free form of social ownership of the means of production and a classless form of society. It protects the rights of the individual, while at the same time providing for the social benefits of the masses of humanity. There is no authority responsible for presiding over how people live; the people decide that. There are no communist party, capitalist or any other bosses under this system. Anarchists believe that any attempt to use a state bureaucracy to rule over society is a limit on freedom rather than a spur to it.

We have been brainwashed by the system to defend the capitalist "free enterprise" system. There is no free enterprise system but rather a system of monopoly capitalism in which the biggest corporations and richest people own everything. Certainly there is no "free government" in America. Government controls; it does not provide freedom. That is why you pay taxes or go to jail, serve in the armed forces or go to jail, register your guns with the government or go to jail—well you get the idea! You are being coerced to toe the government line.

Finally, the United States claims to be the "leader of the free world" and has gone to war many times in the name of "defending freedom" in some other country. In fact, the people are not free in America and they are being used to oppress the peoples of other countries. When the American capitalists talk hypocritically about "freedom" or "peace," watch out! They mean just the opposite and are preparing to attack. They go to war to steal other countries' natural resources or to set up a pro-American regime.

Authority and the state have made warfare against various nations or peoples throughout history from the Roman Empire down to the United States today. Probably the most serious question facing our species is if we will continue to survive in peace or be destroyed in a nuclear war. The United States poses the greatest threat of war in the world. American capitalists jockey for world domination, playing a geopolitical game with nuclear weapons as trump cards. This is a form of state terrorism and international lunacy, playing with millions of people's lives, here and abroad. But so long as there is a nation-state, there will be war and the threat of more wars. Anarchists want to outlaw war, along with the state that causes it.

2

Capitalism and Racism: An Analysis of White Supremacy and the Oppression of Peoples of Color

In America, hundreds of years ago, the white government and political system were created for the enslavement and exploitation of the labor of Africans, the destruction of the Native peoples already on the land, and domination of other peoples of color. It was a colonial regime for white supremacy from inception.

Most of the white working population have been directly controlled as a class, but nevertheless united with the state. Yet, the fate of the privileged white working people has always been bound with the condition of the African slaves, and other internally oppressed peoples of color. Although they have tried, whites cannot be truly free without the freedom of Black people and other peoples of color. They have certainly been given privileges and material incentives, making them much better off than the despised racially oppressed internal colonies of Blacks and peoples of color, but even this was by design. Their entire higher quality of life is because of this collaboration with the capitalist state. The greatest hypocrisy of American life has always been the holding up of this idealized white racist society before the world as somehow "the deserving citizenry of a united democratic nation."

Going as far back as the American colonial period (1619–1776) when Black labor was first imported into America, Black slaves and indentured servants had been oppressed right along with whites of the lower classes. But when European indentured servants joined with Blacks to rebel against their lot in the late 1600s and destabilized the entire British-controlled colonial system, the propertied class decided to "free" them by giving them a special status as "white citizens" and thus a stake in the system of oppression. They became exploited, while the Africans were outright enslaved. Even after a bloody revolution against the British colonial authorities, white ex-indentured servants were used to protect the slave system. In the South, they were ultimately manipulated to hate, fear and despise all Africans, even though many times white workers or poor people were no better off; but, again, they were white and were now "citizens," no longer indentured servants. That "whiteness" was a badge of honor and a means of social control.

How were white workers and indentured servants enlisted in their own exploitation, even down to today? Material incentives. They could get better jobs, live in better houses, not be subjected to arbitrary police rule, or other discrimination. They had legal rights, even if many were limited to control by the big landholders at this stage. They were "white" people, Americans, better off than Blacks, Mexicans or others, who were actually still part of colonized races. This invention of the "white race" as guard dog and protector of the most brutal forms of racial slavery of the Africans went hand-in-glove, and is how the upper classes maintained order during the entire period of slavery. The rich could say: "Let's hire the poor and working class whites as slave-breakers or plantation overseers; they will do our dirty work for us."

The rich reasoned that even poor whites wanted to be part of a white master race and since their social mobility was ensured by the new system, they would abandon their former allies. They were right. The African slaves were left on their own; this Euro-American social mobility, however, was on the backs of the African slaves, who were still super-exploited and whose forced labor was the foundation of capital accumulation and creation of a white nation-state. The Southern agrarian production method, with the chattel slave system and its challenge to the oncoming industrialism, is the contradiction, which ultimately doomed the Old South, but class collaborationism by white workers has remained as the main contradiction in building a multinational struggle.

Even after chattel slavery was defeated with the American Civil War, racial discrimination continued, in fact the die had long since been cast for the dual-tier form of labor, especially in the Southern states, which exploited the African, but also trapped poor white labor in manual or "stoop" labor, mining, textiles and other industries. When they sought to organize unions for higher wages in the North or South, these white industrial laborers were slapped down by the rich, who used semi-enslaved Black labor as their primary mode of production and even later as strikebreakers. The so-called "free" labor of the white worker did not stand a chance.

While these things were happening to Africans in the United States of America, other people of color were being subjected to similar oppression: the land of the Mexican people was being stolen by white colonists through war and terror, imported Chinese were forced to work under dreadful conditions to establish the railroads linking East to West and the white government and its cavalry were mass murdering the Plains Indians, finishing a job started a century before when the White man came to the North American continent and violently evicted the then Southern-based Cherokee tribes, creating a white republic on stolen land in Virginia, the Carolinas, Tennessee and other territories.

Although the capitalists used the system of white skin privilege to great effect to divide the working class of the North, the truth is the capitalists only favored white workers to use them against their own interests, not because there was true "white" class unity. Never lose sight of the fact the capitalists didn't want white labor united with Blacks or other oppressed non-white peoples against their rule and the system of exploitation of labor. *The invention of the "white race" was just a scam to facilitate this exploitation.* White workers were bought off to allow their own wage slavery and Africans' super-exploitation; they struck a deal with the devil, which has hampered all efforts at class unity for the last four centuries or more.

Especially during the early industrial period, the continuous subjugation of the masses depended on competition and internal disunity to keep them from organizing unions and even when they did, make sure that it was either all-white or under white bureaucratic control. Therefore, the white workers and the unions upheld racial discriminatory hiring and promotion policies from the beginning at many industrial plants. Although there were no doubt widespread virulent racists among them, many white workers bought into this racism naively, thinking it was just a price they had to pay for jobs, and that things would improve on their own. But once started you cannot control racism; as long as discrimination exists and racial or ethnic minorities are oppressed, the entire working class is oppressed and weakened.

This is because the capitalist class is able to use racism to drive down the wages of individual segments of the working class by inciting racial antagonisms and forcing a fight for jobs and services. What I mean is that this division is a development that ultimately undercuts the living standards of all workers, creating more poverty generally. Moreover, by pitting whites against Blacks and other oppressed nationalities in society, the capitalist class is able to prevent workers from uniting against their common class enemy. As long as workers are fighting one another over the crumbs from the rich man's plate, capitalist class rule is secure. Especially as long as one wing of society accepts racist exploitation, ghettos, legal job discrimination and other forms of social oppression against the other, it is much easier to rip everybody off.

This "wedge" political strategy is why we are in this situation today and how this corrupt system stays in power. White workers go along with so much of this garbage, thinking it is in their best interests not to fight it. Of course, it is never very simple to make people recognize this and such unity can only be built in a movement fighting actively against racism and exploitation. You cannot blindly holler, "look at what the bosses are doing [!]" when there is so much racism and class collaboration in the white working class itself. This is why white radicals have never been effective just issuing moral appeals to white workers, and have never built a mass anti-racist movement united with Black/POC communities.

If an effective resistance is to be mounted against the current racist offensive of the capitalist class, the utmost solidarity between the poor and workers of all races is essential, but especially among various peoples of color. My position has always been one where rather than the usual road of a white-dominated path to "unity," as laid out by the white left, I believe an alliance of oppressed peoples of color is really the way forward in this period. This does not mean that we do not have group differences or will always agree on individual issues between various non-white ethnic and racial groupings. But our shared history of oppression and desire for liberation equip us for a new type of unity and lays a path to unite with advanced elements of the white working class.

We must point out to those white people who say they oppose the system: that the way to defeat the capitalist strategy is for white workers to defend the democratic rights won by Blacks and other oppressed peoples after decades of hard struggle and to fight to dismantle the system of white skin privilege. White workers should support and adopt the concrete demands of the Black/POC movement and should work to abolish the white identity entirely. These white workers should strive for multicultural unity and should work with Black/POC activists to build an anti-racist movement to challenge white supremacy. They should stand in absolute solidarity with the liberation movements in those communities that arise. (This must be done in tandem with any wage demands, but most white radicals dismiss this as "divisive.")

However, even though we call on white workers to support our struggle, it is also very important for them to recognize the right of the Black movement to take an independent road in its own interests. That is what self-determination means. It does not mean deferring our struggles to that of white radicals or other segments of the white community, with the hope of some mindless "unity" in the future. It has not yet even been proven that the most progressive or "radical" whites are up to the task and since racism is so deep, that they would be able to break away. But we offer them a way forward, in support of and as part of a new movement.

RACE AND CLASS: THE COMBINED CHARACTER
OF BLACK/POC OPPRESSION

Because of the way the American nation-state has developed with the exploitation of African labor, the genocide and theft of the lands of indigenous peoples and the maintenance of Africans in America as an internal colony, they and other non-white peoples are oppressed both as members of the working class and as a racial grouping/nationality. It's not just a question of mere prejudice among the white population or minor discrimination—it's settler colonialism.

As Africans, Chicanos, Native Americans or other people of color in America, we are a distinct people, hounded and segregated in U.S. society. By struggling for our human and civil rights, we ultimately come into confrontation with the entire capitalist system, not just with individual racists or in certain regions of the country. The truth soon becomes apparent: Blacks/POC cannot get our freedom under this system; we have to fight for total liberation. Our struggles can serve as the basis of a battle to overturn the entire system. Based on historically uneven competition and slavery, capitalist exploitation is inherently racist and fundamentally oppressive. The entire corrupt system has to go, not just a few bad features easily remedied by more reforms or the passage of more lenient civil rights legislation. Yet that is what has happened since the end of the Civil Rights/Black Power period.

It's interesting that even though the white government tries to get light-skinned Latinos, Asians, Blacks or others to commit "racial suicide" by passing as white or multiracial and "integrating" into white society, the fact of racial oppression in their own lives ultimately will not let them get away with it. They simply must be the people of color they are, even if it means suffering racial discrimination; they ultimately do not want to be part of the ruling group of a white oppressive society. That is why we see various types of cultural nationalist currents and movements for democratic rights erupt among peoples of color all over the world, from Brazil to the United States, London to Toronto, Sydney to San Francisco, which even includes the lightest-skinned people of color. They are rejecting the white world and white middle-class conformity, if not the capitalist system itself. The real question is whether it can become something more than a movement for civil rights, or racial and cultural pride.

Now the 1960s Civil Rights movement had the potential to go in the direction of revolutionary social change. The potential was there for either road. In fact, the major weakness of the Martin Luther King-wing of the 1960s Civil Rights movement was that it allied itself with the white liberals in the Democratic Party and settled for civil rights protective legislation, instead of pushing for social revolution. This limited the movement to winning reforms and democratic rights within the structure of the capitalist state. That is where we have remained for the last 50 years. Now predictably, these gains are being threatened by the rise of racist conservative movements like the Tea Party.

This self-policing by the middle-class leaders of the movement is an object lesson about why the new movement has to be self-activated, autonomous, and not dependent on charismatic personalities and politicians. The Black Power movement, which came along later had some weaknesses of its own, in that it stayed stagnant in the cultural stage for several years, with poetry societies, performance groups and other cultural groups which celebrated the Black identity and denounced "the Man," but took no action to fight for Black Liberation. The Black youth in the ghettos of America were screaming "Black Power! Black Power!" as they torched the cities and confronted police brutality, but not until groups like the Black Panther Party, the League of Black Revolutionary Workers and local "Black militant" groups became active was there a radical political tendency complementing and challenging the cultural activists.

So, there is always a trajectory for such movements. They can go forward or backwards, accepting reforms, engaging in narcissism, or fighting for an entirely new society. But if such a Black movement does become a social revolutionary movement, it must ultimately unite its forces with similar movements among Native Americans, Chicanos, Puerto Ricans and other oppressed peoples of color, who are in revolt against the system. Such a united movement of activist peoples of color could radicalize even broader sectors of the white society, such as students, youth, laborers and others, thus undermining the consensus upholding white support for the government across class lines.

In fact, for a large part of the 1960s the Civil Rights/Black Liberation movement even acted as a catalyst to spread revolutionary ideas and images of liberation and hope of a new society to millions, which coaxed forth the various opposition movements of that period, not only the various ethnic liberation movements, but even the Vietnam anti-war movement and the New Left; as well as the Women's, Queer and other white radical social movements we see still around today.

This is what we believe has the most potential to happen again, radical Autonomous movements acting as revolutionary "incubators" of broad-based struggles, although it is not enough to call for mindless "unity" as much of the white left does. Their "unity" just means white leftist control and leadership of the overall struggle.

So we cannot sit around waiting on white working people to join our movements, or running to join white-dominated organizations. White people are still not in the same desperate circumstances as Blacks, Latinos or Native Americans, nor want to see the system defeated now as long as it serves them. For instance, it was only after the Black Civil Rights movement, Cesar Chavez's United Farm Workers movement and other Black/POC movements came into existence and gained popular support that whites even became supportive of them in some later fashion. They jumped aboard a moving train.

AUTONOMY AS A REVOLUTIONARY TENDENCY

Because of the dual forms of oppression of non-white workers and the depth of social desperation it creates, Blacks and peoples of color must strike first, whether their potential white allies are available to do so or not. This is self-determination and that is why it is necessary for oppressed workers to build independent movements to unite their own peoples first. Malcolm X was the first one to really explain this. This self-activity of the oppressed masses of color when it reaches the radical stage is inherently a revolutionary force and is an essential part of the social revolutionary process of the entire working and poor class.

As Blacks and other oppressed peoples of color, we are living though some of the most perilous times in both American and world history.

The white empire is declining, but in its desperation to cling to power, we face police murder and brutality, mass imprisonment of youth of color, racial profiling, degrading poverty and unemployment, repressive anti-terrorist legislation and new wars of conquest and yet we do not hear the voices of organized peoples of color in their millions in North America. Instead, we are part of "someone else's agenda" or "someone else's political organization," but it is time now to build our own and speak for ourselves. We must not only demand our "rights" in a Western capitalist society, but fight to build a new world.

The Black, Brown, Yellow, Red and other oppressed peoples of color on the face of this planet earth have been subjected to genocide, racism, warfare, slavery, torture, economic exploitation and other forms of oppression heaped on them by the Western imperialist countries. For centuries, we have sought to resist, individually and with anti-colonial/ liberation and other struggles in our countries, but now we have to build a united front of peoples of color everywhere, fighting the same enemy, the same battles. The whole world is now a ghetto, a 'hood, with poor/ working-class people of color in Brussels, London, Paris, New York, Los Angeles, Durban, Detroit, Lagos, Beirut and cities throughout the world living the same lives of economic, social and cultural deprivation.

So, it is time to get our peoples organized in the barrios, the ghettos, the hamlets, the "quarters," hovels, college dorms, high schools, churches, prisons and other places we find them. We need to organize a federation of autonomous people of color and begin to practice a lost art among activists these days: community-based organizing for grassroots people's power. We must challenge ourselves to become serious organizers and activists in our own communities, to link up with others and someday build a powerful movement that can change the world. And we must make ourselves both a strong voice in the Anarchist scene and an alternative in the radical social change movement generally, instead of just marginal or token Black, Brown, Yellow or Red faces in small numbers inside white radical tendencies. Autonomy means independence.

ANARCHISM + BLACK REVOLUTION = NEW BLACK AUTONOMOUS POLITICS

Although Anarchists do not believe in vanguard political parties, the reality is that because of the peculiarities of the United States of America's social development and especially racial slavery, Africans in America and other peoples of color with a shared history are predisposed to lead at least the beginning states of a social revolution, thereafter enlisting or being joined by potential allies in the white working class. Africans in America constitutes a "class vanguard," a class capable of radicalizing society with its struggle against racism and capitalism. Most white radicals at least give lip service to understanding this, especially since the Black Power and Civil Rights struggles unfolded in the 1960s, although they still hang onto the "white working class hero" ideology of the past, to try to deflect these issues with a backward class argument. We cannot simply wait around for white people to "get it" and become active in our cause.

For years, the white radicals argued that since whites are the numerical majority in society, it is they that should lead all social struggles. Even though Blacks and people of color are a "minority" of the total population, they are estimated to be the majority in a few decades. There can be no successful social revolution in the United States without Black and non-white people not just taking equal part in a white-dominated movement, but in fact leading the way. The U.S. class system is based on racialized social, economic and political oppression. With such a race and class divided society, to ignore this basic fact is a sell-out or capitulation to white supremacy. Rather than reducing all contradictions to class alone, like most white radicals continue to do, we must understand the workings of racism as part of the structure of overall oppression.

In fact, for white radicals to ignore this means that they themselves are engaging in white chauvinism of the worst sort and betraying the very idea of social revolution. Though they think they should lead everybody or have all the answers, social history of the United States has proven too many times that white middle-class radicals cannot even lead working-class whites, let alone the captive nationalities to freedom. Because of their almost total ignorance about race and class issues, white Anarchist radicals don't even know what questions to ask and therefore can't come up with the right answers. So we organize in our own name and for our interests in a Black/POC Autonomous movement, rather than depend on them.

The new autonomous politics is made up of the libertarian socialist core of anarchism and many of the tenets of revolutionary Black nationalism, such as was stated and practiced by the original Black Panther Party. This combination of elements makes up something so new that it has not been fully defined before now. We will attempt to more sharply define what it is that we have been talking about for so many years and also place it within an historical context so that it can no longer be dismissed as an eclectic "mish-mash" or "corruption of (both ideals)" as the purists would claim. Yet, it should not alarm Anarchist ideological "purists" when we speak of an Autonomous movement of Anarchists of color.

First, the early Anarchist movement in America always reflected the cultural, social and political ideals of the community that produced it. Thus, we had a Germanic-dominated anarcho-syndicalist tendency during the 1880s called the International Working People's Association, which was strong in Chicago, Pittsburgh and a few other industrial cities; a Jewish Anarchist movement in New York and other cities during the 1900s—which lasted until the 1980s, wherein some whole newspapers were printed in Yiddish; an Italian movement also flourished in New York, New Jersey and other urban areas in the 1920s to the 1930s and so on. One European ethnic group after another produced unique American Anarchist social movements, which culturally and politically reflected those communities.

So the question then becomes why should anyone be surprised to learn that there would be Anarchist movements of Pacific Islanders, African Americans or Latinos among other peoples of color? In talking about Anarchist ideals and Autonomous movements, we are not talking about "orthodoxies" which cannot be revised, we are talking about ideas which will be picked up, used by millions of oppressed peoples and adapted to their purpose and circumstances. But many of the white Anarchists have shown nothing but fear and loathing.

Black Autonomy is not Black nationalism. First, we use the term 'Black" to refer to all existing peoples of color and not just Africans or the descendants of Africans all over the world. First, all life began in Africa. Second, we believe in self-determination, but not any form of racial superiority. Third, we do not negate class differences between rich and poor within any nationality, those among us who seek to be our neo-colonial masters, the "Negrosie," are our enemies as much as the European racists; fourth, we do not seek to build a nation-state for our own separate peoples; and fifth, we subscribe to the major tenets of anarchism and anti-authoritarian politics, although we redefine many of those to deal with our oppressed condition and ideas of liberation.

Interestingly, it was Fred Hampton and the Chicago branch of the Black Panther Party which first conceived of a "Rainbow Alliance" of revolutionary organizations of various ethnic and racial groups way back in the late 1960s. Hampton was no integrationist and although he remained a strong Black revolutionary, he began to unite white radicals, with progressive elements of the Black community, Latinos, Asians and others into a grassroots political movement to organize in their own communities, and then unite their local political associations into a city-wide grassroots alliance. He openly referred to this as a dual power institution to challenge the established white power structure and empower the poor masses of the Daley political machine. However, he was assassinated in December 1969, before he could really put his program into play. And yet it is something that still needs to happen.

We go further now and say that there should be a movement built of autonomous peoples of color, linked to the Anarchist movement, but existing as an independent tendency. There have been short-term alliances between ethnic and racial groups, but there has never been a real attempt to actually create a revolutionary organization of peoples of color. But what is needed is a radical break from the narrow race nationalism of "our people first and only" to a new radical consciousness of race and class, which embraces those peoples of color and oppressed peoples of diverse ethnic backgrounds that share views of autonomous political action. Many Black nationalists and doctrinaire white radical groups alike would be opposed to this, for reasons of their own.

But the Anarchist purists and Black chauvinists both will just have to shudder, because a new movement is on the verge of happening now and there is nothing that anybody can do to stop it. There are anti-authoritarian activists of color of every ethnic group and hue, who are taking the first slow steps toward building a tendency within the Anarchist movement, or even venturing out as autonomous anti-authoritarians. They have taken those ideals which I and others have put out there and made them into a class weapon reflecting the African, Asian or Latino experiences on this continent and thus taken the first steps to free their peoples and their class.

This great sector of oppressed colored humanity has said we have had enough: Enough racism! Enough poverty! Enough degradation! Enough oppression! They also know they will have to fight their own fight, if they want to be free. Nobody from the white world is coming to save them. Although they know the revolutionary project to defeat this system of capitalism and enslavement requires millions of other allies who will help them, it is people of color who will decide the agenda, the timetable and the tactics for obtaining our liberation. Too long have others spoken for us without our best interests at heart.

The new Black/POC autonomous politics differs from European anarchism in that we know that we are oppressed as a distinct people and as workers. Currently, European-dominated anarchism places its greatest contradictions with the state alone, with the state's ability to hold back a free lifestyle and yet this is exactly what we cannot limit our critique to. This is a white worldview based on many members' privileged upper middle-class background in capitalist society. Some Anarchists and other white radicals argue that we should not "buy into" any race differentiation at all, less known ideals of autonomy. To them we say: yes, we realize that historically constructed "races" have been created under this system, which determines both manner of life and death under this system and that the state upholds this race/class system. Yes, we know that it is no accident that it is this way all white. Yes, it is also true that individual white workers have not commissioned racism and we do not perceive people as enemies. However, we also know how this system really works for white supremacy, and that all classes of whites have been the beneficiaries of our oppression, and that white class collaborationism is part of the social control mechanism of the state. The fact is that it is the whites who should be the ones deconstructing whiteness and confronting white racism, while we fight for freedom and liberation in our own way!

Therefore, we vehemently disagree with the socialists, communists and those Anarchists who say that the oppression of all workers is identical under this system. This does not reflect reality at all. We say that we are a class of super-oppressed people of color historically downtrodden equally because of our racial oppression under this system, not just our social class as workers. Even a cursory glance at history and everyday social reality proves that one's place in this racist society rides on the outcome of skin pigment or ethnic makeup. If you are non-white you are treated one way; if you are white, you are treated another. So racism is a class doctrine, used by the state for social control of workers of color. In fact, racism is the actual class relationship in North American society.

I have pointed out before that so-called "white" people are a contrived super-nationality designed to help the capitalists keep workers of color in their place and safeguard the status quo. So rather than see the white industrial working class as a potentially revolutionary class, instead we see it as an opportunistic, collaborationist body which must be redefined and reorganized if is to constitute a reliable ally for workers of color and have any ability of fighting in the interests of a new working class. As it stands now, they are fighting for white rights, not for the rights of the entire class of the poor and workers.

As autonomous workers of color, we of course disagree with Marxists and other so-called radicals who claim that an authoritarian political party and strong leadership cultism is necessary to produce a social revolution. But we go further and say that neither they nor the white Anarchists can lead us as a people of color (or even themselves) to our freedom, even though they have been conditioned as Europeans to command and rule over people of color and the lower classes. We vehemently reject their mis-leadership and authoritarian rule over us, or their old ideals of white industrial workers as a proletarian class of saviors.

BLACK AUTONOMY IS NOT SEPARATIST

However, we also have differences with the Black (and other race) nationalists, although we may share many basic ideas with them on cultural autonomy. We also believe in and treasure many of the traditions and history of our peoples, but believe it must be demystified and made into a culture of resistance, rather than personality cults or escapism from the reality of fighting racism. Further, we categorically do not believe in any "race nationalism," which demonizes white people and advocates some sort of biological determinism. We are not xenophobic; so do not entertain any race mythology about European peoples as either a superior species or as devils. And although we recognize the necessity of autonomous struggles in this period, we can work with white workers and poor people around specific campaigns. A major point of our differences is that we are not seeking to build a Black nation-state.

In fact, we believe the same class politics of "haves and have-nots" will show itself within any type of Black nation-state, whether it's an Islamic, secular New African or African socialist state, and that this will produce an extreme class differential and economic/political injustice among those oppressed peoples of color. We can look at a succession of dictatorships and capitalist regimes in Africa to let us know this. We believe that a bourgeois class and political dictatorship is inevitable and that a people's revolution will break out under such a Black nationalist government. Look at what is happening today under the former apartheid government, now under Black rule, united with the white capitalist class. The Black bourgeoisie and business class have been elevated as the nominal ruling class, while the same economic forces are exploiting and oppressing the African working class and poor. Millions are homeless, unemployed, exploited at law, wage, labor, jobs, and are landless. Capitalist Black Power has not freed Black people even after apartheid has been defeated. Can the capitalist imperialist financial institutions any less control a Black nation-state in America? Sovereignty is not an option in such a world dominated by this system. A new Black nation-state on a North American land territory does not mean freedom any more than do the ones in Africa, Asia and Latin America.

We also believe that under the capitalist system that now exists, most manifestations of Black nationalism have never been a truly revolutionary doctrine, but rather such movements have asserted themselves most forcefully as a defensive doctrine for the protection of the Black middle class. It is not even a movement to fight white racism, but rather an interest group politics which can battle for equal political power for Black businesspeople or the professional class under this system, not to remove it.

So, a Black nation-state is not the answer to our problems as an oppressed people, in fact it leads us back to slavery, just as it has not led to freedom for any of the world's people. Just flag independence. It replaces the white master for the Black master. We are not immune from the laws of social change; the state is an oppressive institution by its very nature.

In addition, those who argue for a Black state almost never tell how it will be obtained and many of their arguments that have been presented are intentionally vague and fanciful. Who really believes that America will just grant an Islamic state to the Nation of Islam, or give up five Southern states to the Republic of New Africa just because a small faction calling itself a "government in exile" exists and advocates for it? Who can even prove most people want it in the first place? Why, it would require years of a bloody struggle and a major organizing drive. And what are we to do until that great day comes (?); the Black nationalist groups never tell us, but we can presume we are to blindly follow behind their leaders and pay our dues to their organizations. This is opportunism and treachery, leading us down a blind alley.

In addition, the only revolutionary nationalist group to even talk about conducting a plebiscite to find out what form African people in America believed our freedom should take was the Black Panther Party.

They recognized that it was up to the masses to make such decisions, not vanguard organizations in their place. Like the Panthers, we believe that even before racism or capitalism are defeated, we can begin now to wage a protracted struggle against capitalism and its agents and that the only nation-state we should be concerned with is the corrupt American state still oppressing us and most of the peoples of the world.

In common with the Student Nonviolent Coordinating Committee, the leading militant organization of the earlier Civil Rights period, Anarchists believe that the role of the organizer is not to lead people, but to empower them and let them take over their own local struggles. We also believe that such communities are virtual colonies or semi-colonies, which are under the military and political control of the state. But we do not believe that a national liberation movement alone can free us and that the real task is to dismantle capitalism itself. Our liberation struggle is part of a broader struggle for total social change.

Many middle-class Black nationalist groups are tied to the Democratic Party or the Green Party and do not offer any real radical alternative. First, we do not believe in conventional or electoral politics in any form and reject coalitions led by liberals and social democrats. Finally, like the Panthers of the 1960s and contrary to today's Nation of Islam and the Afro-centric movement, we believe in a class analysis and understand that there were historical, socio-economic factors that accounted for both slavery and racism, not because whites are "ice people," "devils" or other such nonsense. The main motive was money, the enrichment of Europe and the "New World." This capitalist system produces racism/white supremacy. It is this capitalist system that must be destroyed to get rid of it, not create an allied "rump republic."

Therefore, this is who we are, autonomous peoples of color, fighters for anarchism, self-determination and freedom for our people and all oppressed people. The Panthers proved how dangerous Black revolutionaries can be to this system. Now we will finish the job of putting capitalism in its grave. No freedom without a fight!

3

Anarchism and the Black Revolution

Some—usually comfortable, conservative, Black, middle-class professionals, politicians or businesspeople, who rode the 1960s Civil Rights movement into power or prominence—will say there is no longer "any reason" to struggle in the streets during this period for Black freedom. They say we have "arrived" as a people and are now free or "almost free." They say their only struggle now is to "integrate the money," or win wealth for themselves and members of their social class, even though they give lip service to "empowering the poor." Look, they say, "we can vote, our Black faces are all over TV in commercials and situation comedies, there are thousands of Black millionaires and we have political representatives in the halls of Congress and State houses all over the land." In fact, they say, there are currently over 10,000 Black elected officials, several of whom preside over the largest cities in the nation and since 1990, there was three African American governors. Now, we have elected and re-elected a Black President, and so now surely we are free. That is what they say. But does this tell the whole story? No, it is all symbolic representation and wealth building that doesn't trickle down to the working people and the poor.

The fact is we are in as bad or even worse shape, economically and politically, as when the Civil Rights movement began in the 1950s. One in every three Black males is in prison, on probation, parole, or under arrest; at least one-third or more of Black family units are now single-parent families mired in poverty; unemployment hovers at 16.7 percent for Black communities;[1] the drug economy is the number one employer

---

1. Black male unemployment was listed as a combined rate of 16.7 percent during the first term of President Barack Obama (2009–12). During the so-called "Great Recession" of 2007–09, Black male unemployment was as high as 22.2 percent, and Black female unemployment as high as 17.2 percent. It was double digit unemployment until 2019, until the presidential term of Donald J. Trump when it dropped to 5.5 percent briefly, then upwards to 16.7 percent

of Black youth in the poor ghetto areas and most substandard housing units are still concentrated in Black neighborhoods. Blacks and other non-whites suffer from the worst health care; and Black communities are still underdeveloped because of racial discrimination by municipal governments, mortgage companies and banks, who "redline" Black neighborhoods from receiving community development and housing funds and small business loans, all of which keep our communities poor. We also suffer from murderous acts of police brutality by racist cops, which has resulted in thousands of deaths, wounds and beatings; along with internecine gang warfare resulting in numerous youth homicides (and much grief for their families).

What we suffer from most and what encompasses all of these ills is the fact we are an oppressed people—in fact a colonized people subject to the rule of an oppressive government. We really have no rights under this system, except those which we have fought for and even that are now in peril. Clearly, we need a new mass Black protest movement to challenge the government and corporations and expropriate the funds needed for our communities to survive.

Yet for the past 30 years or more, the radical Black movement has been on the defensive or invisible. Due to political assassinations, mass frame-ups in the court system and other attacks driving many activists into permanent exile, as well as cooptation, bribery and betrayals of the Black Liberation movement of the 1960s by various leaders, it is safe to say that yesterday's Black revolutionary movement suffered a devastating series of setbacks and today's movement has now become almost comatose as a result. It is just fighting for piecemeal reforms for the Black middle class, rather than to radically transform the whole of society. Well, some dare say that this may be because the Black struggle is just now getting its stuff together after being pummeled by the state's police agencies, but I believe it is because the Black middle class and its intellectuals have taken over the radical Black left.

Black unemployment, when general unemployment rose to 14.7 percent in 2020 at the highest stage of the coronavirus economic collapse of the American economy. Since that time, various reporting agencies have stated it was 9.2–10.3 percent in 2021. Sources: Pew Research Center; U.S. Bureau of Labor Statistics; and the Current Population Survey: years 2007–09, 2011–15, and 2019–20, along with ALFRED electronic archival economic service (since 2006); see also Economic Policy Institute for 1992–2021, which states Black unemployment as 16.7 percent in 2020, and continuous historic Black unemployment consistency at 10–15 percent.

Of course, although police murder, subversion and brutality were the main blows, I believe there were other factors that led to the destruction of the 1960s Black movement in this country. The internal political contradictions that arose in the major Black revolutionary groups themselves, like the Black Panther Party, Student Nonviolent Coordinating Committee (SNCC or "snick" as it was called in those days) and the League of Revolutionary Black Workers, played a serious role. The problems with their internal structure(s), the lack of inner-organization democracy, failure to stay connected with the grassroots communities, political splits among the leadership and overall inexperience in dealing with government repression, all accelerated their destruction.

Of course, many others blame this period of relative inactivity in the Black movement on the lack of forceful leaders in the mold of Malcolm X, Martin Luther King, Marcus Garvey, etc., while other people allege the "fact" that the Black masses have become "corrupt and apathetic," are on drugs, or just need "Jesus in their lives" or the "correct revolutionary line."

Whatever the facts of the matter, it can clearly be seen that the government, the capitalist corporations and the racist ruling class are exploiting the current weakness and confusion of the Black movement to make an attack on the Black working class and poor, especially the youth, and are attempting to strip the gains won during the Civil Rights era. In addition, there is a resurgence of racism and conservatism among broad layers of the white population, which is a direct result of this right-wing campaign. This is a time when we must entertain new ideas and new tactics in the freedom struggle.

The ideals of Black Autonomy, based on anarchism, are something new to the Black movement and have never really been examined by Black and other non-white activists. Put simply, it means the people themselves should rule, not governments, political parties, or self-appointed leaders in their name. Anarchist-Autonomy also stands for the self-determination of all oppressed peoples and their right to struggle for freedom by any means necessary.

What road is in order for the Black movement? Continue to depend on opportunistic Democratic hack politicians like Obama or the same old group of middle-class sell-out political "leaders" of the civil rights lobby, such as Al "the Charlatan" Sharpton? Will one or another of the authoritarian white radical Leninist sects, who insist that they, and they alone, have the correct path to "revolutionary enlightenment," fool us, or will we finally build a grassroots revolutionary protest movement of our own to fight the racist government and rulers?

The Black middle class has no answer. Only the Black masses can finally decide the matter, whether they will be content to bear the brunt of the current economic depression and the escalating racist brutality, or will lead a fightback campaign. Anarchists trust the best instincts of the people and human nature dictates where there is repression, there will be resistance; where there is slavery, there will be a struggle against it. The Black masses have shown they will fight and when they organize in their millions, they will win!

A CALL FOR A NEW BLACK PROTEST MOVEMENT

The Black Autonomists recognize there has to be a whole new social movement, which is ultra-democratic, on the grassroots level and is self-activated. It will be a movement independent of the major political parties, the state and the government, or control by white radicals. It must be a movement that, although it seeks to expropriate government money for projects to benefit the people, does not recognize any progressive role for the government in the lives of the people. The government will not free us and is part of the problem rather than part of the solution. In fact, only the Black masses themselves can wage the Black freedom struggle, without a government bureaucracy (like the U.S. Justice Department), reformist civil rights leaders like Jessie Jackson, or a revolutionary vanguard party on their behalf.

Of course, at a certain historical moment, a protest leader can play a tremendous revolutionary role as a spokesperson for the people's feelings, or even produce correct strategy and theory for a certain period (Malcolm X, Marcus Garvey and Martin Luther King, Jr. come to mind) and a "vanguard party" may win mass support and acceptance among the people for a time (e.g., the Black Panther Party of the 1960s), but it is the Black masses themselves who will make the revolution and, once set spontaneously in motion, know exactly what they want. The people must empower themselves.

Though leaders may be motivated by good or bad, they will ultimately act as a brake on the struggle, especially if they lose touch with the freedom aspirations of the Black masses. They will be bought off, beat off, killed off, or imprisoned. Leaders can only really serve a legitimate purpose as an advisor and catalyst to the movement and should be subject to immediate recall if they act contrary to the people's wishes. In that kind of limited role they are not leaders at all—they are community organizers. Community organizers can help to build a movement, but they cannot truly lead.

The dependence of the Black movement on charismatic leaders and leadership (especially the Black bourgeoisie in this period) has led us into a political dead end. We are expected to wait and suffer quietly until the next messianic leader asserts him or herself, as if he or she were "divinely missioned by God" (as some have claimed to be). What is even more harmful is many Black people have adopted a slavish psychology of "obeying and serving our leaders," without considering what they themselves are capable of doing in their own communities.

Thus, rather than trying to analyze the current situation and carrying on Brother Malcolm X's work in the community against racial oppression, they prefer to bemoan the brutal facts, for year after year, of how he was taken away from us. Some mistakenly refer to this as a "leadership vacuum." The fact is there has not been much "movement" in the Black revolutionary movement since his assassination and the virtual destruction of groups like the Black Panther Party. We have been stagnated by middle-class reformism and broad-based misunderstanding among the people. We are desperate for almost anything or anyone claiming to be a "racial champion."

We need to come up with new ideas and revolutionary formations in how to fight our enemies. We need a new mass protest movement. It is up to the Black masses to build it, not leaders or political parties. They cannot save us. We can only save ourselves and our communities.

WHAT FORM SHOULD THIS MOVEMENT TAKE?

If there was one thing that should have been learned by Black revolutionary organizers in the 1960s, it's that you don't organize a mass movement or a social revolution just by creating one central organization with one leader, such as a vanguard political party or a radical labor union. It is a target for government repression and such leaders can be killed or imprisoned, thus breaking up the organization or setting back the movement. Such movements must have mass support and draw their strength from participation by the poor and grassroots forces. It is the Black community, and grassroots generally, which gives life to all its campaigns, even a revolutionary movement. In fact, such revolutionary movements have to be organic, that is, grow right out of the neighborhood struggles, rather than be something imposed from above.

Even though Anarchists believe in revolutionary organization, they see it as a means to an end, instead of the ends itself. In other words, the Anarchist groups are not formed with the intention of being permanent organizations to seize power and set up a dictatorship after a revolutionary struggle. Instead, such groups act as a catalyst to revolutionary struggles and try to take the people's rebellions, like the 1992 Los Angeles revolt, to a higher level of resistance. Grassroots power is seized and put in the hands of the people, but not in a corrupt domineering organization like a political party of middle-class theorists.

Two features of a new mass movement must be the intention of creating dual power institutions to challenge the state, along with the ability to have a grassroots Autonomist movement that can take advantage of a pre-revolutionary situation to go all the way.

Dual power means that you organize collectives and communes in cities and towns all over North America, which become, in fact, liberated zones, outside the control of the government. Autonomy means the movement must be truly independent of capitalist or white radical political control and thus a free association of all those united around common goals, rather than membership as the result of some oath or other pressure. Most of the white radical boring theoretical parties use mysticism to brainwash and mislead people; they don't want to teach them to think for themselves, "just follow our line."

So how would white Anarchists intervene in the revolutionary process in Black neighborhoods or support our struggles? Well, obviously North American or "white" Anarchists cannot go into Black communities and just proselytize, but they certainly should express support with non white Anarchist-Autonomists and help them work in their own communities of color. White Anarchists have access to a lot more material resources and are in position to take support actions people of color cannot take for themselves.

But we are definitely not talking about a situation where Black organizers go into the neighborhood and win people to anarchism so they can then be controlled by whites and some domineering white political cult. This is how the Communist Party and other Marxist-Leninist groups operate, but it cannot be how Anarchists work. We spread Anarchist beliefs not to "take over" people, but to let them know how they can better organize themselves to fight tyranny and obtain freedom. We want to work with them as fellow human beings and allies, brothers and sisters who have their own experiences, agendas and needs.

The idea is to get as many movements of people fighting the state as possible, since that brings the day of freedom for us all a little closer. For Anarchists of color (Autonomists) we are working in our own neighborhoods, with people we care about. The communists and other radical politicians manipulate people for their own gains; we are part of the people ourselves.

There needs to be some sort of revolutionary organization for Autonomists to work on the local level, so we will call these local groups Local Organizing Collectives. Each one of these Collectives will be Black/POC working-class social revolutionary committees in the community to fight for both our democratic rights and freedom as part of the worldwide social revolution that we want to see unfold. The Collectives would have no leader or "party boss," and would be without any type of hierarchal structure, it would also be anti-authority, opposed to politicians or the government. They exist to do revolutionary work and thus are not debating societies or a club to elect Black, Asian or Chicano politicians to office. They are revolutionary political formations, which will be linked with other such groups all over North America and other parts of the world in a larger movement called a federation.

A city-wide federation is needed to coordinate the actions of such groups; to let others know what is happening in each area and to set down widespread strategy and tactics. (We will call this one, for want of a better name, the "Black Autonomy Revolutionary Federation.") A federation of the sort I am talking about is a mass membership organization which will be democratic and made up of all kinds of smaller groups and individuals. But this is not a government or representative system I am talking about; there would be no permanent positions of power and even the facilitators of internal programs would be subject to immediate recall or have a regular rotation of duties. When a federation is no longer needed, it can be disbanded. Try that with a communist party or one of the major capitalist political parties in North America! Their leaders are entrenched for life.

REVOLUTIONARY STRATEGY AND TACTICS

If we are to build a new Black revolutionary protest movement we must ask ourselves how we can hurt this capitalist system and how have we hurt it in the past when we have led social movements against some aspect of our oppression. Boycotts, mass demonstrations, rent strikes, picketing, work strikes, sit-ins and other such protests have been used by the Black movement at different times in its history, along with armed self-defense and open rebellion. Put simply, what we need to do is take our struggle to a new and higher level: we need to take these tried and true tactics (which have been used primarily on the local level up to this point) and utilize them on a national level and then couple them with as yet untried tactics, for a strategic attack on the major capitalist corporations and governmental apparatus. We shall discuss a few of them.

A Black Tax Boycott

Black people (and all people) should refuse to pay any taxes to the racist government, including federal income, estate and sales taxes, while we are being subjected to exploitation and brutality by racist cops, starved and imprisoned by the government. The rich and their corporations pay virtually no taxes; it is the poor and workers who bear the brunt of taxation anyway. Yet, we receive nothing in return. There are still huge unemployment levels in the Black/POC community; the unemployment and welfare benefits are paltry; the schools are dilapidated; public housing is a disgrace, while rents by absentee landlord properties are exorbitant—all these conditions and more are supposedly corrected by government taxation of income, goods and services. Wrong! It goes to the Pentagon, defense contractors and greedy consultants, who like vultures prey on business with the government. We have yet to see any "peace dividend" from the end of the Cold War—that money is still in the hands of the Pentagon. So don't expect the end of the War in Afghanistan to be used to stabilize Social Security, or as part of an anti-poverty program.

The Black Autonomy movement should establish a mass tax resistance movement to lead a Black tax boycott as a means of protest and also as a method to create a fund to finance Black community projects and organizations. Why should we continue to voluntarily support our own slavery? A Black tax boycott is just another means of struggle that the Black movement should examine and adopt, which is similar to the peace movement's "war tax resistance." Blacks should be exempted from all taxation on personal property, income taxes, stocks and bonds (the latter of which would be a new type of community development issuance). Tax the Rich!

This so-called "Black Tax boycott" can be used as the starting phase of a mass boycott against the government and the capitalist corporations generally. We should think about a mass boycott against the Koch enterprises which are funding right-wing attacks on social programs like Social Security and Medicare/Medicaid, as well as Teachers Unions, public sector workers, while also seeking to defund all programs for the poor and unemployed.

A National Rent Strike and Urban Squatting

Hand-in-glove with a tax boycott should be a refusal to pay rent for dilapidated housing. Historically, these rent boycotts have been used to great effect to fight back against rent gouging by landlords. At one time they were so effective in Harlem (NY) that they caused the creation of rent control legislation, laws preventing evictions, regulations against unjustified price increases and tenant rules requiring reasonable upkeep by the owners and the property management company. A mass movement could bring a rent strike to areas (such as in the Southeast and Southwest) where poor people are being ripped off by the greedy landlords, but are not familiar with such tactics, as part of a national campaign. Unfair laws now on the books, so-called Landlord-Tenant laws (where the only "right" the tenants have is to pay the rent or be evicted) should also be liberalized or overturned entirely. These laws only help slumlords stay in business and keep exploiting the poor and working class. They account for mass evictions, which in turn account for homelessness. We should fight to rollback rents, prevent mass evictions and house the poor and the homeless in decent affordable places.

Besides the refusal to pay the slumlords and exploitative banks and property management companies, there should be a campaign of "urban squatting" to just take over the housing and have the tenants run it democratically as a housing collective. Then that money which would have gone toward rent could now go into repairing the dwellings of tenants. The homeless and poor persons needing affordable housing and low wage workers who badly need housing should just take over any abandoned housing owned by an absentee landlord or even a boarded-up city housing project or other government owned building, should repair the place and just move right on in.

Squatting is an especially good tactic in these times of serious housing shortages and arson-for-insurance by the slumlords. We should throw the rich bums out and just take over! Of course we will no doubt have to fight the cops and security guards for the crooked landlords who will try to use strong-armed tactics, but we can do that too! We can win significant victories if we organize a nationwide series of rent strikes and build an independent tenants movement that will self-manage all the facilities, not for the government (with the tricky Republican "Kemp plan[2]" or Housing and Urban Development (HUD regulations[3]), but for themselves! Nobody should have to sleep in the streets when available housing is right there, much of it controlled directly by the government ...

A Boycott of American Business Products

A strong weapon of the Civil Rights movement was a Black consumer boycott of a community's white merchants and public services. Merchants, bankers and other businesspeople, of course, are the "leading citizens" of any community and the local ruling class and boss of the government. In the 1960s when Blacks refused to trade with Southern merchants as long as they allowed racial discrimination, their loss of revenue drove them to make concessions and mediate the struggle, even hold the cops and the Klan at bay. It was also used against Northern businesses to make them cut ties or change segregationist policies by their Southern company affiliates.

What is true at the local level is certainly true at the national level. The major corporations and elite families run the country; the government is its mere tool. Blacks spend over $350–$700 billion a year in this capitalist economy as consumers and could just as easily wage economic warfare against the corporate structure with a well-planned boycott to win political concessions.

For instance, a corporation like General Motors is heavily dependent on Black consumers, which means that it is also very vulnerable to a Black consumer boycott, if one were organized and supported widely. If Blacks would refuse to buy GM cars, it would result in significant

---

2. U.S. Rep. Kemp (R-NY) was the first so-called "compassionate conservative" who proposed a 1980 tax cut for the wealthy while claiming it would provide jobs and income for the poor and workers. After serving in Congress for 18 years, he was secretary of the U.S. Department of Housing and Urban Development, 1989–93.

3. HUD manages government projects and social housing programs for the poor, grouped into Section 8 of the agency's regulations.

losses for the corporation, to the tune of hundreds of millions of dollars. Something like this could even bring a company to its knees. Yet, the revolutionary wing of the Black movement has yet to use anti-corporate boycotts, calling it "reformism" and outdated.

However, far from being an outdated tactic that we should abandon, boycotts have become even more effective in the last few years. In 1988, the Black and progressive movement in the United States hit on another tactic, boycotting the tourist industries of whole cities and states which engaged in discrimination. This reflected, on the one hand, how many cities have gone from "smokestack" industries since the 1960s to tourism as their major source of revenue and, on the other hand, recognition by the movement that economic warfare was a potent weapon against discriminatory governments. The 1990–93 Black Boycott against the Miami Florida tourism industry and the Gay rights boycott against the State of Colorado (1992–94) have been both successful and have gotten worldwide attention to the problems in their communities.

In fact, modern day boycotts have been expanded to cover everything from California grapes, beer (Coors), a certain brand of jeans, all products made in the then-apartheid country of South Africa, a certain meat industry and many other things. Boycotts are more popular today than they ever have been. (In Chattanooga, Tennessee, where I was a civil rights activist on trial for the frame-up "Chattanooga Three" case in 1998–2000, we used an international tourism boycott against the city to make them lose 10–20 percent of their tourism-based funds within two years of the campaign.) A tourist boycott had been going on in Cincinnati for more than three years (2002–05) to protest the police killings of 15 Black men and other acts of official racism in that city, before officials mediated the protests.

Right now, we should think seriously about boycotting the Koch enterprises, because they are the financial sponsors of the racist Tea Party, founded since the election of President Barack Obama, to disrupt his administration. We should boycott them because they are waging an anti-union, anti-people campaign, to destroy Social Security and other social programs needed by millions of poor and working people, and are financing a right-wing offensive to redirect all government authority to the super-rich. This campaign is designed to destroy all regulations preventing capitalist corporations from robbing the country blind, or exploiting workers like outright slaves for the wealthy.

They want to create nothing less than a fascist corporate state, where the rich outright own and run the government, and nobody else has any human or civil rights at all. The Koch enterprises may be super-wealthy, but they produce hundreds of consumer product brands, in addition to oil and gas production, so they can be hurt by an international boycott. That is why they had kept their activities a secret until now.

Dr. Martin Luther King, Jr. recognized the potential revolutionary power of a national Black boycott of America's major corporations, which is why he established "Operation Breadbasket" shortly before an assassin killed him. This wing of his organization, with offices in Chicago was designed to be the conduit for the funds that the corporations were going to be forced to pour money into for a national Black community development project for poor communities. And although he was assassinated before this could happen and Jesse Jackson corrupted the campaign for his own purposes, we must continue Dr. King's work in this matter.

All over the country Black Boycott offices should be opened! We should build it into a mass movement, involving all sectors of our people. We should demonstrate, picket and sit-in at meetings and offices of target corporations all over the country. We must take it to their very doorstep and stop their looting of the Black community. If this were part of a campaign for reparations, it would stand a better chance of winning than lawsuits and lobbying alone.

A Black/POC General Strike

Black and other workers of color are potentially the most powerful sector of the Black/POC community in the struggle for freedom. The vast majority of the Black community are working-class people, as are most workers of color. Barring the disproportionate numbers of unemployed, millions of Black men and women are today part of the workforce of the United States, with similar numbers in the Latino community. Before the 2008 capitalist economic recession, we could say that about 5–6 million of these were in basic industry, such as steel and metal fabrication, retail trades, food production and processing, meatpacking, the automobile industry, railroading, medical service and communications. For instance, Blacks numbered a third to a half of the basic blue-collar workers and a third of clerical laborers. Black labor is therefore very important to the capitalist economy.

Blacks and other workers of color are some of the most militant workers on the job and, because of their employers' vulnerability to job actions, could take a leading role in a protest campaign against racism and class oppression. If properly organized, they would be a class vanguard within our movement since they are at the point of production. In the 1960s, the League of Black Revolutionary Workers began to talk seriously about the possibility of Black workers leading a nationwide General Strike at their place of work as a protest against racial discrimination in jobs and housing, the inordinately high levels of Black unemployment, brutal working conditions and to further the demands of the Black movement generally.

This proposed General Strike was seen as a Social strike, not just a strike for higher wages and over general working conditions; it is revolutionary politics using other means to change society. This General Strike could take the form of industrial sabotage, factory occupations or sit-ins, work slowdowns, wildcats and other work stoppages as a protest to gain concessions on the local and national level and restructure the workplace and win the four-hour day for North American labor, bring an end to privatization of government services and fight unemployment in inner city communities.

The strike would not only involve workers on the job, but also Black/POC community and progressive groups to give support with picket line duty, leafleting and publishing strike support newsletters, demonstrations at company offices and worksites, along with other activities to win demands like an end to police murder and terrorism, bank redlining of Black and people of color communities, environmental racism and poverty, among others.

It will take some serious community and workplace organizing to bring a General Strike off. In workplaces all over the country, Black/Chicano/Asian workers and their white supporters should organize General Strike Committees at their workplaces and Black/POC Strike Support Committees to carry on the strike work inside their communities. Because such a strike would be especially hard-fought and vicious, Black/POC workers should organize Worker's Defense Committees to defend workers fired or "blacklisted" by the bosses for their industrial organizing work. This defense committee would publicize a victimized worker's case and rally support from other workers and the community. The defense committee could also establish a Labor strike and defense fund and even start a food cooperative to financially and materially support such victimized workers and their families while carrying on the strike.

Although there will definitely be an attempt to involve white workers; where they are willing to cooperate, the strike would be under the leadership of Blacks, Chicanos and other people of color because only those workers can effectively raise those issues which most affect them. As I have pointed out, white workers have to support the democratic rights of Blacks and other nationally oppressed laborers, instead of just "white rights campaigns" on so-called "common economic issues," led by the North American left. That is vulgar socialism, and racism in its own right.

White-dominated labor union locals as well as progressive North American individuals or union caucuses should be recruited. They are not the decisive force to lead this struggle, although their help can be indispensable in a particular campaign. It takes major organizing to make them break free of their racist and conservative nature. So although we want and need the support of our fellow workers of other nationalities and genders, it is ridiculous and condescending to just tell Black, Asian or Chicano workers to sit around and wait for a "white workers' vanguard" to decide it wants to fight before they can do anything. This is nonsense. We will educate our fellow workers to the issues and why they should fight white supremacy at our side, but we will not defer our struggle for anyone!

But we will unite with any movement which supports our goals of opposing mass unemployment, structural racism, taxing the rich for social programs, and punishing capitalist billionaires like the Koch enterprises, who are the economic foundation of the New Right. Although such a campaign can begin in the Black community, we need a broad-based movement to really cripple this capitalist economy, and force social spending on our communities.

A CRITIQUE OF THE NEW BLACK PANTHER MOVEMENTS

In 1986, ex-members of the Black Panther Party, their supporters and others met in Oakland, California, for a 20th-year reunion and retrospective of the Black Panther Party. This sparked some interest in recreating some type of Panther projects, if not the rebuilding of the party itself. Also, the 1989 death of party co-founder Huey P. Newton brought together former members and inspired some discussion of building panther-type projects. Now, over 25 years following the first reunion, a variety of groups have appeared based on the politics of the original Black Panther Party, including the New Panther Vanguard Movement and the Black Riders Liberation Party of Los Angeles, the so-called New Black Panther Party (and its various factions nationwide) and also the Black Panther Collective of New York City. The most important issue is that whatever group is set up should not repeat the errors of the past and adopt a new vision and revolutionary ideology.

First, many young activists who are looking for new strategy and tactics in the wake of the defeat of the Black revolution of the 1960s and are making a re-evaluation of the movements of that period, especially the Black Panther Party for Self-Defense, are doing so because of the weakness and corruption of the contemporary Black leadership. Compared to Jesse Jackson and his ties to the Democratic Party, the Panthers were clearly an uncompromising and anti-corporate street force. But many mistakes were made by the original party of that period: too little internal democracy, too much dependence on authoritarian national leaders and far too much male supremacy within the organization (by today's standards), which hampered the movement of that period. And although many of the youth would like to see a new Panther movement, unfortunately, there are many trying to resuscitate the corpse of the long dead Party for opportunistic reasons, instead of breaking new ground with a whole new type of movement.

It is unacceptable to have a group take the name of the Black Panther Party for purposes of building its own organization, but not carry out its program. The challenge must be laid directly at the feet of the group leaders to reform their organizations, or to rename them. They should also be held up to public exposure as phonies and opportunists and pressured to disband their groups entirely. It is a disgrace and a total political sell-out for religious zealots and political opportunists to steal the history of a movement such as this original Black Panther Party, which had such a positive legacy to offset its mistakes. They must now be made to improve their groups or disband.

I will direct my message to them collectively:

Reject Militarism

The New Black Panther movements should reject all attempts to steer them into the direction of romantic urban guerrilla-ism, which appeared at the period of the deterioration of the Black Panther Party in the mid-1970s or the kind of mindless violence favored by street gangsters. Revolution is a social movement; it is an act of war between two classes. The role of small group terrorism and adventurism is a form of vanguard-ism, which should be avoided at all costs. Too many militants were killed, arrested and exiled in the previous Panther formations to let a new movement think it can posture around with guns as a studio prop. In the earlier period, picking up the gun had great political significance in using armed force to resist racist violence, defeat the pacifism of the civil rights leaders and resist police brutality. Now, it's just "gangsta style," macho posturing by wannabe middle-class revolutionaries with no real political objectives except maintenance of an illusion.

Strutting around in black fatigues carrying guns into a school board meeting, church, funeral home or community meeting is not revolutionary activity; it is posturing and highly irresponsible. Who makes the revolution anyway? The masses of people do! They make the revolution, not a vanguard underground or paramilitary force on their behalf. That is one very important lesson for this New Black Panther Party to learn. It is not the movement that should be armed at every stage, but rather the people in defense of their own community. The militia is not the political organization itself, and should be drawn from its own community. And we should arm them not just with guns, but also with revolutionary ideology and service to the community. All the rest is showboating, or worse, will bring on police repression. It does not advance a revolutionary struggle or defend the community—it sets people up. It is intolerable to make the same mistakes as was done in the past, or to risk the lives of activists just for the TV news, or to excite the politically unsophisticated youth.

The original Black Panther Party was a political organization, which understood that it could not put its own paramilitary activities ahead of the masses of people. Most of the shootouts with the police and other confrontations came as a result of attacks by the government, not vigilante activity, gangster crews or street crazies. This is not the 1960s. Picking up the gun without grassroots political support means that the would-be revolutionary movements are just the latest bunch of wild men that the masses of people should stay clear of. The Black Panther Party appeared and was ultimately destroyed and that was a tragedy. Now a new group has appeared, claiming to be their descendants and that is a total farce.

The original Black Panther Party was a powerful organization that represented a radical breakthrough. It was both a political party and militia, which practiced armed self-defense. Regardless of the considerable fighting capacity of Panther cadre itself, the Black community's masses kept the Panthers from being liquidated by armed police invaders when they encircled the party offices in Detroit, Los Angeles, New Orleans and other cities.

Reject Personality Cultism

The new movement should not repeat the errors of central leadership style and dictatorial control of one person or small group of persons. Although Huey P. Newton and Bobby Seale made a great impact historically in creating the originally Party. Many of the errors of party leadership can be laid at their feet and that of the party Central Committee. Many errors happened because they were not infallible, but more so because the Black Panther Party's structure protected them from challenge and accountability. The membership idolized Newton especially and placed him beyond accountability or criticism, even after it became obvious that he had serious personal problems and began to act in an unstable manner due to drug and alcohol abuse.

There must be accountability within every organization claiming to be a revolutionary project. Unfortunately, the new Panther tendencies appear not to have understood this lesson, placing their leadership in a position of unquestioned authority and not empowering the membership and masses of people. These are authoritarian organizations, worse than any errors of the original Black Panther Party. Just as happened within the original Panther party when they made this error of placing too much power in the hands of leaders, this will lead to serious internal problems in these new groups. The first time was a mistake. This time it's by design of opportunists and petty power seekers. It increases the odds that they will fail or be destroyed due to internal squabbling and an undemocratic structure. No single figure or leadership can ever be allowed to repeat the mistakes of previous Black Panther leadership. After it was over, those in the original party understood, as revolutionaries, we do not fight to empower leaders, but to serve the people of our communities, no matter how sincere or well loved any leader may be. Power and leadership has to come from the ranks, not from the top.

The lesson: no one person or vanguard organization will ever be able to lead us to freedom. Revolutionary organizations and leaders come and go, but the masses are always there. We, common people (the so-called "mindless masses") can free ourselves and we should not wait on leaders to appear and decide our fate. Revolutionaries have to be part of the people, not some special force apart from or above them. The masses are not mindless sheep that need someone to boss them around. The sooner that we understand this, the sooner we will be on the road to liberation. We certainly do not need leaders, intellectuals or party bosses to tell us how to make a revolution; we just need to organize our own community and then society generally in our own interests. Here is the challenge to all would-be leaders: revolutionary movements are designed to help the masses organize, or they have no constructive role.

Build a Movement with a More Libertarian Structure and Ideology

The Black Panther Party of the 1960s was based on Marxism-Leninism and revolutionary Black nationalism and although Marxism-Leninism was the most popular radical ideology of the 1960s, it is inherently authoritarian and undemocratic, even though it gave lip service to so-called "democratic centralism." For instance, the rigid structure and a security squad protecting the leaders prevented any member from challenging any political commands of Huey Newton without being branded a "traitor" and then being summarily purged from the group by the Central Committee. This leadership body also controlled the direction of the party and its policies. The cadre system was also exposed as allowing nothing but obedience to authority, rather than revolutionary initiative and should be junked in any new movement along with the party structure. The various new Panther movements are either mistakenly keeping the authoritarian Maoist formations, or even becoming more rigid with Islamic religious dogma, as with the New Black Panther Party.

No individual or clique should ever be invested with the fate and the entire direction of a political movement affecting the lives of a large numbers of members and the community at large. No religious or political dogma that restricts the rights of members should hold sway. Both Islam and Marxism should be rejected as official ideology of the movement. Black Autonomists challenge these "new" Panthers to adopt a form of libertarian socialism as their ideological doctrine and to build a mass movement rather than another vanguard political party. In fact, any vanguard philosophy, of putting the party before the people, is part of what led the original party to many of its errors of prematurely confronting the state's military and police units, as well as led to its ultimate political isolation from the community.

Reject Vanguardism, Build a Mass Movement

Clearly, if the time has come for the re-emergence of the Panthers, it should be as a mass movement, rather than as a sectarian political party. The idea that the movement should be an entity ahead of the people is a serious mistake. According to Huey P. Newton himself, the Panthers isolated themselves within the Black movement by making enemies with those other Black militant nationalists and progressive reform organizations that could have made up a Black Liberation Front. It also failed to cement ties with the white radical and labor movements, demanding that they give concrete anti-fascist support against government attacks, and it did not really form strong ties with other oppressed nationalities. For instance, it allowed its alliance with the Student Nonviolent Coordinating Committee (1967–69) to deteriorate into acrimony, primarily because of the immaturity of the leaders in both organizations.

The biggest mistake due to vanguardism in the 1960s, however, was its failure to build a sustained mass movement that would have taken over after the old Civil Rights movement had been ideologically defeated. Even though the Black Power movement had radicalized large sectors of the Black community, the Panthers failed to win over large masses of Blacks to party programs or membership. This is not to say at all that the party was ineffective. The party was certainly popular and had widespread community support, but its objective was to build the party, not a mass movement. It is time for the "new" Panthers to build a mass movement which can challenge the capitalists for power, then put it in the hands of the people and build a liberated zone in the belly of the beast as the first step to social revolution, rather than go back to small group politics or adopt a sectarian line in the twenty-first century. The new Panther movements cannot just make the same errors, as if they have learned nothing.

Build a Movement to Free Black Panther Party Political Prisoners

With the destruction of the party, hundreds of its cadre were framed on criminal charges or driven into exile. Many are still in prison today.

No movement which wants to have any credibility at all will try to forget those who made the heaviest possible sacrifices and with that in mind, I call on the New Black Panther movement and others based around ideals of the original Black Panther Party to devote a serious amount of its resources to obtaining the freedom in short order of those ex-Panthers in prison and to freeing all political prisoners. There should be political prisoner support collectives all over the country working to free these political prisoners, not just in New Jersey, New York or California. There is no work that is more important, and this can help rebuild the revolutionary movement as nothing else can. We need to let the world know what crimes the American government committed in suppressing the Black revolution of the 1960s. As former Black Liberation Army political prisoner Ojore Lutalo stated: "Any Movement which does not support its political internees, is a sham movement!"

Reject Sexism

The Black Panther Party had women and men share equal roles as warriors and organizers, not just have the women take care of children or stay at home, while the men save the world. But the so-called "new" Black Panther Party is openly sexist; carrying on the backward and misogynist beliefs of the Nation of Islam that women should stay in their place and are an inferior species. All of the main leaders and activists of this "new" Black Panther Party are heavily male and there is a heavy macho culture in the group. This is not to say that there are no women in the group at all, but they play a clearly minor role, just as they do in the Nation of Islam. The original Black Panther Party was not perfect in the way it treated sisters, but was very enlightened for its time, while the Nation of Islam exercised strict sexual segregation throughout the organization and a form of conservative Islamic fundamentalism.

Women should be empowered to be leaders, organizers and equal members of the New Black Panther Party movements. To fail to do this leads to oppression in the ranks of the alleged revolutionary movement, leads to authoritarianism, sexism and a macho cult. It betrays the history of the original movement.

Reject Racism

The Black Panther Party had a class analysis about white racism and oppression, which was different from the Nation of Islam and most other nationalist groups at the time. It understood capitalism and internal colonialism were responsible for the oppressed condition of Black people. The Nation of Islam and others held that they were "white devils" created in a laboratory and racism could not be defeated, so it called for racial separatism in a Black nation-state—a position that the original Black Panther Party never took and to which it was opposed.

Although the Black Panther Party maintained Black autonomy of its organization and independence of its leadership, it never reviled white people as inherently evil and beyond allowing support for the struggle. Yet, the New Black Panther Party only equates all white people as being devils who should be shunned. Its past leader, the late Khalid Abdul Muhammad, called white people "crackers," "white devils" and other terms that have continued with the current leadership. They have also engaged in the worst type of anti-Semitism against Jewish people.

This has caused many former original Panthers to criticize them heavily for what they see as vindictive Black racism in the New Black Panther Party. They reject any ideals of Black supremacy and chafe at the association of their organization name with such backward beliefs.

Reject Youth Cultism and Age Discrimination

Although the original Black Panther Party was an organization of young people, it was not mandated as a policy of the party. According to Huey Newton himself, one thing that separated the party ultimately from the Black community was to cut itself off from a base of support among poor men and women, such as welfare mothers, senior citizens and others. It perpetuated the idea that only the youth could lead a revolution, when most of the world's revolutionaries like Fidel Castro, Ho Chi Minh, Mao Tse Tung were middle aged and older and clearly pointed out the struggle was a prolonged struggle involving many sectors of the population. Further, since the youth are not seasoned, they make many mistakes. They may have youthful physical stamina, but not a determination and understanding born of years of consistent struggle. As veteran fighters, Ho Chi Minh and others were able to advance their people's struggle because they had both experienced and youthful activists. Although it copied many things from the revolution in the Third World, the original party made many mistakes because of its youth and inexperience and this helped the government smash the organization.

It does not appear, however, that the New Black Panther Party has learned anything from these errors. It has even shown disrespect toward original Panthers, disparaged their age and experience, in favor of creating a youth cult. Such cults are inherently weak and based on style rather than substance. They have no political program of their own based in the material conditions of their own period, so they steal the program of the past period, dress it up and call it their own.

Because of this impetuosity and disrespect toward older activists from previous movements, it will fail at its mission to put itself forward as a new Black Panther Party. It is not a revolutionary movement except in name only. It is not grounded in the Black poor and the community generally; it can only attract youth, but not make them into a serious political force. They are not being politically educated and developed, so that they cannot think critically for themselves; instead they are taught to just follow blindly behind the leaders who are the font of all knowledge. This leads to manipulation and abuse of the idealism of these youth, who sincerely want to do something for their people.

Clearly, the leaders of the New Black Panther Party need to reconsider their age discrimination policies and incorporate many of the veteran Panthers as part of the New Black Panther Party leadership, as well as politically educate these youth.

Build an Organization of Organizers

The original Black Panther Party was all about community-based organizing. It set up offices all over the country, created and administered over 30 "survival programs" to provide free food, housing, clothing, medical care and other services and it did extensive mobilizing on the local level in many cities against racism, police brutality, high rents and utility rates and other issues affecting poor and working-class people. It was one of the most effective organizations of the 1960s. It had obtained mass support in a short span of time because of its programs to elevate the impoverished living conditions, the education and culture of the urban Black masses.

By contrast, the New Black Panther Party, which has several factions around the country, has virtually no real community programs at all, except selling their newspaper and distributing old clothes. They do no grassroots organizing, except for photo opportunities, are doing nothing for the urban poor, prisoners, or any segment of the community since the time of their creation. This seems to be a paper group entirely, who are content to wear black fatigues, boots and berets as a revolutionary costume, but not serve the people. One must conclude this is a sham group, doing revolutionary posturing.

They must be challenged to build a real organization and do grassroots organizing in poor neighborhoods and end this charade of building a bogus Black Panther Party. They haven't done anything!

Respect the History of the Original Black Panther Party

No new organization should be allowed to take the name of a previous revolutionary group and then create a group very inconsistent with the historical mission and ideals of the original group. However, that is what the so-called New Black Panther Party is doing. It has hijacked the name, style and public persona of the original Black Panther Party for purposes apparently in opposition to the original group. The New Black Panther Party has even gone so far as to use faked photographs on its website on one occasion, implying that Khalid Muhammad was an original founder of the party, along with Huey Newton and was one of its leaders during the 1960s. This is not true and Bobby Seale is now a critic of the New Black Panther Party, due to this and other bogus actions.

What is going on here? It appears a hostile leadership group (formerly or currently) affiliated with the Nation of Islam has created the New Black Panther Party. This is extremely suspicious because the Nation of Islam was never sympathetic to and had many bitter grievances against the Black Panther Party in the 1960s. In fact, the founder of this New Black Panther Party, Khalid Abdul Muhammad, lived in Oakland, California, for many years and never worked with the original Black Panther Party. He was in fact known to be highly critical of it, and rose to a leadership position in the Oakland Nation of Islam mosque and later became national spokesperson of the Nation of Islam. Muhammad himself made speeches disparaging the original Black Panther Party and its members right before he died in 2001. According to Oakland-based Panthers, he never sought to join or expressed any sympathy or support for the ideals of the Black Panther Party until he was dismissed by the leadership of the Nation of Islam in the early to mid-1990s and sought a new political vehicle for him to head.

Put squarely, it is sheer opportunism for a leader of the Nation of Islam to set up a bogus Black Panther Party based on its backward religious beliefs. It slanders the original group and its members and shows total disrespect for its legacy of revolutionary struggle. This organization in no way upholds the legacy or the belief system of the Black Panther Party for Self Defense, founded in Oakland, California, in 1966 by Huey P. Newton and Bobby Seale. The New Black Panther Party is merely playing on the good name and awesome reputation of the original Black Panther Party to attract support in this period, without doing anything to deserve it.

CONCLUSION: THE PARTY'S OVER. BUILD SOMETHING NEW!

Although we are glad to see there is interest in the original Black Panther Party and in building a new moment, this is not the way to do it. We cannot pretend that the world has not changed and that new tactics are not necessary, but we also cannot allow opportunism and the theft of the name and history to be plundered either. If the party had not been destroyed and had elected new leadership, a new direction would have been evident. The stage of building revolutionary movements based on the Communist Party vanguard model was proven bankrupt by the mid-1970s, as communist movements fell all over the world. The idea of central leadership and cult of personality fell with it, although the Black movement, especially religious organizations like the Nation of Islam continue with that model. But the fact is that Black people worship a variety of religions and have a variety of political views. It appears that only a united front approach would be effective, but a united front is not by nature a revolutionary organization.

Which leads to the question of where would the Black Panther Party have been going had it survived? First, we believe that the political party model would have been disbanded or expanded to a Black Panther Liberation Front, with collective leadership, a mass base instead of a tightly controlled membership and would have brought many of the persons working on many of the survival projects into full membership.

Instead of just inexperienced street youth as members and leaders, there would have to be a recognition that adult activists, whether welfare mothers, community organizers, seniors, industrial workers or others, would have had much to contribute and should have been allowed to join. This Black Panther Liberation Front would have been formed much like the original Palestine Liberation Organization, in that various tendencies in the Black community united with the Panthers' original vision could be brought into one organization. This would include the progressive wing of the Black movement, grassroots organizations and individuals who supported Panther politics. The main thing we must recognize is a Black Panther Liberation Front is a step toward a mass movement. This does not mean Panther politics would not be in command, but rather folks supporting or working as volunteers with the various survival programs and community organizing projects who were not already members would be invited to work as full members.

Obviously, this would have included a movement for a broad-based resistance campaign and armed struggle, but only when the revolutionary forces fostered the conditions and the masses of people were ready to take such a step, rather than premature adventurism and military escapism by an underground force in the name of the people. Only the masses can make the revolution, not leaders or a vanguard political party. That time is past and resulted in our defeat. Now we clearly need a Black Panther mass movement.

The time for a Black Panther Liberation Front, made up of the existing new Panther groups, community groups and other Black radical forces, including original Panther members is what is on the agenda now. We need a mass-based movement, with collective leadership, to involve the broadest level of the Black masses possible to fight colonialism and racism, mass imprisonment of the youth, police brutality and murder, unemployment and homelessness, drug peddling and other social ills of this period. We need to unite our people around a revolutionary political program, not just a nationalist program. We need to understand that our role in this period is not to just establish a nation-state in five Southern states, but to dismantle the existing government and nation that is oppressing Blacks in America and people around the world, and destroy the system of capitalism in the lives of billions of people.

LET'S ORGANIZE THE 'HOOD: INNER CITY ORGANIZING PROJECTS

We must rebuild inner city neighborhoods as a community survival program, even while we work to fight racism and capitalist-colonialism.

We need to build a new society, but until then we need to organize and empower poor folks living in deteriorating inner city communities to rebuild substandard housing and create jobs, food and housing cooperatives. Capitalism is a social system with inherent economic inequalities. Not only do the poor pay more for basic amenities, but also they are made the scapegoat of this corrupt system. They are called a "criminal underclass," "layabouts," "welfare queens" and other garbage by the rich and their ideological agents; even part of the Black working class echoes this propaganda. Then after they have told their lies, the rich fashion new laws to ensure their unjust rule by starving, humiliating, killing, imprisoning, torturing, policing and otherwise keeping the pressure to survive on the poor themselves, and this is especially the case with the Black poor.

This period of widespread social repression is extremely dangerous: one out of every three young Black men and almost 60 percent of all Black female prison inmates are in the so-called "American criminal justice system" (prison, jail or on parole); high unemployment and social disinvestments are destroying the economic base of many inner city neighborhoods; chemical warfare (drugs) is being used to destabilize our communities and keep us from fighting back; an epidemic of police violence takes place each day to beat, kill and torture Black men, women and children and to intimidate the community into fearing white authority—all these and worse are the daily life experiences of poor Black people under this system.

So whatever movement we build cannot be a disconnected cult or vanguard sect that tries to act as a "champion" of the masses, one working with poor communities to mobilize in its own interests. To fight back against these horrific conditions and to also build an infrastructure for survival pending revolution, it is not enough to do as the Negrosie (also known as the Black upper class or Black bourgeoisie) does and call for "Black pride," while poor Black people are starved and brutalized by the government and corporations. There must be some way to ensure their economic and physical survival, all the while fighting a social revolution.

First, we must recognize that we need a new way of confronting our oppressed situation. How do we get started at this?

The Poor People's Survival Movement (part of a broader program called "Let's Organize The 'Hood"), which was first devised by the Black Autonomy Federation, is what is needed in this period for poor and working-class Black people. With it as a component part of our

Anarchist-Autonomist federation and our political program, we will ultimately build a socio-political infrastructure to intervene in every area of Black life: food and housing cooperatives, Black Liberation schools, people's banks and community mutual aid funds, free medical clinics and hospitals, rodent control and pest extermination programs, cooperative factories, a Black Partisan militia to patrol our communities, the establishment of a Black intercontinental electronic communications network, land and building reclamation projects, public works brigades to rebuild the cities, youth projects, drug clinics, a Black alternate currency and many other programs can be made possible with a mass supported Poor People's Survival Movement, because it can potentially mobilize millions of our people around specific obtainable objectives, instead of pie in the sky rhetoric by national civil rights and Black nationalist leaders.

All of these programs in part can satisfy the deep social needs of the Black community, but they are not total solutions to our problems, because although we can build a survival economy now, we have to realize it will take a social revolution to overthrow capitalism and obtain full economic self-sufficiency. We will have to fight to obtain full freedom. For instance, we will have to demand money for rebuilding the city at government expense. We will create our own community public works brigades to rebuild inner city areas, made up of community residents. We don't need a government bureaucracy.

One way to raise money for such a project is to demand an end to taxes of workers and the poor, increased taxation of rich families and major corporations to finance our social programs. That is especially important during the current capitalist depression. But we have to fight in the streets for any concessions or small victories like that.

Even though that would be part of a mass program for the poor, the reality is that this will not happen right away. We just have to build a mass membership group to organize and represent the poor and serve as their organization. Small amounts of donations and other fundraising can serve as the seed money. But then what?

We must begin to go into the poorest, most economically depressed Black and ethnic neighborhoods and not just begin to define their problems, but to feed, clothe and even house people to the limits of our resources, in other ways, build survival collectives as the grassroots basis of the PPSM. This means starting food cooperatives, doing insurrectionary squatting to reclaim buildings for community cultural centers and for housing the poor and homeless, building local coalitions against police brutality, starting an underground newspaper or other grassroots media.

This also means that we must join with the people to fight their slumlords, local governments, unemployment and welfare offices, their employers and other exploiters who fleece and oppress the working poor. The particular neighborhood, the city and the region, means that the nature of the struggle in different parts of the country will be different, but what I want to emphasize is we must start out with a perspective from day one to be part of the people, on the very scale of their problems, instead of a middle-class "revolutionary study society" like most left-wing and Black nationalist formations are today.

Working out a strategy and tactics that can realistically hasten a revolutionary showdown means it is necessary first to understand where the Black Liberation struggle actually stands today. What stage is it in? The truth is that it is in a reactionary period, where opportunist national leaders and politicians still have a hold on the minds of the people. At best we can say that our revolutionary forces are in a rebuilding stage and once this is understood, the solutions begin to fall in place for all its problems. Our task is to create a movement that will bring into the struggle large numbers of the most despised sectors of the Black working class.

In truth, before we can build an effective revolutionary movement, we must rebuild the foundations of a mass movement of the urban Black poor and their non-white allies in the barrios, reservations, prisons, ghettos and other poverty pits. This in turn has the effect of throwing other class sectors into battle; students, industrial workers, clerical workers, the unemployed generally and we can even split the white working class. This process actually started in the 1960s in the wake of the Civil Rights/Black Power and other ethnic liberation movements, but the conservatives have seized the agenda in recent years.

If we can mobilize the Black poor in the urban ghettos as a force against capitalist reaction and the mis-leadership of the Negrosie, we become a serious movement at an early stage of our organizational development. Otherwise, we get sucked into the trap of "navel gazing," issuing grand proclamations, manifestoes and so on that nobody pays attention to but group members. So the task is to clearly link struggles for the pressing immediate needs of Black people with the revolutionary goal of overturning the whole racist system.

That is why the ideas of the PPSM assume such great importance today. The solution lies in formulating and fighting for a program that can help transform the general discontent and militancy of the urban Black masses into an organized, cohesive, consciously revolutionary force. By presenting and fighting for such a program, a small movement can transform itself into an influential power among the masses of people. Although it is not possible to give an "operating manual" for how to organize the PPSM in each city, here is a simple way to look at it: the main strategic and tactical demand is for Black control of the Black community (leading to a large-scale social revolution in the future). This is nothing new, others have written about it and the demand for Black control has been raised spontaneously in thousands of struggles around the United States over the last 40 years. It is obviously a demand that speaks directly to the needs and present understanding of Black people: they want an end to white domination and control over their lives.

At the same time, the struggle for Black control is profoundly revolutionary, because it poses the question of who will have decision-making power over Black people; will we begin to rule ourselves or continue to be under the white capitalist rulers? The realization of this aim of Black Autonomy can build the cities into Black fortresses that will be centers of Black counter-power to the entire white power structure of North America. Our aim has to be to make ourselves ungovernable to the white power structure. Make it impossible for the police to patrol our neighborhood, make it impossible for politicians to assume control on the local level and begin to take over the schools and other government resources and use them for the people. We can't do as the nationalists do, just advocate for reparations or a future nation-state.

As they develop within the Black communities, struggles targeted to win control over specific institutions and agencies can pave the way and prepare increasing numbers of people for the all-inclusive goal of total control of their community and of the existing political system. These partial struggles, carried out around issues such as Black control of neighborhoods, control of the schools, an end to police brutality, decent hospitals under community control and other issues can be extremely important because through them encouraging victories can be won.

One very simple thing we must understand is that most Black people don't belong to social or civic organizations, except for their church or union. They need to feel that they can now belong to something that can produce tangible victories now.

These victories, even if limited to specific areas and issues at first, can help raise the confidence of the community in its own power and lay the basis for broader future struggles. For instance, the following demands could help to promote this process generally:

1. **End police brutality by replacing police occupation forces with a community-controlled Black militia drawn from residents of the community.** This force would not just do "policing," but deal with civil defense, fire safety, food distribution, youth training, community military preparedness, military communications and a host of other neighborhood safety issues. It would not be a colonial force, a repressive police force for the downtown white merchants, or any other tool of the oppressor. It would be a true community defense guard made up of neighborhood residents.

2. **Black grassroots control of all funds allocated to the Black community and control over all plans for renovating and constructing housing and other communal facilities and improvements.** The Black community can only get decent housing, end urban homelessness, start to house families on project waiting lists when it gets access to massive capital. Only the government and major corporations now have access to such resources. We must fight to win these funds for the people, rather than let the bureaucrats and "community development" poverty pimps decide what they want to do with the money to "help" business-people and real estate developers.

3. **Beat back layoffs by the corporations who are cutting jobs, running to low wage areas of the world, by fighting budget cuts by politicians and rich capitalists.** We have got to build local movements that educate the people to these economic crimes and mobilize them to fight back and stop it. We need to sit-in at the offices of corporation meetings, government hearings and other functions to disrupt local life and be willing to take any other action necessary to win our demands.

4. **We should establish Black community councils to create dual power and start to make policy decisions and administer the affairs of the Black community.** These councils should be composed of representatives elected by poor and working-class Black people in various community institutions: such as hospitals, welfare centers, libraries, factories—as well as delegates elected on a block basis. They would then be federated into a local Community Rights Assembly for city-wide or

regional coordination. This would be the beginning of building dual power institutions to challenge the government itself.

5. **Educate, agitate and organize the Black community around the issues of the prisons and the mass lockup of Black youth.** Show how police brutality, homelessness, poverty, unemployment and the drug economy brought on by the exploitative system of capitalism are what's causing the problems in our community. We must certainly down the idea that police and prisons in any way keep safe the Black community, or that the police are there to protect us. We need to show that this government is willing to spend more money to put our kids in prison than send them to college and that we are being confined at a rate ten times that of whites. We must create a mass coalition around this issue, which includes other peoples of color and progressives.

6. **Establish a Black community-controlled food system for self-sufficiency and as a way of fighting to end hunger and malnutrition, including a cooperative trucking network, food warehouses, communal farms, farmers' cooperatives and agricultural unions, inner city food cooperatives and neighborhood unions and other collective associations.** However, this will also include a mass protest campaign challenging the theft of Black farmland by agribusiness corporations and rich white "land barons" and reclaiming it for our projects. This is especially important now that the U.S. government has entered an economic crisis during which it will no longer be able to provide for our needs. We must force the government and the corporations to provide the money for many of these projects, to be administered under our total control. We must mobilize poor people to be a potent class force in this country and disrupt the system until our demands are met. We will need to join with any authentic organization fighting for the poor to build a mass campaign, whether it's the Ontario Coalition Against Poverty, Kensington Welfare Rights Organization, or the countless Black grassroots anti-poverty groups in every city and state.

7. **We must have an independent self-sustaining survival economy to guarantee full employment to our people, even while we fight the racist and exploitative government and its corporate backers.** We demand that the government provide massive economic aid to rebuild the cities, under the control of the people of those communities and we will create public works and building brigades out of the inhabitants of the community. Ghetto housing has to be rebuilt and turned

over to the occupants. Adequate jobs and services must be provided to all community residents, including first preference for all construction jobs in the Black community, instead of the racist job trust system of white-dominated labor unions. We have to unite with progressive unions, poor people's movements and others to build a broad coalition, but we have to push it beyond reformism and conventional politics. We have to demand reparations for the poor who have been ignored by the government and its rich backers.

In conclusion, the question then becomes how to proceed, as I say there is no textbook or manual on how to do that in every community. We should first trust in the neighborhood residents themselves and the local Black Autonomy organizers must be able to make an assessment of their own communities and out of that build a local strategy and set of tactics.

The Commune: Community Control of the Black Community

> How do we raise a new revolutionary consciousness against a system programmed against our old methods? We must use a new approach and revolutionize the Black Central City Commune and slowly provide the people with the incentive to fight by allowing them to create programs, which will meet all their social, political and economic, needs. We must fill the vacuums left by the established order ... In return, we must teach them the benefits of our revolutionary ideals. We must build a subsistence economy and a sociopolitical infrastruc ture so that we can become an example for all revolutionary people.
> —George Jackson, in his book *Blood in My Eye*[4]

The idea behind a mass commune is to create a dual power structure as a counter to the right-wing government, under conditions which exist now. In fact, Black Autonomy believes the first step toward self-determi- nation and the social revolution is Black control of the Black community. The self-activity of the Black community has the potential to shake the entire system. This means that grassroots Black people must form and unify their own organizations of struggle, take control of the existing Black communities and all the institutions within them and conduct

4. George Jackson, in his book *Blood in My Eye*, Barnes and Noble, New York, 1972.

a consistent fight to overcome every form of economic, political and cultural servitude imposed on them and defeat any system of racial and class inequality which is the product of this racist capitalist society. Very simply, we organize to win, not just to fight. We resist until we obtain all the demands of the people and not compromise our freedom away.

The realization of this aim means that we can build inner city communes, which will be centers of Black dual power and social revolutionary culture against the white political power structures in the principal cities of the United States. Once they assume control from the local city governments, such communes could ultimately be an actual alternative to the government and serve as a force to revolutionize African people—and by extension, large segments of American society, which could not possibly remain immune to this process. It would serve as a living revolutionary example to North American progressives and other oppressed nationalities. We saw this very thing begin to happen in the 1960s with the awakening and organizing of Black people in both the major cities and even small towns in the South.

There is tremendous fighting power in the Black community to resist and win our demands, but it is not organized in a structured revolutionary way to effectively struggle and take what is due. The white capitalist ruling class recognizes this, which is why it pushes the fraud of "Black capitalism" and Black politicians, preachers and other such "responsible" leaders. These fakes and sell-out artists lead us to the dead-end road of voting and praying for that which we must really be willing to fight for. I do not mean just a military struggle, but a resistance by any means necessary.

Most Anarchists, not just Black Autonomy, recognize the local municipal commune as a form of free community, independent of the control of the downtown business forces. It is the primary institution of the new society and stands as a living example and an alternative to the old society. But Black Autonomy also recognizes that the rich will not give up without a fight; so it will be necessary to economically, politically and militarily cripple capitalist America. One thing for sure, we should not continue to passively allow this system to exploit and oppress us. We cannot be afraid to take the action necessary.

The commune is a staging ground for Black revolutionary struggle. For instance, Black people should refuse to pay taxes to the racist government, should boycott the capitalist corporations, should lead a Black General Strike all over the country and should engage in an insurrection to drive the police out and win a liberated zone. This would be a powerful method to obtain submission to the demands of the movement and weaken the power of the state. We can even force the government to make money available for community development as a concession; instead of as a payoff to buy-out the struggle as happened in the 1960s and thereafter.

If we put a gun to a banker's head and said, "You know you've got the money, now give it up," he would have to surrender what was in the till. Now the question is: if we did the same thing to the government, using revolutionary means with an insurrectionary mass movement as our "gun," would these still be acts of expropriation? Or is it just to pacify the community the reason they gave us the money? Is it even violence or the threat of violence that is most effective?

Who can really say? Our communities definitely need the money and however we compel it from the government or corporations is of less importance than the fact that we forced them to give it up to the people's forces at all. We would then use that money to rebuild our communities, maintain our organizations and care for the needs of our people. It could be a major concession, a victory, however limited.

We also have to realize Africans in America are not simply oppressed by force of arms, but that part of the moral authority of the state comes from the mind of the oppressed that consent to the right to be governed. As long as Black people believe that some moral or political authority of the white government has legitimacy in their lives, that they owe a duty to this nation as citizens, or even that they are responsible for their own oppression, then they cannot effectively fight back. They must free their minds of the ideas of American patriotism and begin to see themselves as a new people. This can only be accomplished under dual power, where the patriotism of the people for the state is replaced with love and support for the new Black commune and other oppressed people. We do that by making the commune a real thing in the day-to-day lives of ordinary people. This does not happen overnight, after all this is a prolonged struggle of people who have been oppressed for centuries, but it must happen.

We should establish community councils to make policy decisions and administer the affairs of the Black community. These councils would be democratic neighborhood assemblies composed of representatives elected by Black workers and community people in various community institutions—factories, hospitals, schools—as well as delegates elected on a block basis. We must reject Black Mayors and other sell-out politicians, or government bureaucrats, as a substitute for community power. We must therefore assume community control of all the institutions of the Black community, instead of just letting the state decide what is good for us. Not only with just jobs and housing, but also full control over every government institution must be turned over to that community, because only the residents of a community have a true understanding of its needs and desires. These demands for community control are a revolutionary demand to remove the bureaucrats and put power in the hands of the people.

Here is an example of how it would work under the conditions that exist today: we would elect a community council to supervise all schools in the Black community. When I say elect I don't mean in the conventional sense of using a corrupt county or state election board to handle the matter, but rather we would do it on the grassroots level. Just call a meeting of the people, after we have conducted a door-to-door campaign and ask for volunteers.

We would encourage parents, students, teachers and the community at large to work cooperatively in every phase of the new school community council, rather than have an authority figure like a principal and his or her uncaring bureaucratic administration run things as are done at present. The whole Black community will have to engage in a militant struggle to take over the public schools and turn them into centers of Black culture and learning based on our needs, rather than the ideas of a government bureaucrat. This would never happen otherwise. We cannot continue to depend on the racist or Black puppet school boards to do this for us.

But speaking generally about grassroots councils, at some stage, the local council would then be federated, or joined together, on a local level to create a city-wide group of councils who would run affairs in that entire community or region. The councils and other neighborhood collectives organized for a variety of reasons would make up a mass commune. This commune would be in turn federated at the regional and national level, the aim being to create a national federation of Black communes, which would meet periodically in mass assembly meetings. This federation would be composed of elected or appointed delegates representing their local commune or council.

Such a national federation of the local communes would allow community councils from all over North America to work out common policies and speak with one voice on all matters affecting their communities or regions. It would thus have far more power than any single community council could. However, to prevent bureaucratic usurpation of power from this national federation by political factions or opportunistic leaders, elections should be held regularly and delegates would be subject to recall at any time for misconduct, so that they remain under the control of the local communities they represent.

So, the Black community councils are really a type of grassroots movement made up of all the social formations of our people, the block and neighborhood committees, labor, student and youth groups (even the Church, to a limited degree), social activist groups and others to unite the various protest actions around a common program of struggle for this period. The campaigns for this period must utilize the tactics of direct mass action, as it is very important that the people themselves must realize a sense of their organized power. These grassroots associations will provide to the usually mass spontaneous actions, a form of organization whose social base is of the Black working class, instead of the usual Black middle class mis leadership.

Black Autonomy recognizes these community councils as being a form of direct democracy by Black people (or the people of color themselves), instead of a type of phony American "democracy," which is really nothing but control by politicians and businesspeople. The councils are especially important because they provide embryonic self rule and the beginnings of an alternative to the capitalist economic system and its government. It is a way to undermine the government and make it an irrelevant dinosaur, because its services are no longer needed.

The commune is also a Black revolutionary counter-culture. It is the embryo of the new Black revolutionary society in the body of the old sick, dying one. It is the new lifestyle in microcosm, which contains the new Black social values and the new communal organizations and institutions, which will become the socio-political infrastructure of the free society.

Rather than Black supremacy as taught by the Black nationalist groups, our objective is to teach new Black social values of unity and struggle against the negative effects of white capitalist society and culture. To do that we must build the commune into a Black consciousness-raising social movement to build race pride and respect, social awareness and the correct methods to struggle against the capitalist slave masters. These Black communes would be both a repository of Black culture and ideology. We need to change both our lives and our lifestyles, to deal with the many interpersonal contradictions in our community.

We could examine the Black family, Black male/female relationships, the mental health of the Black community, relations between the community and the white establishment and among Black people ourselves. We would hold Black consciousness-raising sessions in schools, community centers, prisons and in Black communities all over North America, which would teach Black history and culture, new liberating social ideas and values to children and adults, as well as counseling and therapy techniques to resolve family and marital problems, all the while giving a Black revolutionary perspective to the issues of the day. Our people must be made to see that the self-hatred, disunity, distrust, internecine violence and oppressive social conditions among Black people are the result of the legacy of African slavery and the present day effects of capitalism. Finally, and most importantly, the main objective of Black revolutionary culture is to agitate and organize Black people to struggle for their freedom.

As Steve Biko, the murdered South African revolutionary, has been quoted as saying:

> The call for Black consciousness is the most positive call to come from any group in the Black world for a long time. It is more than just a reactionary rejection of whites by Blacks ... At the heart of this kind of thinking is the realization by Blacks that the most potent weapon in the hands of the oppressor is the mind of the oppressed. Once the latter has been so effectively manipulated and controlled by the oppressor as to make the oppressed believe that he is a liability to the white man, then there is nothing the oppressed can do that will really scare the powerful masters ... The philosophy of Black consciousness, therefore expresses group pride and the determination by Blacks to rise up and attain the envisaged self:

By the "envisaged self," Biko refers to the Black self, a liberated psyche. It is that which we want to rescue with such a Black consciousness movement here in America. We need to counter Black self-hatred, internalized oppression and the frivolous "party mentality." We also want to end the social degradation of our community and rid it of drug addiction, prostitution, Black-on-Black crime and other social evils that destroy the moral fiber of the Black community. Drugs and prostitution are mainly controlled by organized crime and protected by the police, who accept bribes and gifts from gangsters. These negative social values, the so-called "dog-eat-dog" materialist philosophy of the capitalist system teaches people to be individualists of the worst sort, willing to commit any kind of crime against each other and to take advantage of each other. This oppressive culture is a large part of what we are fighting. As long as it exists, it will be hard to unify the people around a revolutionary political program.

Building a Black Survival Program

There must also be some way to ensure their economic survival while the fight goes on and in addition to providing new cultural role models. It is then when the commune, a network of community organizations and institutions, assumes its greatest importance. We will build a socio-political infrastructure to intervene in every area of Black life: food and housing cooperatives, Black Liberation schools, people's banks and community mutual aid funds, medical clinics and hospitals, rodent control and pest extermination programs, cooperative factories, community cultural and entertainment centers, the establishment of an intercommunal electronic communications network, land and building reclamation projects, public works brigades to rebuild the cities, youth projects, drug clinics and many other such programs.

All these programs satisfy the deep needs of the Black community now, but they are not solutions to our problems, because although we can build a survival economy now, we have to realize it will take a social revolution to overthrow capitalism and obtain full economic self-sufficiency. But they will help us to organize the Black community around a true analysis and understanding of their situation. This is why they are called survival programs, meaning surviving under this system pending a social revolution.

Building consciousness and revolutionary culture means taking on realistic day-to-day issues, like hunger, the need for clothing and housing, joblessness, transportation and other issues. It means that the commune must step into the vacuum where people are not being properly fed or clothed, provided with adequate medical treatment, or are otherwise being deprived of basic needs.

Contrary to the rhetoric of some leftist groups, this will not make people passive or just dependent on us as activists and unwilling to fight the state for their necessities. Rather than always struggling against the government and demanding those things, survival programs inspire confidence in the revolutionary forces and expose the government as uncaring and corrupt. That is more of an incentive for the people to revolt and overthrow the government than boring political pep rallies, giving empty speeches, running for public office and publishing manifestos and resolutions or party newspapers and other garbage (that no one reads but their own members), like most Black and white radical groups do now.

We need to try something new, that being something that worked for the Black Panther Party and other groups in the 1960s. We need to start grassroots projects, unite our people to fight and to do everything that we need to educate, agitate and organize in the communities. That is the only way we'll win a new world. What follows is an example of the kind of survival program I mean:

1. **We must have community control of all businesses and financial institutions located in our communities** and for those businesses not working in our best interests or not returning some of its revenue back to the community, we will seize said businesses and turn them into community cooperatives and mutual aid banking societies.

2. **We must have community control of all housing and major input in all community planning of Black communities.** If a piece of property or house is owned by a slumlord (either a private realtor or government agency), we will seize it and turn it into community housing cooperatives. Further, we oppose Urban Renewal, spatial decomposition, yuppie gentrification and other such racist government schemes to drive us out of the cities. We must have complete control of all planning boards affecting and concerning the Black community. To enforce these demands, we should lead rent strikes, demonstrations, armed actions and urban squatting to drive landlords out and take over the property.

3. **We must have an independent self-sustaining economy to guarantee full employment for all our people.** We demand that the U.S. government provide massive economic aid to rebuild the cities. The government spends billions per year for the Pentagon killing machine. At least that amount should be redirected to meet the needs of America's oppressed communities. Ghetto housing must be rebuilt and turned over to the occupants. Adequate jobs and services must be provided to all community residents including first preference for all construction

jobs in the Black community, when public works brigades are assigned to rebuild the cities. We must fight for Black grassroots control of all government funds allocated to the Black community through a network of mutual aid banking societies, community development corporations and community development credit unions. Again, organizing and mobilizing is the key.

4. **Reparations: the Big Payback.** The U.S. government and the rich class of this country have stolen and oppressed Africans on this continent for centuries. They worked our ancestors as slaves and after slavery they continued to oppress, murder and exploit our people, on down to the present day. We must build a mass movement in our communities to compel the government and the rich to provide the means for our community re-development. They owe us for centuries of abuse and robbery! We must demand that reparations, in the form of community development money and other funds, be provided and placed in credit unions, cooperatives and other mutual aid institutions in the Black community, so that we can start to obtain some measure of economic self-sufficiency. Yet, we know that they won't give the money to us. We must fight them for it, just like we must struggle to overturn the system of wage slavery today.

5. **End police brutality.** We must organize self-defense units to protect the Black community and its organizations and remove the state's police forces. We demand criminal prosecution and jailing of all brutal or killer cops. No jurisdiction for the state's judicial system in Black liberated zones. We need to build a mass movement to oppose police racism and brutality.

6. **We must undertake a large-scale program to train Black people as doctors, nurses and medical paraprofessionals** to make free, quality medical and dental care available to Black people. We must demand that the government subsidize all such medical and dental training, as well as for the operation of clinics, but Black people themselves must establish and run the free medical clinics in all Black communities whether urban or rural. This would include community anti-drug programs and drug rehabilitation clinics.

7. **We must establish a Black community-controlled food system for self-sufficiency** and as a way of fighting to end hunger and mal-nutrition, including a trucking network, warehouses, communal farms, farmers' cooperatives, food cooperatives, agricultural unions and other

collective associations. This must include a protest campaign challenging the theft of Black farmland by agribusiness corporations and rich white "land barons" and reclaiming it for our projects. This is especially important now that the United States has entered an economic crisis that will not be able to provide for our needs, or the needs of its own white citizens. We must force the government to provide the money for many of these projects, to be administered under our total control, instead of by a government agency.

8. **The Black community must have control of its entire educational system** from the nursery school through college. We must establish a Black Liberation educational system which meets the training needs of Black children, prepares them for job training and future economic security, service to their community and gives them a knowledge of themselves and an understanding of the true history and culture of African people; as well as a program of adult education for community people whose earlier educational opportunities have been stunted. We should demand free higher education for Blacks and other minorities at full government expense, including remedial training programs for all who wish to qualify. Both Republican and Democratic administrations have been progressively cutting back on educational funds. Our task is to see that they make these funds available to our children and young people.

9. **We must demand and fight for the release of all Black political prisoners and victims of racial injustice.** We must investigate and review the cases of all such prisoners who are the victims of government political repression and racist frame-ups and lead a mass amnesty campaign for their release. Some of our best revolutionary organizers are rotting away in the prison houses of this land.

10. **The central demand is for Black control of the Black community, its politics and economy.** We have to take over the cities, establish municipal communes and exercise self-government as a vital step. We are the majority in many of the major cities of this country and we should be able to control our own affairs (or at least obtain some autonomy), but as we should now be aware we won't ever get this community social power by voting for some Black capitalist politician, or from passively depending for "salvation" on leaders of one sort or another. We have to do it ourselves if we are to ever get on the road to freedom.

The Black Working Class

The demand for Black labor has been the central economic factor in America; it was Black labor that built the foundations of this nation. Beginning with slave labor in the Old South on plantations, then with sharecropping and other farm labor after the Civil War, successive migration to the North and working mills, mines and factories during a 30-year period (1890–1920) and on down to the present day, Black labor is important to the functioning of the capitalist economic order. Almost from the beginning, Black workers have organized their own labor unions and worker's associations to represent their interests: the National Colored Labor Union in 1869, the National Colored Farmers Alliance (Populist) in the same year, the Brotherhood of Sleeping Car Porters in the 1940s, the League of Black Revolutionary Workers in the 1960s, the United Construction Workers Association and the Black and Puerto Rican Coalition of Construction Workers in the 1970s and on down to the present day with such unions or associations as the Black Workers for Justice and the Coalition for Black Trade Unionists. Some of these were actual trade unions; some were just caucuses of Black workers in existing unions. In addition to Black organized or labor-led federations in the 1870s, there were 90,600 Black workers in the Knights of Labor in the 1880s and at least 100,000 in the Industrial Workers of the World (IWW) in the 1900s.

In fact, the trade unions would not even exist today if it were not for the plight of the Black slave/worker. Trade unionism was born as an effective national movement amid the great convulsions of the Civil War and the fight to end slavery, yet Black workers were routinely excluded from unions like the American Federation of Labor (AFL). Only militant associations like the Knights, IWW and the Anarchist-initiated International Working People's Association (IWPA) would accept their memberships at all. This continued for many years, until the founding of the Congress of Industrial Organizations (CIO) began its campaign of strikes, sit-downs and other protest actions to organize the unskilled industrial workers. Black labor was pivotal in these battles, yet has never fully reaped the benefits. In fact, the labor bosses betrayed them when the CIO was beaten down in the 1950s and reinstated racial discrimination in many of the Southern union locals.

You would think the American labor movement would see it as criminal or racist to ignore these fellow workers today in that fashion. But even now there is no labor organization in the United States which gives full representation and equal treatment to Black workers, though they all give lip service. The fact is that even with some Black labor officials in office with the AFL-CIO or influential in labor locals, Black workers receive far fewer union benefits than white workers and are trapped in the most low-paid, tedious and dangerous jobs, even though they made substantial economic gains during the 1960s. Massive numbers of Blacks are trapped in the highest unemployment sector, and there has yet to be any fightback by organized labor.

Most of the Black masses are in the working class, even though political conservatives nowadays try to claim that the majority is middle class or even upper class. Because of the role they play in production, Black industrial and clerical workers are potentially one of the most powerful sectors of the Black community in the struggle for Black Liberation and in their place of employment. As the victims of inequality in the economy, Black workers have since the 1960s begun to organize for their interests and to protect their rights on the job, even if the union is conservative, racist and won't fight the bosses. They have formed union caucuses and even independent labor unions where necessary.

Black caucuses in the unions are important (which now include Latinos, Asians and other peoples of color and even some anti-racist whites) mechanisms in the struggle for equality. Black caucuses can fight discrimination in hiring, firing and upgrading and for equality of treatment in the unions now, while most white workers still have yet to widely support democratic rights for Black and other oppressed nationalities as part of the labor struggle. Where they are part of organized labor, they should strive to democratize the unions, regenerate their fighting spirits and eliminate white job trust practices. These Black caucuses in the unions should demand:

1. Rank-and-file democratic control of the union, leading to ultimate control of production itself.
2. Equal rights and treatment for all unionists; eliminate all racist practices in the labor movement.
3. Affirmative action programs to redress past racist employment practices and to end racial discrimination based on seniority and other ploys.
4. Full employment for all Blacks, women and other non-white workers.

5. A 20–30-hour workweek with no reduction in pay.
6. The right to strike, including wildcat strikes without union sanction.
7. Speedier and fair grievance procedures.
8. An escalator clause in all union contracts to ensure automatic wage adjustments to keep up with the rising cost of living.
9. Full payment of social Security by employers and the government. Full unemployment compensation at 100 percent + of base pay.
10. Minimum wages at union scale.
11. Prevent runaway shops, phony bankruptcy claims, lockouts, or "strategic plant shutdowns" by companies without notice to unions or to gain advantage in contract negotiations.
12. A public works program to rebuild the Black and other inner city communities and to provide employment for Black and community workers.
13. Worker's self-management of industry by factory committees and worker's councils, elected by the workers themselves.

In addition to the union caucuses, Black working people need a national Black worker's association, which would be both a revolutionary union movement to do workplace organizing, but also a mass social movement for community organizing. Such a movement would combine the organizing tactics of both the labor and Black Liberation movements. It is not designed to drive Blacks out of those unions where they are already organized, but would rather serve as a tool to multiply their numbers and strength and turn their unions into militant, class struggle instruments. This association would exist along with and be a part of existing labor unions, but independent of the orders of labor bureaucrats. There is very little which is progressive about labor unions these days and they certainly are not a revolutionary force The ability to serve as real allies depends on the number of Blacks and peoples of color within a particular union or local.

The League of Revolutionary Black Workers, which organized Black autoworkers during the late 1960s, provides an example of the type of organization needed to challenge and radicalize the entire union movement. The League, which grew out of its major affiliate, the Dodge Revolutionary Union Movement (DRUM), was undoubtedly one of the most militant Black labor movements in American history. It was a Black labor federation that existed as an organized alternative to the United Auto Workers (UAW), which openly engaged in racial discrimination and was making the inevitable step of taking the Black Liberation struggle to the industrial shop floor, the point of production and then capitalism's most vulnerable area.

The League had wisely decided to organize in the Detroit automobile production industry because of the large number of Black workers at the time, which had no real representation. This was an industry where its Black workers were an important part of the workforce and also in the Detroit Black community, where the League united the struggle in the factories with that of the Black struggle as a whole. It quickly became a major force in the workplace and in the streets as many of its cadres organized on college campuses and in the Black inner city areas. It had the potential to become a mass nationwide Black working-class movement, but this potential was stifled through political faction fights among the leadership, lack of a sustained base in the factories, company/UAW/and state repression and betrayals, organized racism and lack of cooperation from white workers and other such reasons.

Although based in the plants among the workers, it was a movement that had middle-class opportunists among its ranks, who were not workers, rather Marxist-Leninist intellectuals. Eventually the League split into mutually hostile factions and died, after less than five years of existence. Then the opportunists Marxists and petty bourgeois intellectuals became lawyers, judges and other left-wing agents of the liberal establishment, while the Black workers had to fend for themselves.

Even though the League was at best a revolutionary syndicalism organization and later a rigid Marxist-Leninist organization (and their adoption of this later authoritarian ideology, with its ideas of purges and unquestioned leadership, directly led to its demise), there is much that Anarchists and radical Black labor activists can learn from the League. The main thing is that Black workers can and should be organized into some sort of independent labor association, in addition to, or even in lieu of, their membership in organized labor unions and especially where the unions are of the sell-out type and/or discriminate against Blacks. In addition, it is much easier for Black workers to organize other Black workers on the job and in their communities in support of strikes and workplace organizing, than white organizers from the major unions.

Simply stated what would be the program of a newly formed National Federation of Black Worker Caucuses?

1. For class struggle against the bosses.
2. To organize the unorganized Black/POC workers ignored by the trade unions.
3. For workers' solidarity among all nationalities of workers.
4. End the wage system and capitalism.

The Need for a Federation of Black Labor Caucuses

From Detroit, Michigan to Durban, South Africa, from the Caribbean to Australia, from Brazil to England, Black workers are universally oppressed and exploited. There is no racial group more borne down by social restraint than Black workers; they are oppressed as workers and as a people. Because of these dual forms of oppression and the fact that most trade unions exclude or do not struggle for Black laborers' rights, we must organize for our own rights and liberation. Even though in many African and Caribbean countries there are also "Black" labor federations, they are reformist or government-controlled. There is a large working class in many of these countries, but they have no usually militant labor organizations to lead the struggle. The building of a Black workers' movement for revolutionary industrial sabotage and a General Strike, or to organize the workers for self-management of production and so undermine and overthrow the government is one of our major priorities. Unions may not be revolutionary, but they have social power and can hurt the capitalist state. Capital and Labor have nothing in common.

What would an international Black labor association stand for? First, since many Black workers, farmers and peasants are not organized at all in most countries, such an organization would be a federation of labor caucuses in existing unions to push them further to the left. Contrary to most labor unions, which segment labor along trade lines, this association would be representing every conceivable skill and vocation. Such an organization means the worldwide unity of Black workers and non-white workers and then, second, it means coordinated international labor revolts.

The real strength of any workers against Capital and the imperialist countries is economic warfare. A revolutionary General Strike and boycott of the multinational corporations and their goods by Black workers and their allies all over the globe is how they can be hurt. For instance, if we wanted to ensure that African workers obtained their human rights, then we use the weight and power of Labor in those countries and by campaigns led by Black workers in the USA and the UK for instance, to wage strikes, sabotage, boycott and other forms of political and economic struggle against those countries and the multinational companies involved. I believe such protests against the Nigerian dictatorship and Shell Oil Company could have saved the life of Ken Saro-Wiwa and the other leaders of the Ogoni people, who were murdered by the military government, egged on by the Shell Company.

In fact, we may have missed an opportunity in Nigeria, but such a labor-based protest movement would even now be a power to be reckoned with. For instance, coordinated actions by trade unions and political action groups in that country have already caused major policy changes. A full-fledged General Strike would likely lead to the total economic collapse of any military dictatorship, especially if such strikes were supported by Black-led workers in North America, much more effectively than a letter writing campaign by Amnesty International. This would not be just middle-class Black civil rights activists, but spearheaded by Black workers.

In addition to asking the Black workers to form their own international labor association and to organize rank-and-file committees within their existing trade unions to push them into a class struggle direction, we want them to do community work. Of course, none of this is intended to drive Black workers out of those unions where they are already active, but would rather serve as a tool to multiply their number and strength in such unions and make them more militant.

Unemployment and Homelessness

As I have pointed out, being the victims of extreme inequality in the economy, Black and non-white workers have already begun to organize caucuses in the unions against discrimination against racist hiring and firing and are also demanding upgrading and promotions. Also, because of high unemployment in their communities and general poverty, they have had to create movements to demand basic services for the poor and homeless instead of on the job issues alone. History has proven that the government will not respond to either workers or the poor until they organize to demand a change and disrupt the system.

We need to look at the severity of the problem: In the first six months of 2011, the U.S. Labor Department's Bureau of Labor Statistics listed official unemployment rates at just over 9 percent of the labor force. Under capitalism, half that figure is "normal" and nonsensically is considered by capitalist economists as "full employment" even though this is millions of people consigned to economic poverty of the worst sort. But the government figures are intentionally conservative and do not include those who have given up actively searching for jobs, the under-employed (who can't make enough to live on), the part-time workers (who can't find a full-time or steady job) and the homeless (now between 4–5 million alone).

Of the millions of people that the government does count as jobless now, only about five million are now given any unemployment compensation or other federal or state aid; the rest are left to starve, steal or hustle for their survival. A person without a job under the capitalist system is counted as nothing. Every worker has the human right to a job; yet under capitalism, workers are dismissed from employment in times of business crisis, overproduction and depression or just to save labor costs through less workers and more speed-up. And some workers cannot find jobs in the capitalist labor market because of lack of skills, or racial or social discrimination.

But the government's official figures lie; private researchers state that the total number of people who want full-time jobs and thus cannot find them, along with the official statistics amounts to nearly 17.3 million persons.[5] Clearly then this is a crisis situation of broad proportions, but all the government is doing is juggling and hiding figures. Yet the figures do show that Blacks, Latinos and women are bearing the brunt of the current depression. The National Urban League in its "Hidden Unemployment Index" (included as part of its annual "State of Black America" report) reports levels of almost 17 percent for Black adults 25 and older and incredible levels of 25–30 percent for Black teens and young adults 17–24 years of age. In fact, Black youth unemployment has not declined much since the 1974–75 recession. It has stayed at an official level of 15–20 percent, but in some inner city neighborhoods of the major cities like Detroit, Chicago, Philadelphia and Los Angeles, the real unemployment rate for young people is more like 30–40 percent. For Black youth the unemployment rate is at least two to three times higher than that of white youth. Capitalism is making economic exiles of Black people as a

5.   About ten million Americans lost their homes during the 2007–11 financial crisis, the so-called "Great Recession." See *LA Times*, September 15, 2018; also the Economic Policy Institute, and the Bureau of Labor Statistics, with similar statistics.

whole. In fact, some researchers report that there are almost two million homeless youth, most of them Black and Latino.

According to economic researchers, while making up 12–15 percent of the total population, Black America represents nearly 40 percent of the United States of America's poorest population. The fact is that unemployment is concentrated in the Black and Latino communities and is greatly responsible for the most destructive tendencies in human relations and deteriorating neighborhoods. Crime, prostitution, suicide, drug addiction, gang fighting, mental illness, alcoholism and the breakup of Black families and other social ills are rooted in the lack of jobs and the denial of essential social services in their communities. Since so many die in the streets or in prison, it is actually racial genocide in the form of social neglect.

Unemployment is profitable for the bosses because it drives down the wages of all workers and helps the employers to keep the workforce under control through this "reserve army of labor," which are allegedly always ready to scab, according to union bureaucrats. Because of pervasive discrimination against Blacks, Latinos and other nationally oppressed workers, including higher levels of unemployment, the jobs they do get are generally on the bottom rung. This is also profitable for the boss and divides the working class to their benefit.

Homelessness is just the most intensified form of unemployment, where in addition to loss of jobs or income, there is loss of housing and lack of access to social services. There are now millions of people who are or have been homeless over the last 15–20 years, because of the de-industrialization of the economy, the capitalist and government offensive to destroy the unions, to beat back the gains of the Civil Rights struggle and do away with the affordable housing sector in favor of yuppie gentrification in the cities.

You see the homeless sleeping on the streets in cities, big and small, and what this reflects is a total breakdown in the capitalist state's social services system, in addition to the absolute economic inequality in American society. This heating up of the class war waged by government and the major corporations shows, more than anything, that capitalism worldwide is undergoing an international financial panic and is really in the beginning stages of a world depression.

Add to the 90 million persons who live below the poverty line and three to five million homeless in the United States, another 3–5 million homeless in the twelve nations of the European Community, along with some 80 million people living in poverty there, with millions more in the capitalist countries of Japan, Korea and other parts of Asia barely surviving and this can only be accurately called a depression. This is on top of millions more in the Third World because of poverty, the legality of colonialism and unequal trade by the rich countries and financial institutions like the World Bank, International Monetary Fund and World Trade Organization.

So although Black workers must organize and fight homelessness and unemployment in the United States, clearly there must be an international movement of workers and poor people to fight this economic deprivation, as part of the overall class struggle. It's not enough to depend on the relatively privileged unions or the middle-class civil rights organizations alone. In every city in North America, the Black/ POC poor communities should organize poor peoples' organizations to fight for unemployment benefits and jobs for the jobless, the building of decent, affordable low-income housing and an end to homelessness, a universal living wage, as well as against racial discrimination in jobs and housing. Such groups would be democratic organizations, organized on a neighborhood basis (to ensure that they would be under the control of the people and against infiltration and takeover by liberal or "radical" political parties, or cooptation by the government), which would be federated into a city-wide, regional and national organization.

That mass organization would be a national Black unemployment league to create a mass fightback movement in this depression. It would be made up of poor peoples' community based groups from all over the country, with delegates elected from all the local groups. Such a national organization could meet to map out a large-scale attack on unemployment, as well as serve as a national clearinghouse on Black unemployment conditions.

On the local level in the Black and poor neighborhoods, it would be the community unemployment councils which would establish food and housing cooperatives, lead rent strikes and squatting, initiate land and building reclamation projects, establish producer and consumer cooperatives, distribute food and clothing and provide for other services: they would establish neighborhood medical clinics for free treatment of the homeless and unemployed, rodent control programs, etc. and they would deal with community social problems (brought on by unemployment) and other issues of interest. They would build hunger marches and other demonstrations and carry the people's wrath to various government offices and to the businesses of the rich.

Not only would the unemployment councils be a way of fighting for jobs and unemployment benefits, the councils would also be a way to obtain community self-sufficiency and direct democracy, instead of depending on city hall, Congress or the President. This radical self-reliance organizing helps lead to the kind of confidence among the masses that makes a Black municipal commune a serious possibility.

One of the most important functions of an unemployment movement is to obtain unity between the employed and unemployed or homeless and workers' solidarity across race lines.

It is important that although we are talking about uniting the poor generally, we want to be sure that our own communities, suffering more than anybody, are in the lead. We will not accept arguments that the poor or homeless folks should follow behind white middle-class radicals, who have never been poor a day in their lives. We want unity, but not exploitation of our people, as has happened too many times in the past.

Finally, the employed and unemployed must work together to struggle against the Boss class if they are to obtain any serious gains against low wages and poverty during this period of economic crisis. The unemployed, who would even walk the picket lines with workers and refuse to scab just to get a job, could support workers who are on strike or protesting the boss. In turn, workers would form an unemployed caucus in their trade unions to allow union representation of these workers and also force such unions to provide food and other necessities, make funds and training available to the unemployed, as well as throw the weight of the unions into the fight for decent jobs and housing for all workers. The capitalist bosses will not be moved otherwise.

MAKE THE BOSSES PAY FOR THEIR ECONOMIC CRISIS!

Here is what a united movement of workers and homeless people must demand:

1. Full employment (zero unemployment) for all workers at union wage.
2. Establishment of a shorter workweek, so that workers would be paid at the rate for 40 hours of work for 20 hours a week on the job, expansion of job sharing so that more can be employed.

3. End homelessness, build and make available decent affordable housing for all. Repeal all loitering, anti-panhandling and other laws against the homeless.
4. End the war budget and use those funds for decent, low-income housing, better schools, hospitals and clinics, libraries, parks and public transportation.
5. End racism and sexism in job opportunities and relief benefits.
6. Jobs or a guaranteed income for all.
7. Full federal and state benefits for unemployed workers and their families, including corporate and government funds to pay the bills, rents and debts for any laid-off worker and unemployment compensation at 100 percent of regular paid wage, lasting the full length of a worker's period of unemployment.
8. Universal living wage and/or national minimum wage set at prevailing union entry wage.
9. Government and corporate funds to establish a public works program to provide jobs (with full union rights and wage scale) to rebuild the inner cities and provide needed social services. The program and its funds should be under the control of committees democratically elected from poor and Black neighborhoods, to avoid "poverty pimps" and rip-off job agencies, or government bureaucrats.
10. Free all persons in prison for crimes of economic survival; jail corrupt corporate insider traders or racketeers.

These and the demands previously mentioned are merely a survival program and agenda for unemployed workers; the real answer is Anarchist social revolution, the elimination of capitalism and workers' self-management of the economy and society. This is a vital first step, however. There would be no unemployment or social need for wage labor in an Anarchist-Communist society. People can live a decent life without exploiting each other and they do not have to have money to receive decent medical care or housing.

CRIMES AGAINST THE PEOPLE

Today, the rich decide what is or is not a crime; it is not a neutral designation. It is a purely class designation. The laws are written to protect the rich and those who act as agents of the state like the police. But most personal crimes are not committed against the rich; they are usually inaccessible. It is poor and working-class Blacks and peoples of color who are the major victims of violent crime. The Black female is the primary victim of rape and abuse by the Black males in this country. The Black male himself is the leading homicide victim in the US by another Black man like himself and sadly our children are among the leading victims of child abuse, many times by his or her own parents.

We do not like to think of these things in the Black community, but we are battering and killing ourselves at an alarming rate. This is not to deny that the capitalist social system has created frustrating, degrading conditions of life that contribute to this brutality and fratricide, but we would be dishonest and lax in our humane and revolutionary duty if we did not try to correct this problem on the short term and also make Black people assume responsibility for our actions. I am not agreeing with Stanley Crouch and talking some Black conservative or "law and order" garbage here about "personal responsibility" of the oppressed when even worse crimes by the rich are ignored, but rather recognition of fact that we have our own set of problems brought on by the system of oppression.

We have an external and an internal crisis facing us in our community, especially the inner cities. The external crisis is racism and capitalist-colonialism, which works to systematically oppress us and is responsible for whatever internal crisis there is. The present internal crisis is the result of an environment where poverty rules, drugs and violence (both social and physical) are rampant and life is sometimes considered cheap. It is undeniable that crimes and other internal violence are destroying our community. It is undoubtedly self-hatred and the desperate economic and social conditions we live under which make us prey on each other. Drugs, frustrated rage, prostitution and other vices are symptoms of oppression.

We kill, beat, rape and brutalize one another because we are in pain ourselves. Thus, we are acting out anti-social roles defined for us by someone else, not ourselves. In our pain and confusion we strike out at convenient and familiar victims; those like ourselves, perhaps even family members. So these victimizers are "us," ordinary Black people who steal and rob just to survive under this system, because of unequal dis-tribution of wealth. Further, for some of us, in our desire to "make it" in capitalist society we will stop at nothing, including murder. And finally, there are those who do whatever they do because of drug addiction or mental illness.

Whatever the reasons, we have a serious problem we must remedy because it is tearing away at the moral and social fabric of our community. It will be impossible to unite Black people if they are in fear and hatred of one another. It is also obvious the police and government cannot and will not rectify this problem and that only the Black community can do something. Further, neither the courts nor the prison system can prevent the situation from recurring, or protect us from violence. Therefore, what can we do?

The white government has never cared about our well-being. And that has not changed, even with a Black president. Neither the police, prosecutors nor courts have got a handle on this problem and justify crime in our community to bring in more violent racist cops. That will not help. It is the community, through its own organizations of concern, which will have to deal with this problem.

For instance, community self-managed programs to work with Black youth gang members (a source of much violence in the community); rather than the military approach of calling in the police, anti-gang squads empower the community rather than the racist prison bureaucracy and the cops. Also, the community-run drug rehabilitation groups, therapy and counseling groups and other neighborhood organizing help us to effectively deal with the problem of drug addiction and distribution, along with the internal violence stemming from it, and we hopefully defuse it. Most importantly, it involves the community in the effort to find solutions on its own, instead of depending on politicians or outsiders.

But we cannot depend upon counseling or rehabilitation techniques, especially where there is an immediate threat of violence or where it has occurred. So, to ensure peace and public security, a Black community security guard service would be organized for this purpose, as well as to protect against the white power structure itself. This security force would be elected by local residents and would work with the help of people in neighborhoods themselves. This is the only way it would work. It would not be an auxiliary of the current white-controlled colonial occupation army in our community and would not threaten or intimidate the community with violence against our youth or families. Nor would such a community guard protect vice and organized crime. This community guard would only represent the community that elected it, instead of city hall. Similar such units would be organized all over the city on a block-by-block basis. These would be neighbors who know one another, rather than white cops who don't know and don't care for the people.

Yet the Black Autonomists go further and say that after a municipal commune is set up, the existing courts must be replaced by voluntary community tribunals of arbitration and in cases of grave crimes, connected with murder, or offenses against liberty and equality, a special communal court of a non-permanent nature would be set up. Anarchists believe that anti-social crime, meaning anything that oppresses, robs or does violence to the working-class neighborhoods must be vigorously opposed. We cannot wait until after the revolution to oppose such dangerous enemies of the people. The security force would thus have to be armed to be effective.

Since such anti-social crimes are a direct expression of capitalism, there would be a real attempt to socialize, politically educate and reha-bilitate offenders. Not by throwing them into the white capitalist prisons to suffer like animals and where, because of their torture and humilia-tion, they will declare war on all society, but by involving them in the life of the community and giving them social and vocational training. Since all the "criminology experts" agree that crime is a social problem and since we know that 88 percent of all crimes are against property and are committed to survive in an economically unjust society, we must recognize that only full employment, an end to wage slavery and degra-dation, access to decent housing and other aspects of social justice will ensure an end to crime.

In short, we must have radical social change to eradicate the social conditions that cause crime. An unequal, racist society like American capitalism creates its own criminal class. The real thieves and murderers, businesspeople and politicians are protected under today's legal system, while the poor are severely punished. That is class justice for whoever has the money for expensive lawyers and has friends in high places, while most of us go to jail or are shot down in the streets during arrest. This is an injustice and that is what social revolution would abolish.

Understandably, many persons want to end the rape, murder and violence in our communities today, but wind up strengthening the hands of the state and its police agents. They call for even more cops and throwing poor people in jail. This will not get rid of crime, but will let white colonial cops militarily patrol our communities and further turn us against one another. These cops will gun us down in the streets, engage in corruption to protect crime and try to make us accept our own poverty and oppression. We must stay away from that trap. Frustrated and confused, Black people may rob and attack one another, but instead of condemning them to a slow death in prison or shooting them down in the streets for revenge, we must tackle the underlying social causes behind their acts.

Prisons are compact duplicates of the Black community, in that many of the same negative and destructive elements that are allowed to exist in our community and cause crime, especially drugs, are in prison in a more flagrant and concentrated form. To call such places "correctional" or "rehabilitative" institutions is a gross misnomer. Death camps are more like it. These prisons do not exist to punish everyone equally, but to protect the existing capitalist system from you and I, the poor and working class.

Instead of an-eye-for-an-eye punishment, there should be restitution to the victims, their families or community. No revenge, such as the death penalty, will bring a murder victim back, nor will long-term imprisonment serve either justice or the protection of society. After all, prisons are only human trash-cans for people society has discarded as worthless. No sane and just society would adopt such a course. Society makes criminals and therefore must be responsible for their treatment and correction. In fact, white capitalist society is itself a crime and is the greatest teacher of corruption and violence.

In an Anarchist society, prisons would be done away with, along with courts and police (except for the exceptions I have alluded to) and replaced with community-run programs and centers interested solely with human regeneration and social training, rather than custodial supervision in an inhuman lockup. The fact is that if a person is so violent or dangerous that he needed to be socially restrained, he is probably mentally warped or has some physical defect anyway, which causes him to commit violent acts after social justice has been won. If such people are mentally defective, then they should be placed in a mental health facility, rather than a prison where they are dehumanized.

His or her personal human rights should never be stripped and they should not be punished. Schools, hospitals, doctors and above all social equality, public welfare and liberty might prove the safest means to get rid of crimes and criminals together. If a special category such as "criminal" or "enemy" is created, then these persons may forever feel an outcast and never change.

Even if he or she is a class enemy after a revolution, they should retain all civil and human rights in society, though they of course would be restrained if they led a counter-revolution; the difference is we want to defeat them ideologically, not militarily or by consigning them to a so-called "re-education" camp or to be shot, like the Bolshevik Communist Party did when assuming power in Russia in 1917.

There are two major reasons why activists in the Black community, as we move to change society, its values and conditions, must immediately take a serious look and act to change the political debate around crime, prisons and the so-called criminal justice system. Those two reasons hit right home! One is because during any given year, one out of three Black men in this country is in prison, in jail, on parole or probation, compared to just one of every fifteen white men. In fact, Blacks make up 50–85 percent of some prison state populations around the United States (48 percent nationally) making a truism of the radical phraseology that "Prisons are concentration camps for the Black and poor." The national Black incarceration rate is ten times that of whites.

Because the government is building so many prisons at this time and there are two million people currently incarcerated (one million of whom are Black), the time has come to talk realistically about finding alternatives to prison. This government spends over $27,000 per year to send a person to prison, but for that kind of money, they could have them attend New York University or the University of California at Los Angeles, two of the most prestigious universities in the country. Yet, politicians all over the country are using fear of crime to justify building yet more prisons. They are even taking money from the budget, badly needed for schools, hospitals and recreation centers for prison building and operations. No question that we need to fight for a moratorium on new prisons, while we organize for total prison abolition.

Prisons have become the new slavery and the new low-income housing projects for the poor in this period. The government cannot find new jobs for poor people, but they can find new prison space. They have even built a new prison-industrial system that has found a way to make a buck off of prison labor and the massive prison-building binge.

They have started privately owned prisons, with multi-millionaire shareholders, who buy and sell their stock over the New York and other stock exchanges. These private prison companies make their money by obtaining contracts from local, county and state governments and now even many foreign countries. They claim that they can house prisoners at substantial savings, usually derived from cutting back on medical treatment, food and making guards work at lower pay, so they are paid per-head fees by the governmental unit. Since they have no stake in rehabilitation or early release, prisoners serve longer sentences. Since the creation of private prisons in the mid-1980s, there are over 400,000 prisoners in privately run facilities in the United States, and even more if you include Canada and other parts of the world. This is the ultimate sin of capitalism, confining prisoners so that someone can make a profit.

But there are other ways the prison system makes a profit. For one, they can run their own prison industrial services, like the Federal Prison Industries does. UNICOR, its administration, product sales and production division, had over $700,000,000 ($700 million) in sales for the fiscal year 2021 alone, according to their annual report. They make over 2,500 products, everything from guided missile parts for the military to furniture for federal agencies. Yet the prisoners make a mere pittance, usually less than a dollar an hour for work that makes millions for the government. Each of the states has similar companies, some of which produce for the commercial and consumer market, or like Texas, they rent bed space for the federal government and various states to send their prisoners to, especially disciplinary cases that they want "broken" through a harsh penal environment.

We also cannot forget the so-called "factories behind fences," that is, private companies which have set up entire industrial plants behind prison walls to exploit cheap prison labor. Not only does this cheat the prisoners, but it also means that somewhere a worker on the outside is being driven out of a job. I am not talking about some fly-by-night operation. Major companies like Microsoft use inmates to assemble packaging for products. United Airlines uses inmate reservation clerks. These companies split their profits with prison officials and make hundreds of millions. Think they will hire these prisoners when they are released at an outside Sony plant? Then think again. It hardly ever happens.

In addition to the forms of money through inmate confinement itself that I have spoken of and their huge profits, a new form of correctional industry has arisen to make security fencing, food trays, security weapons, electrical wiring and other products to keep the prisons going. There are also correctional construction companies, specializing in the building of new prison facilities. They are making big money off our misery. In fact, everybody seems to be profiting but the prisoners and their families. The poor and low-income workers are being starved because of the capitalist economy, which forces them into crime and then deprives their families of a breadwinner. This is why we must be concerned with issues of crime, courts and massive imprisonment from a position of real concern as capitalist/state repression. This has to all stop, but will only stop with a social revolution to transform society.

It may be your brother, sister, husband, wife, daughter or son in prison, but I guarantee you we all know someone in prison at this very minute! The other primary reason Blacks have a vested interest in crime and penal institutions is because, by far, most Blacks and other non-whites are in prison for committing offenses against their own communities, while corporations and the political economy profit from it.

The high rate of recidivism proves and the so-called authorities all agree that the prison system is a total failure. About 70 percent of those entering prison are repeat offenders who commit increasingly serious crimes. The brutality of the prison experience and the "ex-con" stigma when they are finally released only make them worse and prevent them from obtaining gainful employment, or even a decent house in many communities. It is very difficult to get a job if you tell a potential employer that you went to jail for murder, drug dealing or another major crime.

The best thing I can say about prison is that it makes some of us into revolutionaries. It has produced George Jackson, Malcolm X and other radical prisoners, who have potential to lead our struggle. There are others like Herman Bell, Sundiata Acoli or Marshall Eddie Conway, who can communicate with the youth and our communities in a fashion that no middle-class lecturer or business person ever can.

So, the Black community and the Black Liberation movement must support the prisoners in their fight for prisoners' human rights. We should also fight for the release of political prisoners and victims of racial injustice who are being kept locked up by the government because of their activism in the 1960s–1970s, while part of groups like the Black Panther Party. They could be part of an important Black grassroots leadership to help us at a time of crisis like this.

We should also form coalitions of groups in the Black community to fight the racist penal and judicial system and especially the unequal application of the death penalty, which is just another form of genocide against the Black race. And finally and maybe most importantly, local community groups must begin programs of re-education with brothers and sisters in prison because only through planned, regular and constant contact can we begin to resolve this problem that so directly touches our lives. Basic to solving these crucial problems is community-based organization.

Black Autonomy federations should host community forums on the causes and manifestations of crime in the Black community. We have to seriously examine the social institutions: family, schools, prisons, jobs, etc. that cause us to fuss, fight, rob and kill each other, rather than the enemy who is causing all our misery. While we should mobilize to restrain offenders against the people, we must begin to realize that only the community has the real answers, not the racist capitalist system, with its repressive police, courts and prisons. Only those of us who live in the community and care about the people have the psychology and understanding to deal with our own; now we must develop the will. Believe me when I say no one else cares and, if we don't reach out to help our youth, an entire generation will be destroyed. Now that's as real as it comes!

THE DRUG EPIDEMIC: A NEW FORM OF BLACK GENOCIDE?

Drug dealing is one of the worst forms of criminality and deserves comments all its own. There is a negative drug subculture in the Black community that glorifies, or at least makes acceptable, drug use, even though it is killing us and destroying our community. In fact, every day we read of some junkie in one of our communities dying over an overdose of drugs, or of some street corner drug dealer either dying or being arrested because of a shootout after a rip-off or during a drug deal "gone sour."

The tragedy of the latter is that, these days, innocent victims—children or elderly people—have also been gunned down in the crossfire. The drug addict (the new term seems to be "crack-head") is another tragic figure; he was a human being just like anyone else, but because of his oppressed social environment, sought drugs to ease the pain or to escape temporarily from the "concrete jungles" we are forced to live in, in the urban ghettos of America.

With the introduction of crack, a more powerful derivative of cocaine, which made its appearance in the mid-1980s, even more problems and tragedies of this sort have developed—more addicts, more street gang killings and more deterioration of our community. In the major urban areas there has usually been drug use; what is new is the depth of geographical penetration of crack to Black communities in all areas of the country. Small towns and large cities. But the spread of crack is just a follow-up to massive government drug peddling that began at the end of the decade of the 1960s. In fact, according to newspaper reports, the federal government produced and distributed the first supply of drugs to West Coast dealers.

So the street term that "the White House is the rock house," meaning the U.S. political administration is behind the whole drug trade, but especially crack cocaine, is not necessarily just limited to hip-hop or political slogans, but a fact. The U.S. government has actually been smuggling drugs into this country for many years aboard CIA and military planes to use as a chemical warfare weapon against Black America. Especially in the period of the late 1960s, the inner cities of America were flooded with CIA-imported heroin. But later came other drugs. People in the know even claimed that CIA stood for *Cocaine Import Agency*.

At first, these drugs were (mostly heroin) imported from the so-called "Golden Triangle" of Southeast Asia during the Vietnam War. The CIA had a special airline, Air America, to bring it in. But with the introduction of crack cocaine, there was no need to import drugs into the country at the same extent as before, because it could be chemically prepared in a mainland lab and then distributed immediately on the streets. Crack created a whole new generation of drug dealers and customers for those drug dealers; it was cheap and highly addictive. The CIA and other government security agencies used these drugs as a chemical warfare weapon against our communities, just as the British did against the Chinese in the nineteenth century.

All of this has recently been documented in the U.S. mass media and government reports, but naturally, the president and other high officials will not take responsibility for it. They deny it in the face of real documentary evidence and from participants in the drug trade on the government payroll. But it caused an uproar in the Black and Latino communities, who have suffered violence, death and destabilization for years.

Crack and other drugs are a huge source of profits for the government and it keeps the Black community passive, frightened of each other and politically indifferent. That is the main reason why we cannot depend on the police force and/or the government to stop the drug traffic or help the victims hooked on drugs. They are pushing the drugs to beat us down, on the one hand, and on the other hand, the government is also made more powerful because of its phony "war on drugs" which allows police state measures in Black and oppressed communities. Further, it has railroaded many persons with outright police entrapment and railroading tactics, resulting in the mass imprisonment of Black youth and adults.

The federal government also makes millions upon millions of dollars in government monetary appropriations made to "law enforcement" agencies, which supposedly are putting down the traffic in drugs and obtains substantial revenues through fines and seizures of the property of those convicted. So it is the federal government playing a deceitful role, responsible for our plight.

Most police departments have special units to invade communities where drug dealers are located and most of those raids are in our low-income neighborhoods. But the government's paramilitary drug "strike forces" almost never go after the white bankers or the big business pharmaceutical companies who fund the drug trade, just the street-level dealers, who are usually poor Blacks or Latinos. So, the cops are not our friends or allies and must be exposed for their part in protecting the trade, rather than suppressing it. They are part of the problem, not part of the solution.

Unemployment is another reason drug trafficking is so prevalent in our communities. Poor people will desperately look for anything to make money with, even the very drugs that are destroying our communities. If people have no jobs or income, drugs look very lucrative and the best way out of the worsening economic situation. In fact, the drug economy has become the only viable income in many poor Black inner city communities and it's the only thing that some people perceive will lift them out of lives of desperate poverty. Clearly, decent jobs at a union wage are part of the answer to ending drug trafficking in our community, rather than a dependence on police, courts and the state, but also medical treatment.

Junkies are the victims of the American "drug society," which thinks it's cool to use "recreational" drugs. For instance, we now know children are some of the biggest victims of drug dealing, when they are tricked or forced (by economic necessity) into using or selling it, or they suffer because their parents are thrown into jail for dealing it. But although the users and dealers both are victims, the dealers are something else than entirely innocent.

Here's what I mean: even though that Black brother on the corner selling "dope bags" is a victim himself of the economic and political system which makes him do it, dope dealers are a corrupt, dangerous breed who must be stopped by any means necessary. Many people have been killed or seriously injured for naively trying to oppose dope dealers and make them leave their neighborhoods and they kill each other over "turf."

Therefore, whereas the policy with junkies would be more benevolent and understanding, giving them medical treatment, with dope big-time drug dealers we must be cautious and even ruthless when it is called for. We need to try to win them over, first with an economic and political program to draw them away from the drug trade, but many of the dealers are so violence prone, especially the "big shots" (who are also protected by the cops), they must be opposed by both military and political means.

We are not advocating the summary murder of people, but we are saying if it takes death to bring about a change in the community, so be it! If somebody comes to kill you, then you should defend yourself and your family. The issue of death is an issue of who is doing the dying. It can be direct and exercised against the drug merchant, or it can be indirect and exercised against our youth—if we let it. To be aware of a dangerous situation and not move to change it is to be as responsible for that situation as those who created it in the first place!

Listen, I do not want to simplify this problem by saying just kill a few street-level dealers and that will end it. No it won't and we don't want to do that anyway! The police try doing that all the time and it just brutalizes our community that much more. They are just poor people trying to survive this system, just pawns in the drug game whose lives do not matter to the big capitalists or the government. When the government officials say so, these street-level dealers will be killed or imprisoned, but the drug peddling system will go on. This is a socio-political and economic problem, which can best be addressed by grassroots organizations and social programs. But it's the corporate and industrial backers of the drug trade (not just the street-corner dealer) that not only must be exposed, but must be moved on. In addition to educational, agitational and other actions, there must be grassroots community organizing protected by community militias.

But even these small groups of armed people must have the support of the neighborhoods to function; otherwise people will not know it from another violent gang. Once this social cohesiveness exists among the community, then we can begin to put this proposal into action against the most violent, high-level drug dealers. We just have to realize that it cannot all be accomplished by non-violence and good intentions.

We are addressing ourselves to what can be more or less considered guidelines for dealing with the problem on a neighborhood or community-wide level than at a national level.

We have to take on the government and the cops with a mass movement, because their corruption keeps it all going. Only an organized and aroused community can stop drug trafficking and it is our responsibility however you look at it, which cannot be delegated to others. After all, those junkies are our brothers and sisters, mothers and fathers, neighbors and friends; they are no strangers. We must organize to save their lives and the life of our community. We must establish anti-dope programs in Black communities all over the country. We must expose and counter the government's role as pusher of dope, along with that of the police as protector of the drug trade. Also, we must be prepared to help the drug victims with street counseling, street clinics (where they can clean-up and learn a trade and the socio-political reasons for drug use), propaganda against drug use and other activities.

Since we know the federal government is behind the international drug trade, we must expose this on a mass level to our people and mobilize them in massive protests against the government's scapegoating of poor people in the Black community as "drug kingpins" and then sentencing them to life in prison. It is a fact that the federal government truly is profiting from this matter, politically and economically; if any people are kingpins, they are the ones. These young people must be released and rehabilitated in the community. The repressive drug laws like the mandatory minimum sentences, Rockefeller New York State statutes and federal drug laws must be repealed. They only create more prisoners, not less drugs.

Our greatest weapon has to be truth, with which we will let the world know how the world's greatest criminal has victimized us. In cities all over the world, we need to have mass demonstrations, public tribunals, scholarly studies and article after article printed in the Black, radical and mainstream media to expose this government drug peddling. We even need to get the matter before the international public and accuse the U.S. government of engaging in genocide and human rights violations for both smuggling such drugs to addict our young people and destroying our communities. This is actually a form of chemical warfare by the central government against Black and non-white people in this country especially, since they have concentrated drug dealing in our communities.

This time, we need to charge the U.S. administration of criminal activity and try to get the case before the United Nations International Criminal Court, Human Rights Commission and other bodies for its violations of international human rights. And we need to try to get friendly countries and interested international human rights groups to raise this issue all over the world, so that the U.S. political administration can no longer pretend to have clean hands and be active in suppressing drug smuggling. The failure to do this already is when you realize that there is no real radical Black left movement in this country and the existing movements are just stand-ins. This should have been done yesterday. Here is what is needed:

1. **Set up drug education classes in the community** (for the youth especially), to expose the nature of the drug trade, whom it hurts and how the government, banks and pharmaceutical companies are behind it all.

2. **Exposure of the death merchants and their police protectors.** (Photos, posters, fliers, newsletters, etc.).

3. **Harassment of the dealers**; that is, threatening phone calls, knocking the drug "product," have citizens marching outside their "place of business," and other tactics, but not working with the police.

4. **Set up drug rehabilitation clinics so junkies can be treated, can study the nature of their oppression and can be won over to revolutionary politics.** We must win people away from drug use and to the revolution.

5. **Physical elimination of the dealer**; including intimidation, videotaping their transactions, driving them out of a neighborhood or out of town and whatever other action is necessary.

6. **Mass protest against government drug peddling, demand money to set up drug treatment clinics and prosecute cops and government agencies pushing drugs.** Demand reparations from the government for destroying our communities with drugs.

7. **We should hold international tribunals to expose the role of the U.S. government in pushing drugs in our communities.**

DOPE IS DEATH! WE MUST FIGHT DOPE ADDICTION BY ANY MEANS NECESSARY! DO ALL YOU CAN TO HELP YOUR PEOPLE IN THE ANTI-DOPE WAR!

COMMUNITY CONTROL OF THE POLICE

One of the lasting demands of the Black Panther Party was the call for community control of the local police force in the Black community. This was not a recognition that the police were a legitimate force that would be with us always. It was an attempt to control a military force, which was murderous, out of control and corrupt, but which could not be defeated with simple force of arms at that moment while the capitalist state still ruled. So the calls for democratic control of the police were put forward as a way to put them under civilian control and community-based authority. They are valid demands now, but they are mild now, when the police have become a corrupt, paramilitary death squad.

I am not implying in any way the fiction of "working with the police" to end crime in our communities. As I have pointed out numerous times, it is the capitalist state that is responsible for the poverty and desperation which breeds crime in the first place. They are the real criminals. But it is a reality that the police exist and we must find a way to neutralize them, while we can create a defense force in our own communities. One problem is that with the destruction of the Black Panther Party, you no longer heard calls for community control. Instead, the conservative preachers, sell-out community leaders and corrupt politicians put forth a call for the creation of "citizen review boards" or other advisory bodies, to review the actions of the police *after* they beat or kill someone. They know that these reform groups are useless and designed to just allow the masses to blow off steam when the cops commit their latest outrage. Our concern is preventing violence by the police against our people, while we prevent the victimization of one of us against the other.

The issue here is really that of a political confrontation between classes, one of the powerless poor against the rich and their gendarmes. As long as we do not rule over our own affairs, others will continue to rule over us. These cops are recruited to beat and kill the poor and workers who begin to demand their rights and to dismantle this system. Most people simply do not understand this; they persist in believing that there are "good cops" who will just impartially do their jobs. No such luck.

We must therefore build grassroots anti-racist/anti-cop movements to not only destabilize the state over their police misconduct, but also to educate the masses of people active in those struggles that it is an illusion to depend on the government for any justice, unless it is compelled through a resistance struggle. If you look at the situation now, only when the government is convinced there will be a "riot" or massive rebellion will they rein in and perhaps prosecute their racist, killer cops. It is not just to do simple justice. That's why we fight and organize.

Building police-Community Control Boards would allow us to control the police force and provide a challenge to city government in a way not yet attempted. Rather than boards appointed by the politicians, businesspeople, or other pro-cop elements, they will be elected in districts by the masses themselves. This would allow the possibility of progressive elements out of the community to decide departmental policy and have some ability to punish cops for misconduct. I realize we have to go ultimately beyond all reforms; community control has to encompass more than rallies and hearings. This is not a perfect solution, nothing under capitalism ever is, but it is a distinct improvement over what we have now. We are given no voice in these matters and the politicians and Negrosie leaders just tell our people to "remain calm" while they "investigate" or "figure things out." Of course, they never do anything to bring justice to the situation, just social peace. Our call has to be: no justice, no peace!

A Community Control Board could be an important organizing tool to involve masses of people. They could hold public hearings, expose racism and misconduct, and call for the establishment of binding departmental policies and even the reorganization of the entire force. They could get rid of some of the most corrupt cops and administrators and put the people in command of their activities. I am under no illusion of the nature of the fight to create such bodies, which will be resisted vigorously by the cops and politicians, but if we can get mass community support it will be possible to create this institution and place the government and the police on the defensive. We must restrain the fascist police force by any means necessary.

This will require community-based dual power institutions like not only this police-community control body, but also institutions to challenge other aspects of how the government is run and affects our communities. We want to put maximum pressure on the government for how they undemocratically plan housing for the poor, expend funds for schools in the Black community, create prisons to house poor youth and otherwise politically dominate our communities. Clearly the answer is not the creation of political parties or running community activists for office in the corrupt government, but to create new institutions which challenge the existing government and political system itself. I speak more in depth about this in other sections of this book.

ARMED DEFENSE OF THE BLACK COMMUNE

Our insistence on military action, defensive and retaliatory, has nothing to do with romanticism or precipitous idealist fervor. We want to be effective. We want to live. Our history teaches us that the successful liberation struggles require an armed people, a whole people actively participating in the struggle for their liberty!

—George Jackson, quoted in *Blood in My Eye*[6]

We must organize self-defense units to protect the Black community and its organizations. It is the police and the government who are the main perpetrators of violence against Black people. Every day we read of the police murdering and maiming the people in our community, all in the name of "law and order." This police brutality has included the use of deadly force against children as young as five years old and elderly persons over 75 years old!

After years of mass organizing, we must then begin to disarm and demilitarize the police and force them to leave our community. Perhaps this can be done after a rebellion or insurrection drives them out, or perhaps they will have to be driven out by a street guerrilla force, like the Black Liberation Army tried to do in the 1970s. I have no way of knowing. I just know that they have to go. They are an oppressive occupying army, are not of our community, cannot understand its problems and do not identify with its people and their needs. Further, it is the corruption of the cops that protects organized crime and vice in our community and capitalism with its exploitative economic conditions which is responsible for all crime.

Existing police forces should be replaced with the Black community's own self-defense force, made up of members of our community elected or appointed by their neighbors to that position, or from an existing

6. Jackson, *Blood in My Eye*.

street guerrilla force or political organization if the people agree. They would be subject to immediate recall and dismissal by the Community Control Boards of an area. This is only so that we will have community control of the self-defense force, begin to deal with fratricidal "Black-on-Black" crime and be able to defend ourselves from white racist or police attacks. With the increase of white racist violence today and the possibility of white mob action in the future, usually in the name of "law and order," this community self-defense force is most important. The only question is: can we do this now?

We exist now under conditions of nominal legality and civil rights, but those gains are being rolled back by a succession of conservative governments. And after we do effective organizing, at some stage in the process of building up our community-based forces, it is inevitable that the white power structure will recognize the danger to itself represented by such a free Black commune and will then try to repress it. We must have the self-defense capability to resist. This concept of organizing a self-defense force accepts any level of violence that will be necessary to enforce the demands of the people and workers.

Yet these self-defense forces would not be an elite "party vanguard," a police force, or even a standing army in the usually thought of sense; they would be a neighborhood-based Black peoples' militia, self-managed by the community itself: in other words, the people-in-arms. These militia organizations will allow us to engage in offensive or defensive actions, either in general community defense or as part of an insurrection or underground resistance. If we have the right to govern ourselves, then clearly we have the right to defend our struggles.

But what do we do right now in conditions of legality, to reclaim our community from violent racist cops? Do we sit around and debate the appropriateness of military preparation, when the enemy is in our community now, committing rape and murder of Black people, or do we hit back? How do we even get the idea across to our people, some of whom accept the police even if they criticize them? How do we start to train the community for paramilitary operations? I believe we will have to educate the people about self-defense from the standpoint of it being essential against racist attacks and for self-determination. They should be made to understand we couldn't obtain our freedom or have social peace without the ability to defend our community projects and ourselves. Many Black people already have guns for their personal defense and thus are not pacifists. On a mass scale, I advocate the immediate formation of defense and survival skills study groups, under the guise of gun clubs, martial arts societies, wilderness survival clubs or whatever we need to call them. A thorough understanding of marksmanship, ammunition fabrication, demolition and weapon manufacturing is minimal for everyone.

In addition, we should study first aid pertaining to the traumatic injuries sustained from gunfire and explosives, combat communications, combat weapons, combat tactics for the small group, combat strategy for the region or nation, combat intelligence of police and military activities among other subjects. These subjects are indispensable if we are forced to live underground or during a general insurrection. We are facing extinction from class or race warfare. This government is capable of wiping us out if we just stand by and let it happen. So we must organize the masses of people into a Black Partisan militia.

This is part of what a Black Partisan militia should be teaching the masses of people:

We should put emphasis on the purchase, collection, duplication and dissemination of military manuals, gunsmithing textbooks, explosive and improvised demolitions manuals, police and government technical manuals and pirated editions of right-wing manuals on the subject (since they seem to write the best material in this area) and also begin the study of how to build intelligence networks to collect information on the rapidly growing Skinhead and other totalitarian racist organizations, along with intelligence and counter-intelligence information on the government secret police and law enforcement agencies, like the FBI, CIA, ATF,[7] etc. and on any and every other subject which could be of use to us in the coming struggle

Even though in the United States, development of military skills and self-defense is simpler than many other countries because arms and ammunition are widely available, it is logical to presume the arms situation will soon be so tight so as to make firearms virtually unobtainable, except through an expensive "black market" because of the government's "war on drugs," anti-terrorism legislation and other proposed gun control legislation to prevent street violence, or so they say.

Do you think the sporting goods stores will be open during an insurrection? Therefore, we should learn to use machine tool technology to produce our own weapons. Perfectly adequate firearms may be produced using a minimum of machine tools, everything from pistols to machine

---

7. Bureau of Alcohol, Tobacco, Firearms and Explosives.

guns, providing the individual or group is willing to do the necessary studying and preparation. It is not enough to know a little about these subjects; it is a matter of life and death that one be highly proficient.

I am not advocating the immediate waging of urban guerrilla warfare, especially where there is no mass base for such activities. What I am advocating at this stage is armed self-defense and the knowledge of tactics to resist military aggression against the Black community. It is a foolish and unfortunate trait among Anarchists, the white left and even sections of the Black movement to condemn the study of military skills as "premature" or "adventuristic," or on the other hand, to cast oneself into a blind fury of bank expropriations, kidnappings, bombings or plane hijackings. Too many people in the movement have a death trip approach to guns—they assume if you are not "fooling around," then you should prove your convictions via a suicidal shootout in the streets. It doesn't have to be that way and in fact shouldn't be that way. The Anarchists and Black radicals should learn from the errors and successes of the 1960s.

But the Black movement doesn't even have the luxury of such tepid middle-class debates and must have an armed defense policy because America has a long tradition of government political repression and vigilante paramilitary violence. Although such attacks have been directed primarily at Blacks and other oppressed nationalities in the past, they have also been directed at labor unions and dissident political groups. Such violence makes it necessary to acquire familiarity with firearms and military tactics. In fact, the Black resistance movement I spoke of earlier should think of itself as a paramilitary movement, rather than a strict political association.

We must assert our rights to armed self-defense and revolution, even though it is true that there is a lot of loose talk about guns, self-defense, revolution, "urban guerilla warfare," etc. in the Black and radical movements, but with very little study and practice in handling and using weapons. Some of the same folks think "picking up the gun" means that you pick one up for the first time on the day of a general insurrection or confrontation with police.

This is nonsense and is the real "revolutionary suicide." You could get killed not knowing what you are doing. But many instances attest to the fact that armed community self-defense can be carried out successfully, such as the MOVE resistance in Philadelphia during the 1980s, the Republic of New Africa armed resistance in Detroit and Mississippi during the 1970s, Robert Williams' militia in Monroe, North Carolina during the 1950s, the Deacons for Defense and Justice and the Black Panther cases during the 1960s. Even as important as the act of defense itself is, is the fact that these instances of successful self-defense have made a tremendous impact on the Black community, encouraging other acts of resistance.

INSURRECTION AND CLASS WARFARE

In recent years, we have seen rebellions of poor people rise up against racist violence and police murder. But what is a rebellion and how does it differ from an insurrection? An insurrection is a general uprising against the power structure. It is usually a sustained rebellion over the course of days, weeks, months or even years, which has been organized by grassroots political forces. It is a type of class war that involves a whole population in an act of armed or semi-armed resistance. Sometimes mistakenly just called a rebellion, its character is far more combative and revolutionary. Rebellions are almost totally spontaneous, short-term affairs. But even an insurrection is also not the final stage of social revolution, since revolution is a social process that transforms the whole of society, rather than a single event. But it can be an important demand afterwards.

An insurrection is a planned violent protest campaign that takes the spontaneous revolt of the masses to a higher level. Revolutionaries intervene to push rebellions to insurrectionary stage and the insurrection on to a social revolution. It is not small, isolated pockets of urban guerrillas taking actions, unless those guerrillas are part of a larger revolt.

The importance of recognizing the true differences of each level can define our strategy and tactics at that stage and not lead us prematurely into a full offensive, when the enemy is not yet weakened enough by mass street action or political attacks. The importance of also recognizing the true causes of the revolt cannot be understated. Anarchist revolutionaries intervene in such struggles to show people how to resist and the possibilities of winning freedom. We want to take the people's rebellions against the state and use them to weaken the entire rule of Capital and its white power structure.

We want to create resistance on a longer term and to win liberated zones. To disconnect these communities from the state means that these rebellions will assume a conscious political character like the Palestinian Intifada in the occupied territories controlled by Israel in the Middle

East. Creating the possibility of a Black insurrection means popularizing and spreading the various rebellions to other cities, towns and even countries and increasing them in number and frequency. It also means consciously nullifying the power of the state, instead of temporary revolts against it, which ultimately preserves its power. There must be a deliberate attempt to push the government out of existence and establish people's power. This has not yet happened with the various Black revolts we have seen since 1964, when the first such modern revolt erupted in Harlem, NY.

In the 1960s, the Black communities all over the United States rose up angrily with massive rebellions against the state demanding racial justice. After the Harlem revolt, for the next four years major rebellions shook the United States in the Watts section of Los Angeles, Detroit, Chicago and hundreds of other North American cities. Isolated acts of police brutality, racial discrimination, substandard housing, economic exploitation, "the hoodlum element," a breakdown in family values and a host of other "explanations" have been put forward by liberal and conservative sociologists and others commissioned by the state to whitewash the true causes. Yet none of these revealed this as a protest against the capitalist system and colonial rule, even though the social scientists "warned" of the possibility of a new outbreak of violence.

Once again in the spring of 1992, we saw a massive revolt in Los Angeles, whose immediate causes were related to the outrageous acquittal of four Los Angeles policemen who had brutally beaten Rodney King, a Black civilian. But there again, this was just an immediate cause acting as a trigger; this revolt was not a sympathy revolt for Rodney King personally. The cause of this rebellion was widespread social inequality in the capitalist system and years of police terrorism. This time the rebellion spread to 40 cities and four foreign countries. And it was not just a so-called "race riot," but rather a class revolt that included a large number of Latinos, whites and even Asians. But it was undeniably a revolt against racial injustice first and foremost, even if it was not just directed against white people in general, but the capitalist system and the rich. It was not limited to just even the inner city in the Los Angeles area but spread even to white upper crust areas in Hollywood, Ventura and beyond. This was the beginning stage of class warfare, instead of just a "racial squabble."

We saw yet another rebellion against racism and police terrorism in London, UK, in early summer 2011 after the police murder of yet another

Black man by metropolitan police. The Black community rose up in rebellion, destroyed capitalist property, and "looted" a store of consumer goods they could not afford. Like in most instances, the bourgeois media zeroed in on the "looting," and labeled the whole thing as a "criminal orgy of violence." Sadly, some white middle-class Anarchists repeated this propaganda in their own denunciation of the "rioters." They had no understanding of what was happening, and why they should have been in the streets with these youth, giving them political and military direction. If the so-called Anarchist "Black Bloc" of white youth had joined with inner city Black kids, we may have had a general insurrection of long-standing and major damage to the state and capital.

If an underground military force existed or a militia was assembled out of this united attack of Anarchists and Black youth, it could have entered the field of battle with more weaponry and advanced tactics. As it was, the gangs played that role in Los Angeles in 1992 and London in 2011, and played it very well. Their participation is why it took so long to put the rebellions down, but even they could not prevent the re-establishment of white power in South Central Los Angeles or Black sections of London. Not just because of being militarily outgunned, but because they had no revolutionary political program despite all their rhetoric of having been radicalized. Also, the state came down extremely hard on the rebels. Over 20,000 persons in Los Angeles were jailed, 50 were killed and hundreds more badly wounded, and over 2,000 were arrested and jailed by the UK government and police.

Could a liberated zone have been won, so that dual power could have been established? That possibility existed and still does exist if the people are properly armed and educated, but it is not easy. Mass resistance with heavy military weaponry may have won serious concessions, one of which was to pull back the cops. We don't know if that would have happened and those who said the Los Angeles Police Department did withdraw were engaging in pure speculation. We do know that this is not the last rebellion in Los Angeles and other cities. They may come much quicker now that the genie of urban revolution is out of the bag again. London provided another example of angry poor people rising up over yet another atrocity by the police. There have been hundreds of such rebellions in the USA, UK, France and other countries against police terror and government repression. This is a form of class warfare. If white Anarchists can hail protests like Black bloc attacks on buildings, confrontation with cops at anti-globalization demos, and other acts of political violence, then they need to support these revolts by poor people, the truly oppressed, under the capitalist system, and not lecture them from the sidelines.

ONWARD TO THE BLACK REVOLUTION, AS PART OF A SOCIAL REVOLUTION!

4

Pan-Africanism or Intercommunalism?

The Anarchist ideals lead logically to internationalism or more precisely transnationalism, which means beyond the nation-state as an institution. Anarchists foresee a time when the nation-state will cease to have any positive value at all for most people and will in fact be junked by a social revolution. But that time is not yet here and until it is, we must organize for intercommunalism, or world relations between African/POC in America and other communities, tribes, neighborhoods and their revolutionary social movements around the world, instead of building unity with their governments and heads of state.

The Black Panther Party first put forward the concept of intercommunalism in the 1960s and, although slightly different than what I am referring to with autonomous politics, the original Panther concept is very much a libertarian ideal at its core. Holding that as long as capitalist imperialism exists, there is no possibility of creating sovereign nations, intercommunalism seeks to unite oppressed Blacks in the United States with other oppressed peoples all over the world. All those fighting capitalist colonialism and for a new world should be part of an international revolutionary liberation front.

This is contrasted to "Pan-Africanism," that is supposed to recognize all Africans as part of the Diaspora, but does not recognize the contradictions of neo-colonialism, so that corrupt dictators like Haile Selassie, Jomo Kenyatta and Tom Mboya are held up as legitimate leadership of the struggle, along with "revolutionary" governments and anti-colonial or independence movements. This was similar to the simplistic belief that all Blacks "are the same people" which dominated the 1960s during the Black Power phase. So any sell-out, CIA or FBI pig, politicians, or corrupt elements in our community were not exposed or eliminated by the masses just because they were Black. Some of these Black nationalists believe that any of these African politicians are champions of the freedom of African peoples, no matter how corrupt they are. This is dangerously naive and irresponsible.

Because of the legacy of slavery, continuing economic neo-colonialism and the reality of slavery that dispersed Blacks to every continent, it is feasible to speak of international revolutionary solidarity between Africans in America, Africans on the continent and other peoples of color around the world. We cannot unite with any government, but rather with the masses of oppressed peoples themselves.

Here is how Anarchists of color see the world: it is a situation presently organized into competing nation-states, in military and political alliances. Through international institutions like the World Bank, International Monetary Fund and the World Trade Organization, the capitalist Western nations have been responsible for most of the world's famine, imperialism and exploitation of the economic resources of nonwhite peoples of the earth. But in fact, Anarchists hold all nation-states are instruments of oppression. Even though there are governments that claim to be "workers' states," "socialist countries" or so-called "Revolutionary governments," in essence they all have the same function as a fascist or capitalist regime: dictatorship and oppression of the many by the few.

The bankruptcy of the state is further proven when one looks at the millions of dead after two world wars, sparked by European Imperialism (1914–18 and 1939–45), and hundreds of "brush wars" incited by the superpowers of the West or by Russia in the 1950s and continuing to this day. These include wars between not only the West, but between "workers' states" like China-Russia, Vietnam-China, Vietnam-Cambodia, Somalia-Ethiopia, Russia-Czechoslovakia and others over the last 40 years, who have gone to war over border disputes, political intrigue, invasion or other hostile action. As long as there are nation-states, there will be war, tension and national enmity. Shared political ideology, racial characteristics or similar cultures will not prevent it.

In fact, the sad part about the decolonization of Africa in the 1960s was that the countries were eventually organized into the Eurocentric ideal of the nation-state, instead of some other formation more applicable to the continent, such as a continent-wide free federation. This, of course, was a reflection of the fact that although the Africans were obtaining "flag independence" and all the trappings of the sovereign European state, they in fact were not obtaining freedom. The Europeans still controlled the economies of the African continent and nationalist leaders who came to the fore were, for the most part, as pliable and conservative as possible.

Oh, there was an occasional radical like Patrice Lumumba of the Congo, who demanded full rights and freedom for African peoples, but he was quickly (and brutally) silenced in a CIA-Belgian colonial plot. The countries of Africa were like a dog with a leash around its neck; although the Europeans could no longer rule the continent directly through colonial power, they now did so through puppets they controlled and defended, like Mobutu in the Congo, Selassie in Ethiopia and Kenyatta in Kenya. Many of these men were dictators of the worst sort and their regimes existed strictly because of the support of European finance capital. In addition, there were white settler communities in the Portuguese colonies, South Africa and Zimbabwe, who oppressed the African peoples even worse than the old colonial system. This is why the national liberation movements made their appearances in the 1960s and 1970s.

Anarchists support national liberation movements to the degree they struggle against a colonial or imperialist power; but also note that in almost every instance where such liberation fronts have assumed state power, they have become "state communist" parties or new dictators over the masses of the people. These include some who had engaged in the most epic struggles, but also many based on the most obvious military dictatorship from the start. Their governments are not progressive and they tolerate no dissent.

For instance, no sooner had the MPLA (Movement for the Popular Liberation of Angola) government been in power in Angola than it began to arrest all its left-wing ideological opponents (Maoists, Trotskyites, Anarchists and others) and to forcibly quell strikes by workers for higher pay and better working conditions, calling such job actions "blackmail" and "economic sabotage." And with the Nito Alves affair and his alleged coup attempt (Alves was a hero of the revolution and a popular military leader), there was the first party purge of opponents in the new government. Something similar to this also took place when the Sandinista National Liberation movement took over in Nicaragua in the 1980s. None of this should seem strange or uncharacteristic to Anarchists, when we consider that the Bolshevik Party did the same thing when it consolidated state power during the Russian Revolution (1917–21). It provided the model for all such later regimes.

Countries such as Benin, Ethiopia, the People's Republic of the Congo and other "revolutionary" governments in Africa are not in power as the result of a popular social revolution, but because of a military coup or being installed by one of the major world powers. In addition, one or another of the African states exploits some other country perceived as weaker; for instance, Sudan, an Arab-controlled country, still has African slaves, which are powerless Blacks from the Southern part of the country. Thus, they have been fighting a civil war for 20 years. Further, contrary to many of the romantic reports which dominated Western news reports, many of the national liberation movements were not independent social movements, but were rather under the influence or control of Russia or China as part of their geopolitical struggle against Western imperialism and each other. (This is not to say that revolutionary movements should not accept weapons and other material support from an outside power, as long as they remain independent politically and determine their own policies, without such aid being conditional on the political dictates and the "party line" of another country.)

But even though we may differ with them politically and tactically in many areas and even with all their flaws after assuming state power, the revolutionary liberation fighters (the people in arms as opposed to the vanguard organization) are our comrades and allies in common struggle against the common enemy—the U.S. imperialist ruling class. Their struggle releases the death grip of U.S. and Western imperialism (as Anarchists more precisely call it "Capitalist world power") and while the fight goes on we are bound together in comradeship and solidarity. The movement in Chiapas, Mexico, by the Indians who founded the EZLN, a revolutionary liberation movement, is one that many Anarchists support.

Yet, in analyzing the national liberation movement, we cannot overlook atrocities committed by movements like the Khmer Rouge, a Marxist-Leninist guerrilla movement in Cambodia, which massacred millions of people to carry out rigid Stalinist political policies and to consolidate the country, when it took over in the 1980s. We must lay this butchery and other crimes committed by state communism bare for all to see, right at the feet of world communism and state socialism. We do not favor this kind of revolution, which is just sheer power seeking and terrorism against the people to install a left-wing ruling class. This is why anarchism has always disagreed with how the Bolsheviks seized power in Soviet Russia. They created a police state and Stalin's butchery of the Russian people seems to have set a model for the state communist movements all over the world to follow throughout the years. Now the Soviet state is gone, along with most of the Eastern European governments, but the legacy of authoritarian socialism lives on with their movements in a variety of disguises.

We believe that the national liberation fronts make one basic mistake of many nationalist movements of oppressed peoples and that is to organize in a fashion where class distinctions are obliterated. This happened in America also, where in the fight for democratic rights, the Civil Rights movement included Black middle-class preachers, teachers and others in the leadership and every Black person was a "brother" or" sister," as long as they were Black. But this simplistic analysis and social reality did not hold for long, because when the Civil Rights phase of the American Black struggle had spent itself, class distinctions and class struggle came to the fore. They have been getting sharper ever since. Poor people are demanding to organize in their own name and class interest, because although the rich Blacks and professional class may have prospered since the 1960s, the poor and oppressed have just sunk deeper into poverty and prisons are being used as a social tool to lock up millions.

Although there are Black mayors and other bureaucrats now holding positions in the government, they have no power to change things for their people. They merely serve as pacification agents of the state, what we call "Black faces in high places." Their symbolic representation is supposed to inspire hope or keep the masses of people believing in the system. They are not even a serious concession to our struggle. They are put in office to coopt the struggle and deaden the people to their pain.

This American neo-colonial system is similar to the type of neo-colonialism that took place in the Third World in the 1950s to 1980s, after many countries had obtained their "independence." Europe still maintained control through puppet politicians, economic domination and a command structure of petty bourgeois agents, who were willing to barter the freedom of their people for personal gain. These people have no real power to improve the lives of the masses; they merely preside over their misery. In Africa, some of the most corrupt leaders are/were colonial subjects for the European countries and enjoy no local popularity at all; they just inspire fear through military control and passive acceptance by the masses of people.

So while Black revolutionaries generally favor the ideas of African intercommunalism, they want principled revolutionary unity. Of course, the greatest service we can render the peoples of the so-called "Third

World" of Africa, Asia and Latin America is to make a revolution here in North America—in the belly of the beast. For in freeing ourselves, we get the U.S. imperialist ruling class off all our backs.

As Anarchists of color, we wish to build an international organization against capitalism, racism, colonialism, imperialism and military dictatorship, which could more effectively fight the capitalist powers and create a world federation of Black peoples, a commune. We want to unite a brother or sister in North America with the Black peoples of Australia and Oceania/Asia, Africa, the Caribbean and South America, the Middle East and those millions of our people living in Britain and other Western European countries. We want to unite tribes, nations and cultures into an international body of grassroots and struggling forces, which is what intercommunalism was meant to be.

Only a social revolution will lead to Black unity and freedom. However, this will only be possible when there exists an international Black revolutionary organization and social movement. An organization which can coordinate the resistance struggles everywhere of African peoples; actually a network of such organizations, resistance movements, which are spread all over the world based on a consensus for revolutionary struggle. This concept accepts any level of violence that will be necessary to enforce the demands of the people and workers. In those countries where an open Black revolutionary movement would be subjected to fierce repression by the state, such as Black puppet dictatorships in other parts of Africa, the Caribbean and even parts of Asia, it would be necessary to wage an underground resistance struggle. Further, the state has grown more and more violent, with widespread torture and executions, maximum-security prisons and massive police controls, spying and deprivation of democratic rights, police brutality and murder. Clearly such governments—and all governments—must be overthrown. They will not fall due to internal economic or political problems, but must be defeated and dismantled. So we call for an international resistance movement to overthrow governments and the system of capitalist world government.

The military dictators and government bureaucrats have only proven that they know how to spend money on pomp and circumstance, but not how to dismantle the last vestiges of colonialism in South Africa or defeat Western neo-colonialist intrigues. Africa is still the poorest of the world's continents, while materially the richest. The contrast is clear: millions of people are starving in much of Equatorial Africa, but the tribal chiefs, politicians and military dictators are driving around in Mercedes and living in luxury villas, while they do the bidding of West European and American bankers through the International Monetary Fund. They are part of the problem, not part of the solution!

Our ideas about the importance of intercommunalism are based on a firm belief that only a federation of free peoples will bring true Black Power to the masses. "Power to the people" does not mean a government or political party to rule in their name, but social and political power in the hands of the people themselves. The only real "people's power" is the power to make their decisions on matters of importance and to merely elect someone else to do so in rigged elections, or to have a dictatorship forced down their throats, ain't it. True freedom is to have full self-determination about one's social, economic and cultural development. The future is Anarchist communism, not the nation-state, bloody dictators, capitalism or wage slavery.

BUILDING AN AUTONOMOUS PEOPLES OF COLOR MOVEMENT

Building an autonomous movement of peoples of color, based on Anarchist principles is different than Pan-Africanism or concepts of La Raza, or even socialist internationalism. It means building a movement that goes beyond skin color, language, or even shared history of a people, to build the strongest movement of international solidarity. Most solidarity movements are built around identification with a particular struggle. But either giving useless statements about race unity, or vague statements of support, or subordinating one's own struggle to that of another is *not* what autonomy is about. What we need is an international movement based on shared oppression and commitment to a common struggle.

This has to take us past the primacy of narrow nationalism, or regional struggles and back to the idea of revolution as worldwide social change, an international civil war of poor and oppressed peoples against the capitalist system. I am not referring to just development of a socialist state in one country as happened with the old Soviet Union, regional struggles with African anti-colonialism, or the old 1960s concept of Black Power. The old ideas of political socialism and Pan-Africanism have been lost with nation-statism and Stalinism. Even the ideals of joint forms of oppression have been lost so that many believe that only the United States of America has an internal Black population subjected to racist oppression and that forms of oppression based on caste, ethnicity or other peoples of color are not racism in the same sense. This is a grave mistake and cuts us off from many allies around the world.

In 2001, I was a delegate to the World Conference Against Racism (WCAR), held in Durban, South Africa, organized by the United Nations Human Rights Commission. I represented a group initiated by BANCO, the Southwest Michigan Coalition Against Racism and Police Brutality. Throughout the week of the non-government section of the WCAR, there was lip service by various government officials about ending racism, passing anti-racist legislation and honoring international human rights covenants. It was just so much hot air, although it was important to hear from the oppressed peoples themselves describe what they were going through and the call to build a network of activists resonated among many there. The call for financial reparations and the anti-colonial struggle of the Palestinian people dominated the NGO events, but was ignored or outright denied by the United States and the European Union. But the Dalits of India, the Roma of Eastern Europe, Black Brazilians and African Americans had strong voices at the conference. All of these and many other oppressed peoples were heard for the first time on an international level. Yet, we all felt something was missing.

There was no independent grassroots organizing going on against racism at the conference, instead the South African politicians and NGO professional poverty pimps used it to further their social and political gains. Lawyers, lobbyists and other leftist pimps were on full display. With just a small number of grassroots people (they charged $100 a head to get in!), nobody hardly talked about practical methods of struggle against racism and white supremacy, except for the non-government grassroots groups from the Third World.

What did stand out at the governmental phase of the conference when it started was a perspective that racial discrimination was just one form of oppression which was outlawed by UN treaty, to be handled by government bureaucrats when they were "sensitized to the issue." Clearly they did not want the oppressed peoples to take matters into their own hands. Every time someone would get up and denounce some government, one of that government's representatives would blandly describe it as an "internal matter" which would be "resolved locally." It frightened the hell out of them when we talked about an international mass movement against racism, neo-colonialism and caste/gender/ class oppression. They kept repeating, "let the professionals handle it," meaning lawyers, lobbyists and other middle-class spokespersons. One brother from the United States came up to me and said, "man, this thing ain't nothing but a corporate diversity seminar" and had nothing to do with fighting racism or oppression. He was on the money, but even so it gave radicals the chance to speak out, meet and fight back on an international level.

In fact, inside nation-states (even with so-called "democratic governments"), new forms of oppression were noted at the WCAR meeting: internal colonialism and other forms of oppression of "racial minorities" (nations within nations). With internal colonialism, we are not talking about exploitation by a distant colonial power, but rather the nation-state itself is the exploiter and oppressor of a subject people. Even with the fraud of human rights being bandied about by almost every government nowadays, the fact is governments are more oppressive and murderous today than at any time in history, using widespread torture, genocide and terror by the police and military, along with massive surveillance and subversion of insurgent movements.

The United States and Europe did not want to deal with their history as colonial powers with long years of bloodthirsty terrorism against peoples in Africa, Asia and Latin America and for even maintaining internal colonialism of the descendants of slaves and oppressed peoples in the land of the Mother Country. The biggest fraud of the conference was the scam of dealing with this oppression as a mere "rights" issue, to be resolved either by a legal complaint raising a violation of "constitutional" rights to be handled by the host country's judicial authorities, or to be presented to a toothless body like the United Nations Human Rights Commission.

It could not be more plain how useless all this was, after one particular incident took place. Mary Robinson, then UN High Commissioner for the International Human Rights Commission, would not even give us a copy of the NGO report to the General Assembly at the end of our sessions because she objected to its "militant" language. After that, she claimed to receive so many "death threats" that she had to be escorted by security guards everywhere she went. That was just one more reason why we joined the South African people in demonstrations against the fraud of the conference on the first day of the government sessions.

In fact, as Anarchists, we see the ideals of "international human rights" as a total scam, a lawyer's tool and politician's device to justify nation-statism and capitalism and to allow the continued internal colonialism of various oppressed peoples all over the world. It also allows the creation of more government repression of non-white population groups, such as the criminalization of Black and Latino youth in the United States, military attacks on the indigenous people of Chiapas and in the Brazilian rainforests, along with the suppression of peoples of color all over the world. Somehow the issues of racial oppression never become concerns under the international human rights framework, just as it never seems to be the concern of "civil libertarians' in the United States and other Western countries, unless it can be made into an international legal issue to be "solved" by UN bureaucrats.

Clearly, we need a new agenda: our own, not dominated by capitalist nation-states or authoritarian white radicals. We need to build a network for international solidarity amongst peoples of color who are sympathetic to anarchism, but most importantly a direct action protest and international liberation movement.

I am not advocating for national liberation movements, with all of their known limitations, but rather an anti-authoritarian movement, which does not depend on capitalism, old line democratic socialism, or nation-statist solutions at all. The farce of "state socialism," the idea that nation-states can give us our freedom in a world of imperialist domination and the idea of protecting human rights through partial decolonization, or the passage of unenforceable international covenants against racism, needs to be rejected outright as a total illusion. The UN itself is a tool of capitalism. The failure of old line socialism, whether as state socialism or Stalinist communism, should be heartily denounced, especially now that they are trying to make a comeback in "democratic disguise." They have been disgraced and we should not let them off the hook.

But it also needs to be said that the various national liberation movements based on Marxism-Leninism are being defeated, disarmed and then in many respects becoming part of the very governments they had fought for so long, emerging as a "loyal left opposition" inside Parliaments or national assemblies. The example of Nicaragua and the Sandinista movement is a clear example of what I am speaking of. But, in other instances, they have sunk so low as to become disconnected from the oppressed condition of the masses and just exist as a left-wing death squad, slaughtering anyone who opposes the methods of the movement. Shining Path in Peru is an example of this.

Clearly a new direction is needed. Let's start with these ideas about this new movement and then just flesh it out:

1. Create new links of international solidarity among activists of color, sympathetic to anarchism.
2. Create a new worldwide direct action campaign to win new forms of local and international people's sovereignty, to build new leadership in our movement, which is authentic and grassroots, by the poor and oppressed people themselves.
3. Redefine racism and national oppression to include internal colonialism.
4. Develop a new political agenda, with peoples of color united and in the lead of all revolutionary social struggles for change, instead of dominated by white radicals.

STRUCTURE

First, let me say a proposal is a set of ideals for how things should be. It shows us the possibilities and gives us future projections. It is a planning document and is not engraved in stone. It can be changed, merged with another proposal, rejected in part, or even in whole as unfeasible. It can be helpful because it can give us clarity as to direction, theory or strategy. It can also prevent us from making serious errors, if the wrong course is being proposed from another source, or if we are clearly making mistakes from our current practice.

My thinking on this does not just come from anywhere, but rather from experiences with the Black Autonomy International (1996–present) known as the Black Autonomy Network of Community Organizing until 2007) and now Black Autonomy Federation. One of the things I learned the hard way is you don't organize a mass movement by creating one central organization, but rather dispersed groups devoted to the same cause, especially on the local level. The movement has to be made up of several components that might be spread out over different parts of the country or the world, so that if one is crushed, the others can go on.

I believe that the Black Autonomist movement should be a federation of Autonomist regional and national sections all over the globe, an international organization fighting imperialism and the nation-state, giving mutual aid and support to other peoples to help them obtain their freedom, while we struggle for ours. It won't work as an African American-dominated institution alone; people in this part of the world dominate things too much anyway. I don't mean that African Americans cannot have their organizations of struggle, but rather that our local groups would be part of the international organization of other Black peoples and peoples of color throughout the world. Besides, the tasks and problems of our revolution in the belly of the beast are very different from theirs in the so-called Third World and do not form strict models for us in the industrialized world.

In such a discussion of an international organization, the thing to bear in mind is that this is a concept that can grow out of a popular mass movement, but only when such a movement is strong enough to truly call itself an international mass movement. I believe it is not premature, however, to give a concept about how it could be structured and how it could work to become a central institution for millions of peoples in the world. At any rate, we must begin to think about such concepts now, even while we are a small, unpopular tendency within the Anarchist movement. Again, a proposal is not engraved in stone, but is rather a planning and brainstorming document. So here goes.

Besides the national section of Black Autonomy International (BAI), there are other major component parts to a proposed organization: (a) an armed front called the Black Partisan militia; (b) the administrative arm, called a federation council; (c) International Black Appeal, the fundraising institution; and finally (d) the Organizing Institute.

A BLACK PARTISAN MILITIA

I am not a pacifist, but it would be nice to say that we could accomplish our goals without revolutionary violence, but unfortunately, that is not the case. I don't believe in Anarchist propaganda by the deed, nor any form of political murder of individuals, government officials or civilians as a strategy, but do clearly understand that armed self-defense and underground military resistance campaigns against the state and racist paramilitary forces are an absolute necessity. Yet the left in America is wedded to pacifist tactics and middle-class belief in the government and that it will grant us social justice. They cling to this belief in the face of routine police violence, enforced poverty, racial oppression and other aspects of state terrorism.

All over the world, Black people/POC and the working class are being subjected to oppression by dictatorial governments and the capitalist economic system. This is the case whether we are talking about a military dictatorship in Africa or a racist government in the United States. These governments will not go away of their own accord, but will rather have to be defeated and restructured as political communes; it is also equally clear there must be international solidarity and coordination of our resistance to the largest degree possible.

A Black Partisan militia is an armed militia/underground resistance movement designed to fight a worldwide civil war to destroy capital and the gendarmes of national governments. It would organize these armed units in every village, town, city, state or province, region or country. It allows the people to fight off invaders, bandits, or oppressors of every sort. It in fact makes the social revolution possible and gives masses of people the ability to herald in a new day of unity and freedom.

But in addition to being a resistance movement in times of crisis, it acts as community or village armed rescue force and revolutionary political organization. There is no division between armed force and political force, between the people and the military. In fact, it is the people armed. It works, day-to-day, in organizing to empower the people of each social unit, from the lowest to the highest. It works to break down barriers of tribe, nation or language that split our peoples. The militia is the force that safeguards the revolution and advances it, while the people fight for full autonomy and establish their communal structures. Although made up of cells and collectives at the lowest levels, the partisan militia can be any size and can serve as a mass movement to fight for decent jobs and housing, build food and housing collectives, against racial oppression and most importantly for political independence and economic self sufficiency through armed struggle.

This concept accepts any level of violence will be necessary to enforce the demands of the people, although theoretically a militia is for defense, while an underground force is deemed at a later stage. In those dictatorships where an open radical movement would be subjected to fierce repression by the state for the mere act of organizing, it would be necessary to wage an underground resistance struggle from the beginning, along with the aboveground mass organizing. People's guerrilla warfare techniques should then be used with the aim of disabling and overthrowing the government and establishing worker/peasant/farmer councils for direct democracy by the people and to control industrial and agricultural production.

But even in the Western imperialist countries, with their tradition of a "democratic" form of state, we must recognize the legitimacy of revolutionary violence. When such forms of revolutionary action are required, however, a clear difference should be seen between simple terrorism without popular support or coherent political goals and guerrilla warfare arising out of the collectively felt frustrations and oppression of the common people and workers, which is why we adopt militias on a community basis, rather than purely as an underground movement. The use of military methods would be necessary to counter the violent actions of the state. For instance, if the state attacked our political and social movements, this would make it imperative for revolutionaries to defend themselves by taking armed action, where a dictatorship to strip the masses of the basic democratic rights is being created. In addition, where there was a social rebellion taking place that created a favorable opening for a social revolution, the armed movement would have to go into action. Even a civil war for democratic rights, to claim territory or liberated base areas, would be an opportunity for armed struggle.

Of course, armed struggle is not always a matter of defensive violence. It is in itself a major way to mobilize the masses of people in a general offensive, and in many instances, it is also a matter of survival since we know that the state will try to violently crush any effective Black or revolutionary movement with both subversion (the FBI's COINTELPRO used during the 1960s), as well as murderous repression by the police or army. There is the example of the Black Panther Party to prove this, but every government has or will use repression to put down a revolutionary force, if its existence is challenged. So it is a question of the masses being armed in support of the movement *because they are the movement*, rather than the movement being armed "in the name of the masses" as some sort of vanguard paramilitary which liquidates the role of the masses of our people as a revolutionary force in their own right and makes them into cheerleaders for a group of "revolutionary heroes."

Building territorial communes in a country or a liberated area is just a step to social revolution. It is a dual power institution, and it is not the final phase of social revolution. We must be clear about this. We do not pick up arms merely to fight or defend, but to help us survive and create a new world.

BLACK AUTONOMY INTERNATIONAL FEDERATION COUNCIL

The federation council (FC) would serve as the administrative body of the Black Autonomy movement on the international level. It would, theoretically unite all components of the organization and deal with major political and economic issues of importance to the revolutionary movement and make intercommunalism real. It would directly involve the masses in decision-making, not just national leaders or politicians in a government. People would organize communes or other self-governing entities at the village or neighborhood level, then the town or city level, regional or tribe level, then into a federation of communes on the national or continental level, convening the federation council for decisions on meetings.

The delegates to the FC (we will say two from each region, although any number will do) would be elected to their posts by their compatriots in the village, region or country, but although freely elected, they are not career politicians and have no decision-making power in their own right; they merely attend, investigate, observe, record and then report the facts back to the people. It is the people who make the decisions and make their decision known through their delegates in most instances, but can also bypass their delegates, if they so desire and present a petition to the FC at any time it is in session.

So, in essence, the FC is an international council of Black Autonomy, where delegates from all over the world could meet to discuss and decide important political and economic matters, including the setting of policy for the next year. It would concern itself with food, housing, regional development, military defense and other issues which affect all regions and countries of the world. It would develop strategy to deal with the day-to-day concerns of many of the poor peoples of the world. It would develop a budget and realistic policies for an international survival program while capitalism still exists and following Liberation, would do much economic planning and organization to support the conditions for a new world.

THE INTERNATIONAL BLACK APPEAL

The International Black Appeal (IBA) is the fundraising and material support arm of the proposed organization. It will solicit funds and materials (food, clothing, office equipment, military supplies) for the movement as a whole. It will set up an international non-profit foundation to do direct mail and other forms of fundraising all over the world to raise funds to run the organization and its projects, solicit memberships and other forms of support.

It would also serve as an education society and information bureau to explain the Black Autonomy Federation and its programs. Because of the Internet, social media and other new forms of technology, almost instantaneous communications are now possible between any part of the world at moderate cost. This makes it possible for activists in many parts of the world to keep in contact, do organizing and to do joint planning electronically, but it also lets us enter the "news business" with our own publications and international reporting and even to set up a world information bureau like the Independent Media Centers, a radical news network in various countries. In organizing this IBA, we should not neglect a material aid campaign to buy or send telecommunications equipment to Africa and other poor continents where people cannot get ready access to new technology.

COMMUNITY ORGANIZING INSTITUTE

Although I speak about community-based organizing most thoroughly in Chapter 3 of the book, it is important to talk about a Black Autonomy unit which is responsible for community-based outreach, building a grassroots fightback movement and grassroots counter-institutions. There is only one way to reach the people and that is to go where they are in the poor neighborhoods. The whole world is now a ghetto and poor peoples of color in Paris, France, Detroit, Michigan, Senegal or Jamaica, London and Lisbon and many other places are living the same racist and degrading existence, brought on by the same capitalist system.

Although capitalism itself cannot be brought down on the local level and international movement of the poor and oppressed is possible, regardless of language, national borders or geography, a community-organizing institute would train people to fight their own battles locally, create a federation of the poor (Poor People's Survival Movement) and fight for the rights of the poor and workers. The idea is to make the poor people's movement into a revolutionary movement fighting for a new society, rather than a reform movement satisfied with social insurance or welfare.

REPARATIONS OR LIBERATION?

A variety of Black nationalist currents are involved with the reparations movement. Some are advocates of using these funds for a nation-state, some are bourgeois politicians and businesspeople, some are honest people who believe that this economic approach is the major tactic for our freedom and there are smaller segments who have a variety of reasons. There are also several Black activists who have mistakenly elevated the struggle around reparations demands as the primary contradiction between Black people and the American government. They call for an apology and the payment of financial resources, which would allow the government to wash their hands of the matter finally.

In addition, some Marxist Black radical groups know better, but they opportunistically join in with this approach because they feel it's the best way to create a mass campaign that will attract people to their movement.

Of course, some white people and even some Black conservatives oppose any idea of reparations, claiming there is no way to discern the guilt of the ancestors of slave masters, or that they and their family came to America after slavery, or even that Black people are "not qualified" for reparations, which are specious arguments. These whites and all of white America have benefitted from centuries of Black oppression, regardless of when they came.

Their standard of living is based on a parasitical and exploitative relationship with the condition of Black people. Like Dracula, they have also sucked our blood. Regardless of what such white critics say, I believe we are clearly entitled to such payments; after the trans-Atlantic slave trade, centuries of poverty and oppression, there is no doubt we are due. This should not fool us.

But we don't have many white allies in this struggle; even the great majority of white radicals apologize for this theft by their white colonial slave masters in the West. Some white radicals try to explain it as the result of the "higher production standards" of workers in the West, that is, they "work harder" and have "more technology" and thus more social product. This is fundamentally untrue and misstates the colonial situation and a history of genocide and slavery.

Again, look at the United States of America as our example; the country was created by the stolen labor of the African slaves, the genocide of Native peoples, the theft of lands of the Mexicans and the forced labor of Chinese serfs in the West, which provided the resources to create a white republic, even though some doctrinaire white radicals like to push European immigrant factory workers as the "economic pedestal" for the emergence of capitalism. They claim that the manual labor of slaves and serfs never amounted to much, "primitive accumulation" they call it and only when the "white working man" came to America from Europe, can we talk about producing capital resources upon which a capitalist economic system could possibly be constructed. So not only should we not be compensated, but that our labor never amounted to anything anyway. This pseudo-economic analysis is worse than hardcore conservative racism.

In other words, the Industrial Revolution of the eighteenth and nineteenth centuries is all we should concern ourselves with in any radical class analysis. But then America, as we know it, would not even exist without slave labor and the capital reserves from the forced agrarian method of production. This treacherous argument only advances white supremacist interests and in fact objectifies and minimizes the importance of laborers of color and their years of suffering and enslavement under this system. It is Obscurantism, the hiding of historical realities.

If the white Western world was literally created by the enslavement, exploitation and colonization of the peoples of color in Africa, Asia, Latin America and Oceania, then this would be the reason why the white world is currently so rich and developed and the rest of world is currently so poor. It is purely and simply because of the theft of resources and labor of the peoples of color around the world.

In fact, one of the things pushing forward the present day reparations movement by peoples of color all over the world is this knowledge of the stolen labor and wealth by the white world. So they are now demanding financial reparations from both the governments and corporations of the European countries and the United States. But the reality is that the capitalists will not voluntarily give up their stolen booty just because it is "the right thing to do," nor have they become more "enlightened" since those days.

As I have said before, I believe the demand for financial reparations has to be subordinated to the overall struggle for liberation. We want freedom, not just cash money; we have to destroy the system responsible for our enslavement and the continued oppression of the peoples of the world. We must be firm about that.

Speaking to Black people involved with this movement, I believe that it is not enough to call for apologies or hush money; we have to expropriate these suckers of every stolen dime they have! We need to lead street campaigns that disrupt all of America's cities. We need to force them to give up all capital resources, the land and the remaining industrial means of production. In the final analysis, it will take a mass movement—in other words, worldwide protests and a revolutionary struggle of workers, the poor and oppressed people of color—and probably an international civil war to dislodge them of these resources. It won't be done through Congress, public opinion or lawsuits. We will have to shed blood and dispossess the rich, the same as in any revolution.

Financial reparations can only be part of a liberation agenda, rather than some "pay-off for social peace." Financial reparations alone will not free us as an oppressed people. Almost a billion people are now starving in the world, most in Africa, Asia and Latin America; we cannot be oblivious to this, so the truth is that the purpose of such reparations payments by the United States and Europe has to be to redistribute the wealth of the world to the poor and workers of the Third World and oppressed peoples of color in the West, not create a new class of Black capitalists or a bourgeoisie of color.

The truth is, these capitalist bloodsuckers will be happy to give out a few billions and a land grant to a group of Black nationalist petty bourgeois agents, who are nothing but aspiring capitalists themselves. They will finance the petit bourgeoisie to control the Black urban poor and working class, even with a neo-colonial government. They, in fact, see the creation of a comprador collaborationist Negrosie as a good thing, if it allows them to stay in power and will quiet the natives and the poor with the illusion of sudden wealth. Some of these Black nationalist groups are corrupt enough to go for this. Like Malcolm X said: "These Negroes ain't trying to build no nation, they're trying to climb back on the plantation."

Ungovernable: An Interview with Lorenzo Kom'boa Ervin[1]

William C. Anderson (WCA): What do you think about the current uprisings happening throughout the country in response to police violence?

Lorenzo Kom'boa Ervin (LKE): I think the uprisings are good but we're seeing that they have limitations as a revolutionary uprising. These limitations allow the state to subvert the nature of uprisings as well as the issues as mere reforms. The state and the liberal politicians and others are able to utilize that against the movement. This kind of cooptation has been happening for a while. I've watched 60 years of protests and so-called "riots" and rebellions and uprisings in major cities and small towns like Ferguson, Missouri. I've watched 60 years of them going back to 1964 with the Harlem rebellion in Harlem, New York. It was always something to do with the police. One form or another, they kill somebody, beat somebody, or just come into the community and did some kind of atrocity. And the people responded with a fight back, in the form of a rebellion. Then the politicians and the others claim to be using their issues or their drive to then turn around and propose some liberal reforms, which aren't liberal at all, actually.

What we see is that each time the police terror or racism becomes worse or it just becomes prolonged. So we have to ask ourselves, "Okay we're having protests. We're going up against the man. But are we also not understanding that the role here now is to transform the society as a whole?" We're not trying to just "defund the police" or whatever. The government is not giving anything, and even with the protests pressuring them, they have yet to come up with anything in terms of any kind of program to prevent further atrocities against Black people. There have been thousands of people killed by the police in the United States and the government has given impunity to the killer cops.

---

1.   First published by Black Rose Anarchist Federation/Federación Anarquista Rosa Negra (https://blackrosefed.org/ungovernable-interview-lorenzo-komboa-ervin-anderson/). This interview has been edited for brevity and clarity.

This is a form, in my estimation, of class warfare or fascist policing, and we need to understand that. They are using the most violent statist agents, especially in the Black community and in poor communities. They are using them to beat down any grassroots political opposition as well. They're using them to create a new kind of criminal system where they *are* summarily charging people and putting them in prison for long periods of time with draconian sentences. And this has been going on for quite some time. So, rebellions are great. They're wonderful, it's great to see people standing up. The only thing is (you know my standpoint as an old long-term activist and everything), I try to look at the actual essence of a struggle, not just the fact that it's happening. The orientation of the struggle today is very similar to what I saw in the final stages of the Civil Rights movement. You see them win reforms, but not transform the system itself. That's the difference between revolutionaries and reformers, we want to smash the state entirely.

WCA: What sort of advice would you have for young radicals then who want to transform this society? What advice do you have for those who are politicized and looking for some direction on how to go about doing the things you think need to be done?

LKE: We as activists, as organizers, have to make ourselves and our communities ungovernable. I know you've heard that term before. That means what it says. We have to make it so that we create a new kind of political system of our own, whether it's dual power or revolutionary direct democracy, whatever we want to call it in this period. We need to create that kind of movement, a mass anti-fascist movement on one hand. And on the other hand, we need to have the capacity on a mass scale to build a community-based mass economic survival tendency, based on cooperatives in the ghetto for housing the poor, rebuilding the cities, and taking care of the material needs of the poor. We need to be able to build that. I'm not opposed to some of these groups that are coming about because although not now radical, potentially they could turn into something else. But what needs to happen is that we need to be reaching the masses of urban poor people with these programs. We're not fighting just to have a cult or a group, or some leaders. We're fighting to put power in the hands of the people in a new society. Presumably, revolutionaries know some things in some areas of organizing that people don't know. So we need to be training them, we need to be equipping them to be independent of this political structure. I also think the Black Panther Party was right, we need to have survival programs and we need to be going beyond just what they had. We should be trying to build the survival economy in this period right now.

We should go from this period where there are some people who understand or are practicing mutual aid, but the masses do not. So we need to go beyond "just helping," to working toward some sort of different economy, a survival economy on the way to full on Anarchist communism. Maybe that's the name we know of, as Anarchists, but in some parts of the world, they call it a "solidarity economy" to help them survive capitalism. Whatever it's called, we need to have that so we're not totally dependent on the capitalist state. I don't claim to know it all, but I do know some things and I know one thing that's not going to work— is when you allow the same corrupt, racist cops to claim that they're reformed now or you got the same politicians claiming "Well, this is not the same system, we've never found a way to defund the police, but we're reorganizing it, so be patient!" George Jackson, a radical prisoner in California and member of the Black Panther Party in the 1960s, himself, said that such police or prison reforms are nothing but the further rise of fascism. They help fascism become acceptable to the people.

We've dealt with that for years because you see how the police have been using different kinds of psychological warfare and pseudo campaigns like Weed and Seed, or community policing over the years. That stuff was designed to put the police in power over the community. They were intentional racial profiling and control measures, and we need to understand what's been happening up to this point. This stuff with Trump is just the culmination or the end stage of their building of fascism. They built the prison system which is the biggest in the world. They built that back years ago. They started using paramilitary policing years ago, especially in the Black community. All these things that we see, these forms of what would constitute a fascist state in another country, they don't have to build it. They've already got segments of it built in America.

You have to ask yourself some critical questions like how is this ever being allowed to happen at a time when you've got all these so-called anti-racist, anti-fascists in name. But they don't even do anything to deal with this kind of fascist struggle against capitalism itself. They go and get in the street and fight some drunk Nazi, some low grade kind of organizing campaign. We need more than that in this period, now coming up especially. We need the ability to have a mass base, not just youth but communities, a broad segment of the people. We need that mass base added to a new kind of politics where the people are being put in control, rather than the politicians or preachers or whomever all these people they've chosen. Tell the youth to build movements from the grassroots up. Build resistance movements and build a large enough movement that cannot be controlled by the state so that, as I said before, it's *ungovernable*. And ungovernable means a number of things to people in the movement right now: it means the kind of tactics you engage in in the street, it means how the community is organized that they don't have to depend on these politicians, it means a mass boycott of capitalist corporations, a new transitional economy, and many others things as part of a resistance.

One thing I'll be most anxious to say to people is we can't organize the way we organized back in the 60s, we can't organize the way we organized even 30 years ago, 20 years ago. We've got to break new political ground and have new political theory and new political tactics. These don't come from one person or group alone, it must be decided by the people themselves.

WCA: Can you talk a little bit about why you started Black Autonomy, what it is?

LKE: Black Autonomy was something I started to try to deal with the fact that inside the anarchist movement, there were very few Black people. Black Autonomy was designed also to be a pressure group against institutionalized racism within the anarchist movement. At that time, white anarchists in the USA were not really relating their political direction to the Black community or interested in Black organizers. Truthfully, it was not an anti-racist movement in that period. And I eventually reached the stage where I said what we will have to do is create an African American/ Black tendency within the anarchist movement that is strong enough to stand on its own. And that can challenge the white radical nature of the anarchist movement. That was the same reason I started writing *Anarchism and the Black Revolution*, which was a book that raised the contradictions around race and colonialism and oppression, and called for Anarchists to raise their consciousness. They had never looked at it as a problem or issue before; they never thought about Africans or Blacks in America at all unless they were merely trying to recruit Black people into their tendencies, but even that was not happening when I came along in the early 1970s. I was the only Black Anarchist in the USA and even other parts of the world for years, actually decades.

In the United States, Black people's labor and living conditions have always been different from the white population, going all the way back to slavery. Something that Marx himself has said is the "pedestal" for the creation of capitalism in the USA was Black slavery. I tried to get anarchists to understand and think more critically about it, but they would become very angry and defensive at me for saying this. So we created our own ideological construct and organization that wasn't perfect and it was created under some really tough conditions, but we created it. It was in the face of fear, guilt and hostility by white anarchists. They gave Black Autonomy no real support, began to call us "narrow nationalists" and this and that.

We created what was essentially a Black Anarchist collective first in Atlanta in 1994. You know, myself, and I think there were seven other community organizers, and seven or eight students from Clark College and Morehouse University. They became part of this collective right at that time. Eventually the group built a ten city national federation and a group in London.

We were doing political discussions and so forth in Atlanta on the direction we should take. So, the ones from the street said, "Well, look, we gotta be organizing the Black community against the conditions that are happening to us." And we started organizing around the Atlanta PD police assassination of a brother named Jerry Jones in 1995, and we also started organizing around the attempt by the city government to take the Atlanta transit system away from the poor and working people inside the city and give it to people in the suburbs during the 1996 Olympics. You know, they were going to raise the transit fare so much that people who lived in the city wouldn't be able to pay for it. In 1994, we started the Poor People's Survival Movement, a mass group of poor people who wanted to fight back. And out of that came the Atlanta Transit Riders Union. We were fighting against the city authorities that ran the transit system and we began raising contradictions around race, class, and poverty that had existed for years by city authorities. That was a successful campaign. We were able to beat the transit officials back for years against implementing the fare hike. We made the rich, the city government, and corporations underwrite it, instead of poor people or workers who had no other transit options.

Black Autonomy itself was an anarchist organization, but it also understood that its politics were based around the reality of the oppression of Black people in the United States and around the world. We organized around the things that we still see happening today: mass imprisonment of Black people and murderous shootings by the police or fascist vigilantes. We have been organizing in a number of cities in the 1990s and even in the 2000s. The 2013 anti-klan demonstration in Memphis, Tennessee was the largest anti-fascist demo that year with 1,500 to 2,000 people. We had been organizing a number of cities against police terrorism for years as well.

So Black Autonomy also started organizing and trying to create a dual power political structure trying to create ideas that can reach the youth and trying to combat prisons as an entity. Not just combating judges and all this other garbage, but actually dealing with the prisons being used as a tool of oppression of Black and poor people. And unfortunately, we weren't able to get enough forces around us on that question to build a broad based movement against mass imprisonment. We tried to get groups like the Anarchist Black Cross to help us, but we failed when they united with the authoritarian left.

WCA: Why do you think the current administration is homing in on anarchists and Antifa (Anti-Fascists)?

LKE: Trump needs a scapegoat for one thing. Antifa are willing to combat these fascists in the street and they have been doing so for quite some time. So Trump's able to utilize that "violence" to justify his policies, and he'll become more repressive about it as time goes by. I really do think he wants to prosecute them in federal court for "treason." They want to project Antifa as "enemies of the state." I think he would have used the DOJ and his federal goon squad to try to smash them by now, if it were not for the fact that he has had to run for office and he has not had a totally free hand. And also, I think that he believes, and to some extent it may be true, that a lot of the stuff that's happening in the street is by anarchists that seem to have mass support.

The thing is, for almost 100 years, the government has always seen anarchists as a serious threat for disruption. In years past, there have always been waves of repression against anarchists, for instance the 1919 Palmer Raids. But in recent years, anarchists haven't been exactly doing very much that would warrant this kind of repression. I'm surprised that it's coming now but I'm not surprised in one sense, because we are a convenient scapegoat as the most dangerous tendency on the left. The communists? Oh the communists are all sold out! (*laughter*) They've all sold out and they're running for office or whatever. And to some extent (*laughter*) that's true to be quite honest. I'm not saying in every instance, but you have got a lot of communist elements that are in bed with the state and in bed with the capitalists right now.

The Department of Justice and FBI want to scapegoat the Black protest movement. They haven't been able to do it with the Black Lives Matter movement yet, although, you know, they came up with this so-called state security program some time back where they were going to go after Black activists, you know, "extremists."

WCA: "Black identity extremists."

LKE: That's exactly what they called it, and they tried to use it for intimidation, but for whatever reason they weren't able to get the public support to that extent. He wants to do it with Black Lives Matter. But I think a lot of people have been convinced now that Black Lives Matter is just using non-violent tactics. So the American people are not so much in favor of the idea of the state or the government coming after them like that. It may still happen before or after he leaves office, if the Black protest tendency becomes more radical or switches tactics.

WCA: I wanted to ask you about the increasing popularity of Black anarchism. There are a lot of Black people who are becoming more interested in anarchism. A lot of these Black people are getting interested in your work. Can you speak about this and why you think it's happening? And can you also kind of speak to what you will hope that they get out of your work and Black anarchism?

LKE: First, it was a surprise to me to even find out that there were new anarchist tendencies, Black anarchist tendencies, on the scene. And I only found that out in the last year, this year actually. But on the one hand that speaks to the work we did with Black Autonomy. Whatever mistakes we made and our failure to build a mass tendency years ago, it speaks to that effort. I think if I hadn't written *Anarchism and the Black Revolution* and done other things that I did with the comrades that I worked with in Black Autonomy, people wouldn't even know about the ideas of Black Anarchism.

The other thing is, I stand for a type of anarchism that's a class struggle anarchism. My perspective and my understanding going back reading years ago is that anarchism comes from the socialist movement. It is in fact self-governing socialism or libertarian socialism. The ideas of self-governing socialism and all this came from Bakunin, and the anarchist movement was part of the first international communist movement. So my thing is, if people are going to want to get an anarchist perspective or Black anarchist politic, they have to understand that we have to build a movement that's about struggling for power to the people. That's not just a term of art, but means we are fighting not to just have a party or cult or some authoritarian leadership. We're fighting so the people on the ground, on the bottom, can begin to build a new life for themselves and a new society. There's all kinds of debates on what that society could look like or what transitional stages of fighting and building a new society we have to go through.

I do believe we'll have to go through a transitional stage. But at this point, at this moment, it is about revolutionary community organizing, not just "peaceful protests" to appeal to the government. We must adopt new thinking about resistance and rebuilding communities so that we can be ungovernable by the state. We have to think about people building revolutionary communes and building other forms of independent political entities. Right now we have to think about millions of homeless people coming, and talk about how we give them some place to live. How do we deal with the government to force them to provide those resources and, how do we fight the government to take over housing entirely? We're going to have to do widespread fight back in the form of squatting or just going in physically taking over buildings. With the kind of class warfare that exists in the United States, you will have to pick up the gun if you want to change society. I mean, I'm not saying using armed struggle as an only tactic, but the revolutionary civil war is coming inevitably. The government will make war on you, whether you are ready for war or not.

I acknowledge a mass tendency which uses non-violence at a certain historical stage can push the government back, and that's what's happening right now. Yes, the protest movement is pushing the government back, pushing it up against the wall, but it's not choking the life out of it. What we need is the kind of revolutionary movement that can choke the life out of it and create a new society all together. These organizations we're talking about, are stifled by petty bourgeois consciousness, petty bourgeois organizing, petty bourgeois leadership and so forth creates a certain kind of movement. A certain kind of movement that will not go to the point of "going for it all" as they used to say back in the day. I really think that they have built in limitations on their ability or their willingness to overthrow the state or even talk about it. The funny thing is, we have to continue to think about things just like that, overthrowing the state, not getting some reforms. I'm not gonna tell you that you never should get reforms if you can in the immediate sense. But at this stage, we've gone too far now to just settle for this reformism over and over again especially in this moment. This moment is a revolutionary moment and other things have happened to make it that way, not just the protests.

The system itself is tottering because of the COVID virus and everything that's happening with Wall Street. All these things are happening and it puts the state on the weakest point it ever has been. Even Trump or whomever taking over the state and trying to create a fascist state is not doing it from a position of strength. They're not trying to impose dictatorship from a position of strength, they're trying to impose it from a position of weakness, and fear. So that's why I said we have to build an alternative, radical force, so that it can then work in a way that it never has before to overthrow the entire system. Not just the *Democrats* or the *Republicans*—you know the rulers want that sort of bullshit. They want it, because it's trivial. It means *nothing whatsoever*. In the final analysis, Trump may want a personal dictatorship. But the other guy [Biden], he's an agent for the state and he's an oppressor in his own right. He's helped to get the prison system to the point where it is. His running mate, Kamala Harris,—well she is just as much of an establishment Democrat as he is. She's just as much in favor of using the police and the government against *the poor*. We need to be able to educate masses of people about these things while we're creating an alternative, so they will not be fooled. We need a new society and a new world, not more capitalism.

William C. Anderson is an independent writer from Birmingham, Alabama, and co-author of *As Black as Resistance*.[2]

---

2.   Zoe Samudzi and William C. Anderson, *As Black as Resistance: Finding the Conditions for Liberation*, Chico, CA, 2018.

Index

Thanks to our Patreon Subscribers:

Lia Lilith de Oliveira
Andrew Perry

Who have shown generosity and
comradeship in support of our publishing.

Check out the other perks you get by subscribing
to our Patreon – visit patreon.com/plutopress.
Subscriptions start from £3 a month.

The Pluto Press Newsletter

Hello friend of Pluto!

Want to stay on top of the best radical books
we publish?

Then sign up to be the first to hear about our
new books, as well as special events,
podcasts and videos.

You'll also get 50% off your first order with us
when you sign up.

Come and join us!

Go to bit.ly/PlutoNewsletter